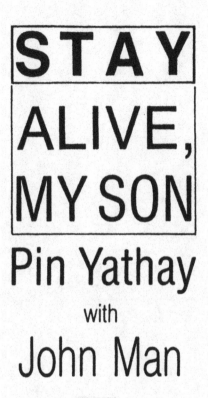

STAY ALIVE, MY SON

Pin Yathay

with

John Man

A TOUCHSTONE BOOK
Published by Simon & Schuster Inc.
NEW YORK · LONDON · TORONTO · SYDNEY · TOKYO

Touchstone
Simon & Schuster Building
Rockefeller Center
1230 Avenue of the Americas
New York, New York 10020

1 3 5 7 9 10 8 6 4 2 Pbk.

Library of Congress Cataloging in Publication Data
ISBN 978-0-6716-6394-0

'Stay alive, my son. Stay alive to escape. Escape to stay alive . . .'
On April 17, 1975, the implacable, black-uniformed Khmer Rouge
guerrillas filed into Phnom Penh to open a new and appalling chapter in
the story of the twentieth century.
On that day, Pin Yathay was a qualified engineer in the Ministry of
Public Works. Successful, highly educated, French-speaking, he had
been critical of the corrupt Lon Nol regime and hoped that the Khmer
Rouge would be the patriotic saviours of Cambodia.
Then came the immediate evacuation of Phnom Penh. All roads out of
the city were jammed with a mass of humanity fleeing the fear of
American air raids. Pin Yathay and seventeen members of his family
drove their cars out of a city that was bleeding to death. They took with
them whatever they might need for the three days before they would be
allowed to return to their home.
But they were never to return. Under the cold commanding eyes of the
new masters they were moved on from camp to camp, their possessions
confiscated or abandoned and as days became weeks and weeks became
months they became the 'New People', displaced urban dwellers
compelled to live and work as peasants. As they moved on again and
again, their days were filled with forced manual labour and their survival
depended on ever more meagre communal rations. The body count
mounted, first as malnutrition bred rampant disease and then as the
Khmer Rouge singled out the dissidents for sudden death in the darkness.
All in the name of Angkar, the 'Organization', the faceless all-pervading
authority of the new Democratic Kampuchea.
Pin Yathay's family was reduced to just himself – now known simply as
'Thay' – his wife and their one remaining child. Wracked with pain and
disease, robbed of all they had owned, living on the very edge of dying,
they faced a future of escalating horror.
'Stay alive, my son. . .' His father's words echoed in his memory,
when Thay and Any, his wife, had to make the heart-breaking decision of
whether to abandon their last son to the care of a Cambodian hospital and
make their desperate break for freedom. The account of that escape
describes a nightmare that defies imagining.
In just three years, the Cambodian holocaust claimed between two and
three million dead and devastated a culture half as old as time.

Pin Yathay came out of the killing fields to write Stay Alive, My Son
*. . . at once a powerful tale of individual survival and a compelling
chronicle of our time.*

This is a true story. I dedicate it to the memory of my children, my wife, my parents and other members of my family, as well as to the memory of millions of my compatriots.

Pin Yathay

CONTENTS

ACKNOWLEDGMENTS

I would like to express my gratitude to various national and international philanthropic institutions for all their actions in favour of the refugees of South-East Asia: the religious and humanitarian organizations, the International Red Cross, the United Nations High Commission for Refugees, the Thai government, and all countries which have accepted refugees from Indo-China.

I would like to offer particular thanks to all the press who alerted international opinion to the Cambodian tragedy and who printed the stories of the survivors. Personally, I am grateful to the following organizations, associations and journals which relayed my appeals: Amnesty International, the International Federation of the Rights of Man, the Coordination Committee for the Khmer associations and groupings in France, the Khmer associations in the USA, the European Committee for Aid to the Khmer Refugees in Brussels, the International Institute of Cooperation (University of Ottawa), the Research Center on East Asia (University of Montreal), the American Security Council in Washington, bulletins and reviews on Cambodian affairs in France, the review of the Khmer community in Canada, *Cambodian Appeal* in Washington, Agence France-Presse (Joseph de Rienzo), *Le Monde* (Roland-Pierre Paringaux), *L'Aurore* (Denise Dumoulin), *Les Temps Modernes* (Pierre Rigoulot); *Le Soir* of Brussels, the *Daily Telegraph* (Michael Field), German Television (Henning Huge), *Bangkok Post*, *Sankei Shimbun* of Tokyo (Seki Tomoda), *Le Devoir* of Montreal (Georges Vigny and Clement Trudel), *Le Droit* of Ottawa (Fay La Riviere), Radio Canada (Radio and Television); NBC News (Jack Reynold), 'Good Morning America' (Jack Anderson), *Washington Star*, Associated Press (Robert B. Cullen), *TV Guide* (Patrick Buchanan), *National Review* of New York (J.D. MacHale).

I am grateful to Charles Ronsac and Lucien Maillard, my publisher and collaborator respectively, for their work on the first French edition of my account.

May all friends, known and unknown, of the Cambodian people pardon me for not being able to cite all their names.

My thanks for their work on this rewritten edition are due to Iradj Bagherzade, my publisher; to John Man for his invaluable collaboration; and to Sophie Clarke-Jervoise, who typed the manuscript. I am indebted to a great many other friends, without whose support and encouragement the publication of this present edition would not have been possible.

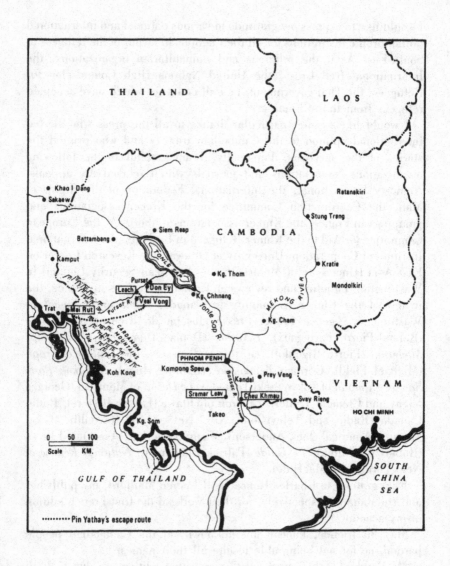

FOREWORD

In April 1975, the Cambodia I had known from childhood became a nightmare. The wheel of the Khmer Rouge revolution, finding enemies everywhere, sought to crush the country, its people and its culture – individuals, families, society, knowledge, beliefs, and every positive emotion, even love itself.

In many respects, it succeeded. Cambodia became a nationwide experiment in totalitarian ideology. Hatred, fear and destruction ruled. Cities, possessions, money, education, and the arts alike were condemned. Millions suffered deportation, hard labour, starvation, and death. The country became one vast concentration camp.

In just two years, I lost everyone I loved – seventeen members of my family and uncounted friends – and everything that was dear to me. I am left only with memories.

In this book, I want those memories to live on. I want the world to know how my children, my wife, my parents, brothers, nephews and cousins were all indiscriminately snuffed out. But, more, I want the world to see my suffering, and my family's suffering as representative of what happened to millions. Through our suffering, I want you, my readers, to see how fine-sounding ideals of justice and equality can be perverted by fanatics to create brutal oppression and an equality of misery.

Such things have happened before. It is said that history is a mirror of the future. I pray that this is not necessarily so. I pray that this book may help prevent such horrors recurring. If it does, in one way at least my family and millions of other Cambodians will not have died in vain.

1 REVOLUTION

I was woken by the noises of war, the whistle and thud of shells. As I lay there, I became aware of other sounds: the murmur of idling cars, the squeak of bullock-carts, the occasional shout. I looked at my watch. Five a.m. I slipped out of bed, went to the window, and stared in amazement. The street was a mass of people and vehicles surging slowly past in the pale pre-dawn light. The whole country seemed to be crowding into town. It was April 17th, 1975, and I knew then that at last the civil war was nearly over.

'Thay, my dear?' Any was awake now, lying quiet in the darkness. She must have been watching me, waiting for my reaction.

'Quick, Any.' I felt tense, not fearful, but exhilarated by the knowledge that the time for action had come. We had to move fast to avoid the fighting. 'It's the end. The Khmer Rouge will be here soon.'

Any accepted what I said instantly. She swung herself out of bed and pulled on her skirt and blouse, moving rapidly but gracefully, settling her shoulder-length hair with a shake of her head. 'What will happen?' she asked.

'Don't worry,' I said, hurrying through to the living-room to gather our things. 'It'll be difficult for a while, then everything will be back to normal.' Our voices woke the children. The two older ones, Sudath, who was nine, and five-year-old Nawath, began to chase each other round the two-roomed apartment that formed our part of my parents-in-law's house. 'But right now we have to get these children dressed, and hurry up into the centre of town before the troops come.'

'Nawath!' she called. Nawath, who was wrestling Sudath on a bed, took not the slightest notice. 'Nawath, you come when you're told!' Any called again, more forcefully. Sometimes I thought she was a bit too harsh on the children, but they were a high-spirited pair, and needed a firm hand. With a quick lunge, she caught the fleeing Nawath and began to dress him, ignoring his protests. The baby, Staud, sat up with a yawn and looked

1

round sleepily. 'Sudath, come on,' I said to the oldest boy. 'Get yourself dressed. Can't you see we're in a hurry?'

It would not take long to pack the little we needed. We had known for a week – since the Americans pulled out on April 12th – that five years of slowly building conflict between Cambodia's insurgent Khmer Rouge and the Republican government of Marshal Lon Nol was almost over. It was only a question of when, and from what direction, the Khmer Rouge would come. Two days before, the sound of approaching battle had warned us to make temporary arrangements for evacuation, in case the house was hit. I had visited my parents and agreed that if the worst came to the worst the whole family would all meet at the house of a cousin, Oan, who lived near the centre. We had all filled our cars with petrol. Now, all we had to do was pack two suitcases of clothes, together with Any's jewellery, our savings and my foreign currency – three thousand dollars in hundred-dollar bills. I grabbed a small radio – that would be useful for news broadcasts – and a cassette recorder, which contained spare batteries. I also threw in a few things that might be useful professionally – technical books on irrigation and terracing and a French-English dictionary, together with pens and paper.

Now Nawath was kicking his feet as Any tried to force him into his shoes. Just at that moment, Any's older sister, Anyung, bustled in, saying that she and Any's parents were ready to go. While Anyung put Staud, who was just out of nappies, into a T-shirt and shorts, Any gathered some biscuits and sweets for the children. I checked my possessions – books, watch, money, identity papers, radio, cassette player – and took a last look round, wondering if after all I should have sent the family abroad. No, I had been as much against the corrupt regime of Lon Nol as anyone. I had nothing to fear from the Khmer Rouge.

Hurrying the family out to join Any's parents, who were already in their Austin, I pushed our baggage into my Fiat, shouting instructions above the sounds of a city in chaos – the rattle of machine-gun fire, the boom of distant shells, and the steady hum and roar of engines. Slowly, we eased our way out of the driveway.

The street, one of Phnom Penh's many spacious boulevards, was a torrent of people, cars, trishaws, bicycles, trailers, motorcycles, and a few bullock-carts piled with people and goods, all streaming past in the pale light of dawn. Some families walked, the fathers wheeling bicycles laden with household possessions, the mothers with infants straddled across their hips. Everyone was clearly anxious, with drawn faces, yet strangely silent. The drivers of the cars seemed unnaturally patient, drifting along at walking pace without even a touch of their horns, something that would have been unimaginable in the hectic rush of Phnom Penh's traffic a few days previously. There were even a few groups of soldiers of the now-defunct Republic walking in threes and fours with their rifles slung across their shoulders, not frightened, but joking among themselves, happy now the war was over.

We had gone about a hundred yards, easing along like flotsam in this river of people, when I heard an explosion. Over to my right, round a corner from our house, a huge column of smoke rose into the air. Within a few minutes ambulances and a fire engine, bells ringing and lights flashing, cut across in front of us, forcing us to a temporary halt.

Despite the sense of urgency in the crowds around us, despite the closeness of the battle, I felt we were in no real danger. Even after years of civil war, even after all my father's warnings about the nature of the Khmer Rouge, I believed everything would again be the way it had been in the Cambodia I had always known, before the civil war started.

I came originally from Oudong, a village twenty-five miles north of Phnom Penh, where my father, Chhor, made a living as a small trader. He was not rich – our red-tiled house had only three rooms and a floor of hard-packed earth – but he and my mother, Loan, were ambitious for me, the eldest of five children. I was sent off to Phnom Penh, so that I could get a good high school education. I was an excellent student. Indeed, when I was seventeen, I was the best mathematician in my year in the whole country.

I gave no thought to politics then. My teenage years formed a sort of golden age of stability compared to what followed. Cambodia was neutral, our ruler Prince Sihanouk was popular, the country seemed to be developing without stress, and the war in Vietnam was a distant murmur. There was no talk of American involvement in South-East Asia.

As a bright student, I was eligible for education abroad on a government scholarship. Traditionally, Cambodian students went to France, but France had become the centre of opposition to Sihanouk, and I, along with several others, was sent instead to Montreal, where I studied engineering.

I returned to Cambodia in 1965, to a new life. I joined the Ministry of Public Works, and got married to my first wife, Thary, living (as usual for newly married couples) with Thary's parents. It was a large house, for her father, Mr Khem, was a well-off official in the Ministry of Finance. Our son, Sudath, was born in 1967. We seemed all set for a rosy future.

Looking back, however, there were portents of unrest even then. Sihanouk was the self-proclaimed father of the nation. Soon tales of nepotism and corruption were rife. Now, moreover, the war in Vietnam was at its height. Sihanouk, eager to stay on good terms with his powerful neighbour, had secretly given his agreement that the North Vietnamese could use the remote eastern areas of Cambodia for the transport of men and arms to South Vietnam. This in its turn drew the attention of the United States. Cambodia's traditional neutrality had been compromised.

In reaction against these developments, Cambodia's own minute band of insurgents, the Khmer Rouge, led mostly by French-educated intellectuals, received a steady stream of support from disaffected Cambodians.

Little of this impinged on our existence. I had worries enough of my own. In 1969, my life was struck by tragedy. Just as we were looking forward to the birth of our next child, Thary, who was just twenty-four, went down with hepatitis. She never recovered. Both she and the baby died in childbirth. For a year, I mourned her, relying on Thary's two younger sisters, Anyung, who was twenty-one, and in particular the nineteen-year-old Any, to help look after Sudath while I was at work.

Eventually, as if it were the most natural thing in the world, I fell in love with Any. She was a beautiful girl, with her shoulder-length black hair and slim figure. At twenty she was happy to assume the burdens of domesticity and had come to love

Sudath as her own. We married. In 1971, our first son, Nawath, was born, and in 1973, Staud arrived.

Through the early 'seventies, I rose to become Director of the Department of New Works and Equipment in the ministry, a position that protected me and the family from the political and economic consequences of the growing civil war. Any had never known any other life but her parents' house, and never questioned my political judgment. We were, I suppose, more than a little complacent, like almost everyone we knew.

Sihanouk's policy of trying to please everyone had by now undermined any semblance of neutrality. There were so many North Vietnamese in the country – an estimated forty thousand – that President Nixon ordered them to be bombed, a secret extension to the war that was to have devastating consequences, for him and us. The effects of the raids were exactly the opposite of those intended – they drove the communists deeper into Cambodia.

In 1970, to great acclaim, Sihanouk was overthrown by the Prime Minister and army chief, Lon Nol, who promised to root out corruption and expel the Vietnamese. Sihanouk fled to Peking, and, astonishingly, declared support for the guerrilla fighters, the Khmer Rouge, his previous enemies. This army of insurgents – increasingly made up of peasants – he now termed liberators, down-playing their communist ideology.

At first, we had high hopes of Lon Nol. But as time went by, it became clear he was not up to the task he had set himself. He had a stroke, and was partially paralysed. The administration and the armed forces remained sunk in corruption and complacency. The army failed to make any impact on either the North Vietnamese or the Khmer Rouge, even with the help of the US. The Khmer Rouge, backed by the Chinese, benefited. The country collapsed into all-out civil war, with catastrophic inflation that forced those of us who could travel abroad to hoard foreign currency, dollars in particular. In 1970, a dollar was worth 60 riels; in 1975, 2,000.

Strangely, in Phnom Penh, because of Lon Nol's obvious deficiencies, we – that is, the professionals and intellectuals – were inclined to believe Sihanouk's line that the underground were nationalists rather than communists. Indeed, their programme, as adopted by Sihanouk's Peking-based National United Front of

Kampuchea, did not mention communism, making much of reassuring phrases like 'the Cambodian people', 'national independence', 'peace', 'neutrality', 'freedom', and 'democracy'.

I, too, joined in the opposition to Lon Nol, forming an organization we called the Bees Club, a social forum for like-minded professionals – bureaucrats, university teachers, officers, and a few opposition politicians. We were against totalitarians, communists and the Lon Nol regime alike, but not supporters of anyone in particular. The Americans we regarded as a mixed blessing – they were anti-communist, but also supported the discredited and incapacitated Lon Nol. We were for a government of national reconciliation, which meant, if possible, a coalition government including the Khmer Rouge.

I certainly did not believe the Khmer Rouge were anything but patriots, for I knew many people who supported them, and some who had joined them. My father, who saw and spoke to countless refugees before moving to the city with the rest of the family in 1972, repeatedly said I was wrong. I used to tell him not to be so pessimistic, insisting he was just swallowing government propaganda. After all, I said, Sihanouk had his own men in the guerrillas and would never support the sort of people who killed their own countrymen and destroyed pagodas. Some might be communists, I said, but they were first and foremost Cambodians like us.

There was a feeling, in early March 1975, that there would be a change of government, that the Khmer Rouge would force Lon Nol out, but we assumed this would lead to the orderly establishment of a new regime. Somehow, I imagined Sihanouk would be part of the political solution, whatever it was.

True, many people did pack up and leave, and there were reasons enough to be fearful if you were a high official who owed your position to the Lon Nol regime. But on April 1st, Lon Nol was persuaded to leave, thus removing the final obstacle to a negotiated settlement and leaving the government nominally in the hands of Long Boret. With the old regime as good as dead, I knew I had nothing to fear. I was merely an engineer. There was no need for us to leave the country. I looked forward to the end of the war, and to playing my part in the new Cambodia.

* * *

It took two tedious hours immersed in this mass of humanity to cover the couple of miles to the Psar Silep quarter, the residential area over towards the river. This was the heart of the city, Phnom Penh at its best – broad, leafy streets and detached, French colonial-style villas. It is an open city, spacious, with plenty of room for trees and gardens between the drab glass-and-concrete blocks. This was where my cousin Oan lived, in a fine two-storey house protected by a head-high brick wall with a metal gate. It was a good meeting place, for Oan was alone in his big house, his wife and son having left the country with his wife's parents some weeks earlier.

While my parents-in-law and Anyung went on to take refuge in the home of an aunt on the next block, I turned the Fiat into the side-street where Oan lived. In the house, I was surprised to see a mass of relatives – Oan with his two sisters and their families, my two sisters, my two brothers, their families, and my parents – about thirty people altogether. Everyone crowded around, clearly relieved to see us. They had all been there for an hour or so already, and were getting anxious about us.

As the children ran off to play with their cousins in the garden, the women began to prepare some food, all except my sister, Vuoch, who remained to talk with the men. At twenty-one, Vuoch was the intellectual of the family. She was in her third year at the university studying engineering, a most unusual choice for a Cambodian girl. She cultivated a severe expression and simple styles of dress, as if determined to escape from the traditional feminine role in our country and assert herself in a man's world. She was as warm-hearted as her older sister Keng when talking to my mother, or Any, or the children, but she was certainly more easily distracted: at the merest hint of a political discussion, she would be drawn irresistibly away from whatever she was doing, with a little smile, and a promise to return in a minute or two.

On a side-table, a radio was on, but there was no news, just the continuous blaring of military music. With a dismissive wave of his hand at the radio, my brother Theng asked what I thought was happening in the town. Theng was only two years younger than me, married, with two boys and a baby girl, but he deferred to me in political matters, not only because I was older but because I did after all have a position in the ministry. He was a primary school teacher, still living with my parents, and was anyway far more interested in basketball than politics. He had the build for it, which made him a useful fellow to have around when there was physical work to be done. Oh, I said knowingly, officials on both sides would be working out a settlement and. . .

'Why don't they announce it on the radio then?' Vuoch butted in.

'Yes, it's odd,' I said, without looking at her, not wishing to be too direct with her. 'Anyway, no need to worry. We'll soon have a new government with Prince Sihanouk back in power. You'll see.'

'Well, he'd better not make any of the same mistakes again.'

There was a brief silence. To break the mood, someone said: 'What do you think, Sarun?'

We all exchanged glances. Poor Sarun. He had been a teacher until two years previously, when he had a motorcycle accident in which he received a severe head-injury. He had never been the same since. Once an extrovert, always ready with a joke, he had become moody and unpredictable. Most of the time, he was as timid as a child, and lucid enough, but sometimes he became violently angry, or would go off on some tangent totally unrelated to the subject under discussion. Of course, the school hadn't been able to keep him on, but he could never understand why. One thing remained unchanged: his love for his five-year-old daughter Srey Rath and his wife, Keng.

'What do I think?' Sarun said, with his usual bland smile. 'I don't know. But with Sihanouk back in power, maybe I'll get my job back. What do you think, Thay?'

He believed himself to be the victim of some terrible conspiracy, and it would never do to get into a discussion about it now. I smiled, and shrugged.

'What are you smiling at, Thay?' Keng's mildly accusing voice came from the kitchen door. 'Sarun is sure to get his job back when things settle down. Now Sarun, dear, perhaps you could fetch Srey for me? The food's almost ready.'

We all admired Keng. Her loyalty and protectiveness were a godsend to Sarun.

Luckily, at this point we were interrupted by a squeal of brakes and the clatter of a bicycle falling roughly against a wall, and there at the door stood my strapping young cousin, Sim. He looked round, with a broad grin on his face, as if he had just come back from a joy-ride round town.

'Sim!' said Oan, in surprise. 'What are you doing here, without your parents?'

'Oh, aren't they here? I thought. . .' He broke off, with an exaggerated frown.

'Come on, Sim,' said my father, who knew the boy of old. Sim, at eighteen, was still at high school, but he was no intellectual. He was always dashing round the streets with friends, and his relatives were a little tired of his escapades. Somehow, though, he always managed to get away with it. No one could resist his smile and his protestations of innocence.

'I thought they'd be here, uncle. I went off to watch a house on fire, and then I couldn't find them, so I came on here. I'd better go and find them.'

'No, no, silly boy. They'll be all right. You stay here. It's too dangerous to go out again.'

And there we settled, sitting wherever we could, eating the rice, meat and fruit provided by Any and the others in the kitchen. Above the muffled noise of the refugees crowding past the end of the side-street and the strident music from the radio, we began again to discuss what was going to happen. I repeated my conviction that there would be a political solution. Mostly people agreed or kept silent. If Theng was reticent, my other brother, Thoeun, was even more so. He had been raised away from home, lived with his parents-in-law, and felt himself to be something of an outsider in the family. Vuoch had had her say. Any, as always in a large group, retreated inside herself, looking round with large eyes at whoever was speaking. Oan, too, contributed little, although we were in his house. He was well-off, but not because he was particularly quick-witted. He had been lucky enough to marry into a rich family – his father-in-law owned several theatres – and was a bit out of his depth in political discussions.

But my father was not so reticent, repeating his pessimistic warnings about the Khmer Rouge being communists. He was a tall, sturdy man, sturdy in character as well as physique, patient, of few words and much respected for his good sense. But his dire predictions irritated me. I had heard them all before. Again and again I told him not to worry.

'It's all rumour, father, just propaganda,' I said, trying not to show impatience. 'Look at the programme, there's nothing in it about communism. Some of those people are my friends. They would not lie. Why should they? Ours is a rich country. They would not have to do anything harsh to feed the people.'

My father fell silent. It was my mother who now spoke. She looked frail, being several inches smaller than her daughters, and she had spent her whole life in our village, raising the family. But when she chose to speak, you could see where Vuoch's combative spirit came from.

'You show some respect to your father, Thay,' she said, quietly but firmly. 'We have talked to people who fled, people whose families were killed, whose houses were burned. The Khmer Rouge are hard. They're communists, like Mao's people in China. If they rule, it will mean the end of our religion. You can forget about happiness.'

'Oh, mother!' I said. 'What do you mean, communists? Some of them may be, but they know the Cambodian people are too religious and too much in love with life to accept communism. They're patriots first and communists second. They will abide by the will of the people.' I knew that I was right. After all, my contacts gave me privileged information. Besides, I had been abroad, and had a wider view. And what could my parents, a mere village trader and his wife, possibly know about the real position?

For an hour or so we talked, interrupted now and then by the shouts of the children and the occasional boom of a distant shell. Then suddenly, around ten o'clock, the military music on the radio was interrupted by a voice, a shrill new voice we had not heard on national broadcasts before: 'Attention, please! Stand by for an important announcement!' Everyone hushed everyone else and called relatives in from the kitchen and the garden. I beckoned Any, who hurried in after a quick glance at Nawath, playing happily in the garden with his cousins.

Silence fell.

Over the radio came the frail voice of the Buddhist Patriarch, Huot Tat. We all looked at each other, and smiled reassurance.

Huot Tat was not only the country's highest religious authority, the very symbol of stability; he was also a member of our family, my father's uncle.

I felt particular attachment to him. He had taken a close interest in my education, and it was, I'm sure, as a result of that contact that I had as a student begun to find strength in the tenets of Buddhism. It seemed to fit my aspirations and character. Salvation, Buddha taught, lies in oneself. God can do nothing unless you are willing to take the initiative. All virtue and all evil will have their effects, either in this life or the next, but you are always free to improve yourself, to 'make merit', to refine your moral sense, by praying for guidance and clarity of vision, by performing good actions and by making the best of the skills and virtues you have been given. I had certainly done my best, thanks in no small measure to the influence of Huot Tat.

So I was as eager as everyone else – perhaps more eager – to find reassurance in the words of this venerable old man, whose status was unquestioned, whose guidance and blessing would inevitably be sought by the new regime.

'Don't be alarmed,' he said. 'Stop fighting. Peace is coming now. Our country has passed through a difficult time. We must rebuild.' That was all, and all that was required.

Then another voice came on the air, that of General Mey Sichan, the Chief of Staff of the Republican armed forces. 'All soldiers should lay down their arms,' he said, 'to avoid a bloodbath while the negotiations are continuing with our brothers.'

It's all over, I thought. 'Wonderful,' I whispered to Any, giving her a hug. We all smiled round at each other in relief.

But a second later the general's words were swamped by a confused babble. Then another voice broke through, forcefully, as if someone had seized the microphone: 'The war is won by weapons and not by negotiations! The government forces have surrendered! The underground forces have triumphed! Now the war is over!'

Then sudden, unnerving silence. No music, just static. Our smiles vanished. Someone switched the radio off and on again, testing it. Nothing. We stared at each other, wide-eyed.

In the silence, I became aware of the murmur of voices and roar

11

of engines from the street. We and our neighbours were securely locked in our houses, but outside tens of thousands of people were crowding into the centre of Phnom Penh. Where were they going? I could only suppose they intended to camp in the pagodas, in the university, and in the grounds of the public buildings until the fighting was over.

An hour passed. The children went on playing, while the adults talked quietly amongst themselves. Then in the distance we heard cheers. Sim leapt outside to see what was going on, and then rushed back in, shouting 'It's the Khmer Rouge!'

So it really was over. We all hurried out to open the gates and watch.

Up and down the street, the houses and windows were dotted with white. People were hanging out shirts, sheets, towels, anything white they could find. Then the crowd began to surge down the street away from us. It became clear that they were going to watch some sort of procession on the Preah Monivong, a main route from the south that crossed our side-street about a hundred yards away. Waving Any to stay with the children, I and several of the others shouldered our way through the crowd to the front. There, I saw my first Khmer Rouge soldiers.

The roadway was clear, with the crowds pressed back along the sidewalks. Down the middle of the road, in single file, divided into squads of about fifty, walked a line of soldiers such as I had never seen before. The sight was soon to be familiar across the world from film and photographs, but we had no warning of what they were like. They were all in black, in simple pyjama-like uniforms, without decoration, but neatly buttoned. They wore black Chinese caps and Ho Chi Minh sandals – sections of car tyre kept on with strips of inner tube. Some carried AK47s, others had rocket launchers. All of them had chequered *kramars* – headscarves that they wore round their necks or over their caps. They were not walking in step, but there was nothing sloppy about them. They just stared straight ahead, unsmiling. Not one of them appeared to be over the age of eighteen. I had had no expectations, and felt no surprise, certainly no sense of impending doom, but there was something disturbing about those stony-faced teenagers, all the more so when I saw the welcome they were receiving. City people followed the columns, clapping and cheering in an outpouring of relief, all fear gone. But the crowd's enthusiasm made no impression on the grim youngsters. They just stared straight ahead, blank, impassive as automatons.

We were all too relieved, however, to read any significance into their behaviour. The war was over. We had come through unscathed. No wonder the young people hugged each other and waved their pieces of white cloth. Far from feeling fear, I – all of us – were reassured by the passivity of the Khmer Rouge. It was astonishing that the fighting should have stopped so suddenly, that against all our expectations the centre of the city should have been penetrated without violence.

Only once did I feel a pang of fear. From a side road emerged a military truck driven by a Republican soldier, perhaps on his way home, delighted not to be fighting any more. A Khmer Rouge held up his hand, signalling him to get out. The man, unarmed, leaped down and fled. One of the Khmer Rouge, clutching his weapon, sprinted after him and caught him. He pinned the soldier against the wall, and levelled his rifle at him. Then, after a long moment, the Khmer Rouge calmly ordered the soldier to take off his uniform jacket, abandon his vehicle, and leave. The man did as he was told, and the Khmer Rouge turned away. I relaxed again, feeling more certain than ever that things would be all right.

We returned to Oan's house elated, chattering, joking, making plans. I said I would be taking my family back home. Others said they would go to the beach to celebrate. Everything seemed about to return to normal. Any's parents, in their Austin, stopped by on their way home. We were on the point of leaving ourselves when Oan said, 'Why not stay to lunch?' Why not? My parents-in-law would look after the house until we got there. The children were playing in the garden. It was only eleven o'clock in the morning. There was no hurry. We stayed on, laughing and talking.

We were having our lunch, and I was already wondering whether I would be going to work as usual the next day, when a man entered, breathless. He was the caretaker of the house belonging to Oan's parents-in-law, who lived about a mile and a half away, back along the route of the Khmer Rouge advance. When they had left Cambodia some weeks earlier with Oan's wife and child, they had entrusted their house to this man, now standing in our doorway, frightened and dishevelled. 'The Khmer

Rouge made us get out of our houses! They told us to leave the city! All of us!' he said, obviously distraught. 'What should I do?'

Instantly, the mood changed. We stopped eating, and began to bombard him with questions:

'Are you sure?'

'Why?'

'You must have misunderstood!'

'We didn't hear them say anything like that.'

Was he playing some sort of a joke? An evacuation, what an extraordinary idea!

We had to find out more, and went out to ask our neighbours what was happening. They too had heard rumours of an evacuation. But nothing had come over the radio. The official silence seemed to justify continued optimism.

We no longer knew what to do. Should we all leave Oan's home? We desperately needed more information to make some sort of a plan. I suggested we consult our uncle, the Patriarch Huot Tat, who lived in the Onalom Pagoda, a couple of miles away, by the river. He was bound to know what was going on. We would get advice from him, as well as receiving a measure of protection.

No one could think of anything better to do. All of us packed into our three cars – my Fiat, my brother Theng's Peugeot and Oan's Mercedes. Once again, we joined the slow procession of fugitives. The streets were still jammed. Now, those heading towards the centre of town from the outskirts had been joined by crowds of others who had been thrown out of their houses. People looked stunned, but there was no confusion and no noise, just a mass swirling slowly forward, a current of pedestrians, cyclists, trishaws and cars. From time to time a shot rang out in the distance. These reminders of war kept us alert, for we had no idea who was shooting at whom. Suddenly everyone was very law-abiding and courteous, scrupulously obeying the rules of the road, afraid, it seemed, of causing accidents, afraid of being noticed.

Only once in the next hour did I see any Khmer Rouge, when thirty of them came out of an adjacent street, marching silently in single file in the middle of the road, pretending to be unaware of the crowds around them. Cars and pedestrians pulled to one side to let them past. They marched by without paying us any attention, as if to avoid being contaminated by us.

The Patriarch's pagoda was set in its own compound, a tall two-storey temple with a steep yellow-tiled roof, and a number of smaller roofs lapping like eyebrows over the pillared porches. It stood back from the river-bank, overlooking the vast expanse of water formed where the Mekong and the Tonle Sap, meandering down from the north, met before winding off to the south in two huge branches, the Mekong proper and the Bassac. Round about, among trees and flowering gardens, were a number of buildings in which the saffron-robed monks lived.

We parked the cars, took the children, and went to the Patriarch's residence. After leading the family into the large entrance hall, a tiled area without walls which was already packed with perhaps a hundred people, some of us – my parents, myself, Oan, and my brothers – went into the Patriarch's reception room.

There, sitting on a bench, was the Patriarch, a surprisingly sturdy figure for his eighty-five years, his shaven head held high, his broad face that of a much younger man. Dressed in his yellow robe, one shoulder bare, he was surrounded by a crowd of monks and civilians. Apparently dozens of other people had had the same idea as us, coming here to find out what was going on and seek the protection of the Patriarch. I recognized two of the men at once, General Chhim-Chhuon, former aide-de-camp of Marshal Lon Nol, and General Mao Sum Khem, Chief Operations Co-ordinator for the Republican armed forces. Both these men, formerly so bombastic, now seemed humble and uncertain. Other men in civilian clothes were clearly their bodyguards. We knelt down amidst the others on the floor, and made our three-fold obeisances with our hands held together in front of our foreheads. Then we sat back cross-legged, listening to the conversation.

There seemed to be two main questions: how should the Republican officers behave towards the victors? And why had the civilian population been obliged to evacuate their houses – for it seemed from reports that the whole city now was being evacuated? The Patriarch was urging calm. Perhaps, he said, there was no general evacuation. The Khmer Rouge programme had never made any mention of mass deportations. 'It is not logical there should be an evacuation,' I heard him say. 'Remain calm and wait for orders.'

The Patriarch asked a monk to telephone first to the President of the Cambodian Red Cross and then to Chau Sau, the General Secretary of the Opposition Democratic Party. Between them, these two should have been able to provide some information. But no one seemed to know anything, except that the Hotel Le Phnom and the French Embassy had been designated as neutral territory by the Red Cross.

Someone called for silence, pointing to a transistor radio on the table beside the Patriarch. The government station was on the air again, with a very brief message. All ministers and all senior officers of the armed forces were called to the Ministry of Information that afternoon at four p.m. 'Now you know what to do,' the Patriarch said. 'I will send my own representative there as well.'

After the generals and one of the monks had left, we wandered back and forth asking each other what it all meant, wondering whether to stay or go to the French Embassy or the Hotel Le Phnom. The Patriarch remained sitting cross-legged on his bench, waiting calmly.

As the afternoon drew on, the waiting became unbearable. I agonized over whether we should leave, but a strange foreboding, a lack of certainty, the possibility of being caught up in the evacuation, the impossibility of making any plans, all prevented me from suggesting that we go. At one point, to relieve the tension I asked the Patriarch's permission to call the French Embassy. When I asked for asylum and said that I was at the moment seeking refuge with the Venerable One, the voice at the other end said it was impossible for any Cambodian to enter the French Embassy. The gate was guarded by the Khmer Rouge. 'Even if the Patriarch himself came to the door,' the man said, 'the Khmer Rouge would not let him through.' I put the phone down, shocked that any Cambodians might not recognize the Patriarch's authority. For the first time I began to realize that we were trapped.

I tried to call my parents-in-law and Anyung at home. No answer. There was nothing to do but wait. I wandered back and forth, trying to reassure Any, telling her about the calls, exchanging a few words with the children. They were happy enough, playing with children of their own age and running in and out of the house.

At dusk, about six p.m., the Patriarch's representative came back. I followed him as he wove his way through the crowds to the Patriarch, who raised a hand for silence. I tried to read some good news into the messenger's face. It was a blank.

There were many senior Republican officers and ministers present at the meeting, he said, including the Prime Minister, Long Boret. The monk had sat next to a Khmer Rouge officer who had addressed him in respectful tones. The officer had extolled the virtues of the Khmer Rouge and said that now reconstruction could get under way with the help of former officials, intellectuals and technicians. When the monk asked about the evacuation, the officer shook his head. Such an order made no sense. Why order the evacuation of able-bodied men just when the economy was to be set to rights? 'He told me: I can give you my word of honour that I have never heard of this order. It is an imperialist manoeuvre. Their agents want to sow the seeds of panic in the population.'

Relieved, I went out to reassure Any that the rumour of an evacuation was not true – only to hear reports from refugees still streaming into the pagoda that it was still in progress. I became increasingly puzzled and alarmed. Either the officer was misinformed, or he was lying. No, no, the monk said, when questioned by Oan, the officer could not have been lying. But perhaps he had not been quite as knowledgeable as he seemed.

Night fell. I tried a second time to call my parents-in-law. Still no reply. Had they been driven out of the city already? I imagined the worst: Any's father and mother and her sister Anyung tossed out into that stream of refugees, with nowhere to go. I exchanged glances with Any, wondering if she shared my anxieties, and smiled reassurance at her.

Worn out by the long day and the worry, we ended up bedding down on mats on the pagoda's tiled floor, all thirty of us, divided into families, the children – even Nawath – awed into obedience by the novelty and confusion. I tucked my radio under some clothing and tuned in to Voice of America in Cambodian to see if there was any news. Nothing. I switched off, but found it hard to sleep. There was constant coming and going as new people arrived, looking for space to lie down, each arrival providing additional confirmation that the evacuation was still proceeding. Hundreds crowded into the pagoda and its compound, even as many thousands more were heading past, out of town.

Soon after most of us were asleep – it must have been about nine-thirty p.m. – a Khmer Rouge officer entered the hall, a pistol in his hand. He was about my age, in his early thirties. In the harsh glow of the electric lights, he looked round at us suspiciously, pointing his pistol around at the drowsy figures on the floor as if expecting to find opposition. Then his gaze fell on half a dozen bicycles and three motorcycles parked by the entrance.

'Who do these motorbikes belong to?' he shouted. No one spoke. He returned his gun to his holster, went over to the bikes and seized a blue Honda which looked brand new. It was chained to two other motorbikes. Twice he repeated, 'Who is the owner of this motorbike?' and then 'Angkar needs it!'

Angkar – the Organization: it was the first time I had heard the word used in this way.

Still nobody answered. The officer shoved the motorcycle to the ground, took his gun out, and put it against the security chain, aiming down the corridor. He shot twice, in quick succession. The chain split apart. The noise in that silent, crowded hall, with children sleeping all around, was a fearful shock. Children woke and looked around, dazed. Seconds later, the officer had gone, with the motorcycle, leaving us in stunned silence. Any looked at me. I gestured for her to keep quiet.

After a minute, Any muttered to me, 'How can he do that?'

'What can we do?' I replied.

My father gave me a long, steady look.

'Well, maybe they're not all like that,' I said to him, defensively, still talking in a whisper.

Fifteen minutes later, two other soldiers came in and seized the other two motorcycles without saying a word.

It was clear to me, and to all of us, that these actions were far more than mere theft or appropriation. The Patriarch had an importance that far exceeded his religious role. He was respected in even the remotest villages of Cambodia, yet here, in quick succession, we had seen three people who apparently had no idea where they were, let alone any respect for the Patriarch himself. It was the first indication we had had that the moral values of centuries were about to be overturned.

Before falling asleep again our eldest, Sudath, asked, 'Father, when are we going home?' I remained silent. It was Any who replied, 'Sleep, my child, we will be home tomorrow.' I couldn't believe it any more. Nor, I'm sure, could she.

2 EVACUATION

Long before dawn, all of us woke together. Slowly, leaving the children asleep, we began to pack. No one said much. We were sure that we would soon be ordered out, along with everyone else. And indeed, even before it was fully light, three Khmer Rouge soldiers appeared at the door. The room fell silent.

'Comrades! You have to go now!' one of them said. His words chilled me, not so much because of the order – that merely confirmed what we had expected – nor its tone, which was not impolite. What shocked me was that once again the Patriarch had been ignored. 'We have to purify the town!' the officer went on. 'But don't take much with you, it's only for three days. You have to leave because the Americans will bomb the city.'

There was no thought of arguing, for there was nothing on the radio to contradict what he said. As we finished packing, talking about what to do for the best, I said that if evacuation was inevitable, we had better go back to Oan's place and pick up blankets and cooking utensils. Any wanted to fetch more things from our home and check on her parents, but I told her it would take too long, and might even be dangerous, to go right back across town. At all costs, we had to stick together. If we became separated, there was no knowing how or when we would meet again.

When we were ready, I led the family back into the Patriarch's room to pay our last respects.

He was sitting on his bench, surrounded by yellow-robed monks.

'You have to go now,' he said quietly, as we made our obeisances. 'Be careful.'

'What will you do, grandfather?' I asked.

'Don't worry about me, I am too old to go anywhere. I must stay whatever happens. Take care of yourself, your family and your children. Do nothing wrong.'

As he spoke, it struck me that I might not see him again. That thought, and the old man's serenity in the face of danger, brought tears to my eyes. 'Children, pay your respects,' I said. As they

20

bowed goodbye, the Patriarch stepped forward and placed his hand on both their heads in turn. 'My child,' he said to each, 'I wish you a good life. Be good.'

As we made our way out of the pagoda, across the compound, to the cars parked in the crowded street, I found myself pondering the officer's words. American bombings? The Americans had left us to our downfall on April 12th. If they had wanted to bomb the Khmer Rouge, they would have done so then, before the collapse of the city. Why do it now? And why send us out for just three days? If the Americans *were* going to bomb the city, why wouldn't they do it for longer than that? I could make no sense of his words.

Driving back south, towards Oan's place, we found ourselves heading against the current of people, the same expressionless pedestrians carrying bundles of belongings, laden bicycles, motorcycles, trishaws, cars. This whole sector of the city seemed to be moving north. But after half a mile or so, the crowds began to thin out. Apparently, those to the south had been told to move off southwards. Now there were only a few stragglers. Before our eyes a city was dying, its life draining from its now almost lifeless heart.

It occurred to me we might be running a risk, driving in the wrong direction like this. But the exodus was not being strictly patrolled. As we headed into the empty areas, we caught sight of only one group of soldiers, and turned down a side-street to avoid them. Two or three times, a Jeep or a private car filled with Khmer Rouge passed in the opposite direction, driving at high speed. No one took any notice of our convoy.

We reached Oan's at about eight a.m. Though most of the houses in the area were empty already, a few of our neighbours remained, not yet ready to leave. Oan and I checked with one family who had just left their home. Their orders had been similar to ours. An American bombing was imminent. Everyone had to leave for three days. To arguments and prevarications, the Khmer Rouge had replied quietly and reasonably: 'Why make a fuss about three days? Why make a fuss about family members? Don't worry about your things. We have lived for years without family to liberate you. Three days is nothing. After that you will return. Don't worry.'

In addition to the clothing we already had, we began to collect together food, blankets and kitchen utensils, the women discussing among themselves what would be best for the children. There were several people whom neither Any nor I knew intimately – Theng's wife, Lao; Lao's mother; Aeng, Thoeun's wife, who was five months pregnant; Aeng's parents; Oan's sisters and their families. But already, under my mother's firm direction, the women were working well together. Clothing, my mother insisted, that was the most important thing. The refugees who had come through Oudong had told her that in the Liberated Zones – those controlled by the Khmer Rouge – clothes were the only objects that had any real value. Again, I tended to dismiss her advice. After all, I said, we were only going for three days.

Three days: there was something reassuring in those words. Although I couldn't believe in the imminence of an American bombardment, I and all the others accepted the three day story. It sounded a good grace period, time in which we would adapt to the new regime, and the regime to the problems of planning reconstruction.

While we worked, deciding who would have what, some of us took turns hurrying back and forth to talk to passing families. Each of them had their own story, the dramas and tragedies of a city in disarray. One family said their teenage son had gone outside to cheer the victors and had vanished. Some people had been separated from their families, and were heading out of town alone. Some heads of families who had gone on errands across town the day before had never returned. An old woman with her three grandchildren described how the children's father had taken their mother to hospital, and had not come back. It seemed everyone was being evacuated north, south, or west away from the river, depending where they happened to be when the Khmer Rouge arrived. We had been lucky not to run directly into a patrol clearing the area round the pagoda.

At one point, Any asked me to call our house again to check on her parents. Again, no one answered. Should I go there to see what had happened? No, I couldn't risk being separated from Any and the children. Still, I argued with myself, why was I so worried? We were, after all, only leaving for three days.

EVACUATION

All of us – all thirty-two, for I counted them carefully – packed into three cars, Any carrying Staud in the front with me, the other two children in the back with my parents and Keng's little girl, Srey. Keng herself sat on the pillion of Vuoch's motorcycle. The others piled into Theng's and Oan's cars. Packing in the bundles of food and clothing, I was glad we had all had the foresight to fill up our tanks and buy those extra cans the day before. One of Oan's relatives had a motorcycle, and offered Thoeun a ride. My young cousin, Sim, rode his bicycle.

In convoy, we turned on to the broad, tree-lined Preah Monivong Boulevard, heading south past two- and three-storey office blocks and graceful villas. Once again, we found ourselves in a crush of people, the same slow moving mass of pedestrians and vehicles. Like everybody else, our aim was only to get out of the city. We had no idea where we were going to spend the night.

Not far from the house, we saw two corpses, Republican soldiers, face down on the pavement. Nobody took any notice of them. Yesterday we had heard an ambulance rushing to a fire. Today, apparently, there were no public services.

Then, a few hundred yards further on, I saw Khmer Rouge waving people out of their houses. Men and women were crying. Travelling at walking pace as we were, with the windows open, we could hear them in their doorways pleading with the Khmer Rouge, their hands together above their foreheads, begging for a few more minutes to wait for a child, or a mother, or collect a few more possessions. The Khmer Rouge were unmoved, though always polite. I heard snatches of the same arguments: 'You shouldn't cry . . . three days is nothing . . . you will see all your family then. . .' No threats, just the steady stream of implacable orders. Only once did I hear a Khmer Rouge show a hint of impatience – 'Hurry up! A day has already gone by and the Americans may bomb us at any moment!'

As I scanned the crowds, in the faint hope of seeing my parents-in-law, or someone who knew them, I saw a few people I knew must be senior officials, engineers, or teachers. There were even some doctors and nurses, still dressed in white. No one, it seemed, had escaped the round-up. One young man was carrying his sick father on his back. Women carried babies on their hips,

the lame limped on crutches. Twice I saw patients in wheeled
hospital beds being pushed along by relatives. Some people had
small bundles of food or clothing, some carried a chicken or a
duck slung over their shoulders, some had nothing but the clothes
they wore. One little boy of seven or eight was wandering
through the crowd, crying pathetically for his mother, staring up
at every adult, hoping to see someone he recognized. There was
a feeling of indefinable tension, as people looked around
desperately for friends and acquaintances and lost family
members. Deprived of everything by which they had until a few
days before defined their lives, they seemed to be seeking any sort
of reassurance, linking themselves to passing strangers with
gestures and glances.

In amongst the pedestrians and bicycles were the trishaws and
cars, all laden with families, and some piled high with
possessions. Small Citroens and ancient delivery vans overflowed
with bundles of clothing, curtains and incongruous but treasured
items – cookers, sofas, cupboards, and in the back of one van a
pig. Some of the larger cars, the Mercedes and the Peugeots, were
filled with the symbols of former wealth: televisions, tape-decks.
The back of one family estate was entirely taken up by a huge
refrigerator. Why were we going? Where? From one car to
another, we exchanged comments and questions, reassuring each
other that this was only for three days.

By now, it was about ten o'clock, and the heat was building up,
for in Cambodia April is the hottest month of the year. It was
towards the end of the dry season, and there had been no rain for
weeks. The city, or at least this part of it, had become one gigantic
traffic jam, the cars and motorcycles held back by the crush of
slow-moving pedestrians. It seemed to me, as the temperature
rose in the car, and the sweat dampened my shirt, and the children
dozed after their disturbed night, that this snail's pace was an
unconscious way of resisting the Khmer Rouge orders. No one
complained, but it seemed that by delaying our departure from
Phnom Penh we were all trying to give ourselves a better chance
of returning.

We had covered no more than half a mile when I heard a
gun-shot. We all looked round, craning our necks to see what was
happening. Almost at once, there was another shot. Up the street,

on the steps of a villa, lay the body of a young man. He was about eighteen, with long hair – a student, I guessed. Some fifteen yards away from him, a soldier stood, smoke still wafting lazily upwards from his AK47. Everyone around asked each other what had happened. Within a minute, word reached us that the boy had forgotten something in his house. He had turned back, in defiance of the soldier's order, and was about to re-enter his house when the soldier shot him. The soldier had exclaimed: 'This is what happens to recalcitrants.'

Curiously, the scene did not provoke any violent response. As we heard the news, we fell silent, turned, and continued on our way.

By one o'clock, we were crawling towards the Law Faculty, a huge modern three-storey building about a hundred yards long, set back from the road. Here we might have an opportunity to rest. I pointed at the Faculty with its parking areas, still relatively clear, and received nods of agreement. We were all hungry and could do with a break. Slowly, we eased our way through the crowds into the forecourt and parked. There were no objections from the few black-uniformed Khmer Rouge, who were merely watching the exodus, without orders, it seemed, to hurry us along. The place was already buzzing with people who had had the same idea.

Gathering up our food and some of our belongings, we found an empty spot in the hall of the main building, a huge veranda on the first floor. We settled down back from the edge in the shade. As the women began to make a meal from the cooked food that we had with us, Oan, my father and I decided that this would be as good a place as any to stay for the three days that we would be away from our homes.

After eating, we fetched blankets, mats and cooking utensils from the cars, set up camp and tried to rest. Everyone was in desperate need of sleep, everyone, that is, except the children, who had been sleeping in the car. Sim, as usual, started a game, dashing off and urging the children to chase him, until my father told him to behave himself. But by then all six of the children – Nawath and Sudath, Theng's two boys, Thoeun's daughter Sarah, and Keng and Sarun's little girl Srey – were chasing each other round the columns of the hall, in among the other families, with their piles of possessions. They couldn't be allowed to make such a disturbance. Srey, Sarah and Sudath came when they were called, but Nawath was having too much fun with Theng's two sons, Visoth and Amap, to pay any attention. Any, cradling Staud in her arms, called him again as he rushed past – 'Nawath, you come here this instant! Do you want a smack?' – glancing round with an apologetic smile. In the end, it was Vuoch who broke up the game, seizing Nawath and whispering threats of such terrible punishment that he was reduced to wide-eyed silence. Any smiled her thanks, and at last there was peace.

While the children rested, the hall became increasingly crowded. It was lucky we had arrived early. Later arrivals had to settle down either at the edge of the veranda, or outside on the grass. It was going to be a rough three days. The toilets were already crowded and filthy, and there were only two taps working. But there was no anger, no pushing and shoving. Everyone seemed content to make do as best they could.

During the course of the afternoon, I noticed crowds of people carrying cans and bags of food from a large building, the roof of which was visible above the surrounding trees. Soon, everyone knew what was happening. The building was a large municipal cooperative food store. The door had been left open, and people were just helping themselves. The few Khmer Rouge, as detached as if watching animals, made no move to stop them. In the end, the pilfering degenerated into a free-for-all. My two brothers, Theng and Thoeun, went over to see what was happening. By the time they got there, the place was teeming with people, snatching food from the shelves. They managed to grab two bags of rice, a few pounds of sugar and some soya beans. Later we learned that the crush had become such a scramble that two people were killed, suffocated when bags of rice weighing a hundred kilos each fell on them.

That evening, after nightfall, two or three armed Khmer Rouge made rounds, checking by shining their torches right in our faces. I had my radio wrapped in clothing to form a pillow, intending to get some objective news, and did not dare to switch on. Instead, we talked in low voices, falling silent whenever we saw their torch-beams darting about near by.

EVACUATION

The next day the pillaging by the crowds camped in the forecourt and street worsened. Many turned on local homes. People were wandering past laden with whisky bottles, transistors, and cameras. A new economy was being formed before our eyes. The pillagers were not necessarily after the goods for their own sake, but for sale at exorbitant prices. The money was then used to buy food from those who had it, at equally exorbitant prices. Near us, I saw a Chinese trader, alone and rather pathetic – we assumed he had become separated from his family – sitting holding a bag full of money. It was all that he had brought with him. He had no clothes, no rice, no personal belongings, but he did not seem to be worried. He could buy everything he needed. I even bought a few little things myself – soya sauce, corn, two jars of Nescafé, and five cans of condensed milk. There was no confusion and no violence, but I found these scenes depressing. The Khmer Rouge had promised to look after our homes. Was this the best they could offer?

Over the next two days – the 19th and 20th – with nothing much to do but wander round and exchange gossip, I was surprised to see an occasional acquaintance, people I had met professionally once or twice. Actually, this was not quite such a coincidence as it may appear, for Phnom Penh's community of officials was not a large one, and a high proportion were heading out of town in the same direction. They were puzzled, but not despairing. One man, a young engineer, eagerly explained that he quite understood the actions of the Khmer Rouge. They had to take stock of the situation, and the more help we could give them the quicker things would be back to normal. Anyway, whatever happened, he said, people like us would be all right. We were the technocrats, after all, and were indispensable to any regime.

I even bumped into my former boss, General Thappana Nginn, the former Minister of National Defence and of Public Works, who was camped outside under a tree, with his family and his subordinate, Colonel Long Man. Both were in civilian clothes, having shed their uniforms in an attempt to be inconspicuous. They weren't the only ones to abandon any military effects that might suggest a connection with the previous regime. The grounds were already littered with abandoned military ponchos and ground sheets.

I asked the general for his version of recent events. How had the Republicans fallen so quickly? The general, a solidly built man in his fifties, glanced around to make sure that he was not overheard, and began to speak in a low voice. The Republicans, he said, had been duped by the Khmer Rouge. According to him, two top Republican personalities had been in contact with Khmer Rouge leaders, and then persuaded the government to recruit two hundred Khmer Rouge, armed to the teeth, who were said to have deserted the ranks. These two hundred Khmer Rouge soldiers were sent to the front to incite their former colleagues to defect. Of course, exactly the opposite had happened, said the general in hushed tones. The Khmer Rouge had persuaded Republican soldiers to give up, promising them a general amnesty after the Khmer Rouge victory.

That wasn't all. Apparently, the Soviet Union had said to the Republican leaders that if the US left, Russia would provide new arms and equipment, help reinstate Sihanouk as Head of State, and mediate between the Republicans and the moderate faction of the underground to create a coalition to resist the more radical – the Maoist – wing of the Khmer Rouge. The Khmer Rouge, in exchange for a ceasefire, had agreed in principle to negotiate. That was why the Prime Minister, Long Boret, had not fled when the town fell. But it was all a trick, the general insisted. The day they seized power, they renounced their promises. Long Boret and his ministers were all being arrested and many might already be dead. The Russian Embassy had already been closed and the Russians forced to take refuge in the French Embassy.

Listening to him, I felt I was beginning to understand. Only a few hours before, I had heard a strange story which I had dismissed as no more than one of the many rumours I had heard that day. I had been chatting to another Republican officer, and asked him, as I asked many people, why the collapse had been so rapid. Oh, he said, it wasn't just the Republicans' fault. The Americans had deliberately accelerated the country's downfall. 'We had secret codes for communicating with our units,' he explained. 'Each time we tried to contact our troops, we heard the voice of a Khmer Rouge officer. Apparently, the Americans had handed over our codes to the other side.'

It sounded ridiculous. Why should the Americans deliberately betray their allies? But now, listening to the general, it all began to make a weird sort of sense, for the two stories complemented each other. The Americans were faced with disaster anyway. But they knew the Khmer Rouge to consist of two factions – the radical pro-Chinese and Sihanouk's moderates, now apparently being wooed by the Russians. From the American point of view, it would surely be better for the country's new rulers to be pro-Chinese than pro-Russian. So the Americans might well have attempted to undermine the plot to form a pro-Russian coalition.

Listening to the general speak, I began to feel quite angry. I saw now how impotent we had all been amidst the diplomatic haggling. Our former leaders had been more concerned to preserve their power than protect ordinary people. And here, right in front of me, was an example of the incompetence and self-delusion that had led to this mess.

But my anger died quickly. Weren't we all, especially the technocrats, in some way responsible? Wheeling and dealing was the business of politics. But we who should have known better had acquiesced. Our leaders may have deceived us, but we had deceived ourselves. And anyway, whatever the general had done, he was now as much a victim as I was.

After a long pause, I asked him if he wasn't afraid of being recognized, even in his civilian clothes. Apparently the thought hadn't occurred to him. He glanced round furtively and went off immediately to find his family. I saw them later with bulging suitcases heading towards the main building to take refuge in the crowd.

To no avail. I learned later that the Khmer Rouge arrested him and his subordinate and led them off, arms tied behind them. Neither of them were ever seen again.

By late afternoon on the second day, the Law Faculty was in chaos. The taps had run dry, though we still had water left in our bowls from the morning, and there was no more food available nearby. Each family was thrown back on its own resources. The Khmer Rouge wandered about in twos and threes without paying any attention to us, doing nothing to help. Everyone simply continued to wait, believing, as I still did, that the next day or the day after we would all be allowed to go home.

* * *

On the morning of the fourth day, however, three Khmer Rouge began to make their way through the crowds, telling us simply that we would have to move on now. They were as polite as ever, and as implacable. None of us dared ask: Why are we going on, when you said we would be going back?

Well, I said, we would just have to go. The decisions about what to do and when seemed to have fallen on me. Oan wasn't good at expressing opinions, Theng and Thoeun as usual deferred to me as their older brother, and my father preferred the role of adviser to man of action. Our only hope, I said, lay in obeying. There was no water, no food and no information, no basis on which to argue with the Khmer Rouge, even if we had dared. We really had no choice.

Once again, our little convoy of three cars, escorted by Oan's brother-in-law and Vuoch on their motorcycles and Sim on his bicycle, committed itself to the stream of refugees heading out of town.

At the junction of the two main boulevards, Preah Monivong and Preah Norodom, there should have been two possibilities open to us: to cross the Bassac River by the bridge, or travel alongside the river. We found the bridge closed with a tangle of barbed wire. On we went, still at walking pace, heading south along the river.

The mood had changed, I noticed. Now the distinction between rich and poor seemed to have vanished completely. If any of the once well-to-do women were wearing silk blouses, these were now as grubby and sweaty as peasants' cotton shirts. In one large car, I saw a plump middle-aged woman who had surely been used to a life of ease, yet her face bore no trace of make-up, and her hair was a mess. Like the rest of us, she wanted to identify with the poor.

As we eased forward, still in first gear, I saw a young man waving and smiling at me, nodding deferentially. He was an orderly at the Ministry of Public Works. The sight of him made me suddenly apprehensive. If any Khmer Rouge spotted us, they would immediately know I had once been in a position of authority. I beckoned the man over to the car window. 'Don't do that, Sry,' I said, quietly, glancing round. 'Things are different now. We are all the same. Just pretend we're old friends.'

EVACUATION

Because the well-off had abandoned the evidence of their wealth, this sluggish, silent column had a terrible uniformity. There was none of the nervous energy that had infused the first day of the evacuation. No one looked around now, or tried to force their way through the throng, or made impatient gestures. There was hardly a horn or bicycle bell or shout to be heard, nothing to punctuate the low roar of engines, the shuffle of feet and the squeak of wheels. We flowed as steadily as blood from an open wound. Behind us, Phnom Penh was dying.

We travelled all day, stopping only briefly to eat some rice by the roadside, covering a mere four or five miles. That evening, as we entered the suburb of Takhmau, clouds rolled in. The dry season was about to end with the first of the year's torrential downpours. We'd better shelter here for the night, I said, pointing to the local high school, or we'll be drenched. Again, we were lucky. About fifty of us refugees took over two adjacent classrooms. We had hardly spread our blankets when the storm struck. Standing at the window, we saw people who had set up camp by the side of the road scattering in all directions to shelter under trees and roofs, abandoning their bicycles and trishaws. At least the rain brought relief from heat and thirst. As water began to pour off the roof, we ran to the edge of the veranda with our bowls and filled them all to the brim.

The next day, on we went again, the same unremitting pace in first or second gear, the same mass of pedestrians and trishaws pressing southwards. Alongside us or between us, sometimes easing forward, sometimes dropping back, rode Vuoch, Oan's brother-in-law and Sim, keeping us in touch with each other, passing little messages back and forth as we made sure the others were in good spirits.

Any and my mother began to talk. Crammed in with the children, they drew strength from each other. My mother had always been pleased that I had married Any – 'She's a good girl,' she used to say, 'And she really loves Sudath' – and it was good she could show it directly, whispering encouragement and reassurance about Any's parents and Anyung. Any certainly needed it: this was the first time she had ever been separated from her parents. Perhaps it was because of my mother's support that Any was able to accept whatever happened with such equanimity. When we stopped, Nawath always demanded biscuits, and Any always made sure the other children had some as well.

That day we made only about ten miles. It was the same the next day. We were in the country now. On our left lay the river, and on our right, scattered wooden houses on piles, set among orchards. In this depressed and silent throng, only the young people – those who had cheered the Khmer Rouge entry into Phnom Penh and had then found themselves separated from friends and family – were unaffected. They formed small groups of two or three, feeding themselves by running off to pick fruit from orchards, or looting houses.

At night, we rested under the stars, some of us in cars, some on the ground or camped in abandoned houses. At each stop, Oan's family built one fire, while we built another. My mother, assisted by the other two older women, organized Any and the other four younger women to cook and distribute food. No one said much. We were all too taken up with the business of cooking, or setting up camp, or controlling the children, who insisted on treating camping out as a great adventure.

Slowly the crush of refugees eased. Now we began to get an inkling of what the evacuation of the city really meant. People had sunk into themselves, exhausted, depressed, concerned only to keep moving. The further we travelled from the capital, the more exhaustion claimed the sick, the injured, the lame and the old. They sat staring at the passing throng with empty eyes, seeming to accept their fate impassively. Increasingly, we began to see bodies left beside the highway, until we were no longer shocked by the sight. Cocooned in our cars, we hardly ever talked to other family groups.

Twice, however, we saw the bodies of women hanging from trees. Suicides. That shocked me. Suicide is condemned by Buddhist doctrine. On the scale of human life, the higher the life form, the greater one's obligations to it. Human life is the greatest of all gifts, and to throw away one's own was the greatest of sins. Nothing could have better shown the despair of the people.

Everywhere we saw traces of war. Many houses had been blown apart, and burned. All were abandoned. Republican fortifications – wooden emplacements protected by barbed wire and sandbags – were still standing. Bomb craters dotted the countryside. Sugar-palm trees had been blasted to shreds by shell fire.

Then, as the miles slowly slipped by, cars began to run out of fuel. The sides of the road were increasingly littered with abandoned vehicles. Some pushed their useless machines, clinging (as we all did) to the trappings of status. Some of the cars no doubt contained small fortunes in clothing, electrical goods, wads of dollars and packets of jewels, but there was no aura of wealth now about these people. The men in sweat-stained shirts and the women with worried looks and puffy eyes. We passed a middle-aged man, who only a few days before had been working in an office, heaving sweat-soaked at a huge grey BMW; alongside him was his wife, still in a tight skirt and high heels. Out of the corner of my eye, I saw her bang her hand on the bodywork in frustration and wince in pain at a broken nail. How soon, I wondered, would we be in a similar position? Which of our cars would run out of petrol first? Would we, too, resort to pushing, to save what we could?

Like us, everyone was stripped of their past, borne up by the one remaining reality: family. Those with families had a source of encouragement, strength, help, food, and hope for the future. Those who were alone – especially the old – seemed to drift, lost and hopeless.

On the seventh night, while we were making camp, spreading mats on the ground, the motorcycles standing beside us, a Khmer Rouge soldier of about twenty approached, carrying a rifle. Hoping not to draw his attention, we all looked away.

'Excuse me, comrades,' he said politely, pointing to Vuoch's bike, 'whose motorbike is that?'

Silence. No one answered.

'Whose motorbike is that?' he asked again, without raising his voice. Then: 'Angkar needs it.'

Vuoch hesitated for a moment, then got up and went towards him. 'The motorbike is mine,' she said, putting her hands protectively on the bike's handlebars. 'It's all that I have left to carry the baggage. Why don't you take the bicycle instead?'

Sim stood up, eyes wide, aghast at the idea of losing his means of transport.

'Angkar needs that motorbike,' the soldier repeated, ignoring them both. Then, as polite as ever, but with a sinister emphasis, he said, 'Angkar *proposes* to borrow it from you. Do you accept, yes or no?'

'I'm sorry, I cannot let you take it.' She was always inclined to be a little too forceful for her own good. 'I need it. How else can I carry my baggage?'

The soldier's eyes widened. He unslung his rifle, said, 'You dare say "no" to Angkar?', cocked the rifle and stared at Vuoch. Then, suddenly, he fired into the air right in front of her face.

We, of course, had heard everything, while pretending not to. Now we all leapt to our feet in shock. Vuoch's façade of bravado collapsed. She burst into tears, hiding her face in her hands, then ran to my mother, who took her in her arms. The soldier glared round at us all, as if daring us to move. I was frozen with fear.

Not my father, however. 'Comrade,' he said calmly, taking a slow step towards the soldier, 'You may take the motorbike. Pardon my daughter. She is too young to understand.' With a final glare, the soldier settled his rifle back on his shoulder, slowly untied Vuoch's baggage, handed it carefully to my father, mounted, kicked the engine into life, and rode off, leaving Vuoch staring after him, angry, fearful, and for once in her life helpless.

Day by day, we witnessed scenes of increasing desperation. A man separated from his wife and children came begging for rice, holding his hands through the car window, 'I can pay! I have riels!' No one wanted his money. In just a few days money had lost its meaning. Then came others, simply begging, many of them in tears. Even though Buddhists would normally give generously, we refused them all, except an old lady with her grandchild, to whom I gave a handful of rice. It could have been my own mother out there, and my heart went out to her. But as she went on down the line of people and vehicles, my mother said from the back seat, 'Don't do that again, Thay. Think of your own family first.' I didn't reply, but I knew she was right. From now on, selfishness, caring for one's own family to the exclusion of others, would be one of the keys to survival.

EVACUATION

Still further on, in an abandoned village, I again saw the solitary Chinese man who had left the city with a bagful of bank notes. He was thinner now, his clothes tattered, and he was trailing his bag of money behind him dejectedly. I saw from his face that he was a broken man. He had lost family, business, possessions, and now even his money was useless.

That night, as we set up camp, we saw a small crowd of people down by the river. The Chinaman had thrown himself in and drowned, leaving his bag full of useless riels on the river-bank.

3 THE LIBERATED ZONES

On April 26th, nine days after the fall of Phnom Penh, we entered the Liberated Zones – those country areas which had been under the control of the Khmer Rouge for some time. The houses, largely untouched by war, were inhabited by peasants, or the 'Ancient People', as the Khmer Rouge called them. We, the deportees, were the 'New People' – a lower and despised order.

Not that we were aware of our new status yet. We had been stripped of practically everything that defined our status – houses, possessions, money, running water, comfortable beds – and had been living rough for a week. But as a family, we had been protected from the worst of the exodus by our cars and our supplies of food. The children were used to the rhythm of travel, watching the slow-moving throng of refugees and sleeping away the heat of the day.

We entered Prek Toch, the first village in the Liberated Zones, in late afternoon, as the sun cast long shadows from the scattered sugar-palms over the rice fields and the grassy banks of the irrigation canals. Here, in one of the dozens of thatched wooden houses, raised on stilts to protect them from the Bassac's frequent floods, at least some of the refugees could hope to sleep under cover. People scattered among the houses. Oan pointed to a likely one, and said he'd see if the owner would take him and his six dependants in. I, with four times that number to look after, searched around and settled on a huge wooden house with a tiled roof. Perhaps because it was so imposing, no one else had thought of approaching it. Inside, I found a man in a sarong, who looked up in surprise as my head appeared round the door. Diffidently, I asked if we could stay.

'How many?' he asked.

'Twenty-five,' I replied.

'All right,' he said, to my amazement, 'Why not?'

Later, feeling at ease with each other, we began to talk. It turned out that he was not exactly a true Ancient, but a landowner. He confessed he had no love for the Khmer Rouge. In a low voice, as Any and the four other women, supervised by my mother, prepared food and looked after the children, he asked me and my father how the evacuation of the capital had really occurred. His question attracted Vuoch's attention, and she drifted over to join us, murmuring an excuse to my mother.

My account seemed to add to our host's pessimism.

I tried to reassure him. 'Look at me,' I said with a confidence I did not feel, avoiding Vuoch's critical eye. 'I am a deportee, yet I have not given up hope.' Three days, we had been told. Well, three days was not long. Undoubtedly, Angkar would need several weeks to accomplish the enormous task it had set itself. Then we would return.

In trying to convince him, I was trying to reassure myself. I still thought we would be returning soon. After all, I was a technician, an engineer, who would be useful in the reconstruction of the country. Besides, I wanted to impress my host, to make him see how important it was to treat me well in preparation for the better days ahead.

He made few comments. As we sat chatting, with the women settling the children down on mats for the night, he probably thought me naively optimistic. He must have known the Khmer Rouge even better than my father, who was also listening, and saying little. Looking back, it seems extraordinary that we found a man who had preserved such generosity in the face of such adversity.

Next day, I saw that some of the refugees, those with small families, those who could work, remained in Prek Toch. But nobody there would want to provide a permanent roof for Oan's family, let alone all of the rest of us.

Besides, there were other reasons to keep moving. I had driven along this road many times, and knew the next village was a richer one. And I had a half-formed plan that I shared with Any and my father. If we were forced to continue, if things did not improve, if it seemed that we would not after all be allowed back to Phnom Penh soon, then we could perhaps slip over the border into Vietnam and register as refugees. Since I still surreptitiously listened to the Voice of America's Cambodian language service every night, I knew the Americans had not left. At least there we would be safe until the crisis had passed.

We moved on, making better time now that the road was

clearer, weaving through the cyclists, pedestrians and few remaining cars.

Around midday, our convoy approached an abandoned pagoda, which had clearly become something of a centre for refugees. Hundreds of people were milling about in its compound, boiling rice for their families. Perhaps it would be possible to replenish our food supplies. I waved at the others to park by the side of the road, lifted out Nawath and led the way into the main courtyard of the pagoda. I noticed that a loudspeaker system had been rigged up, and pointed it out to the others. Perhaps, I said, we could learn what was to happen to us.

While we were eating, sitting in the shade of a large tree with a crowd of others, there came an announcement for employees of the Cambodian Electricity Company and of the State Waterworks Department, requesting that they present themselves to the local authorities for return to Phnom Penh. I saw half a dozen men go smiling to the Khmer Rouge officers.

As they returned to their families, however, their expressions had changed. I asked one of the men what had happened. The Khmer Rouge had ordered them to go to Phnom Penh without their families. Why this arbitrary separation? Apparently the families would follow later. When one or two of them had wondered out loud whether they and their families would meet up, the Khmer Rouge soldiers had expressed surprise: 'What are you afraid of, comrades? Surely you know where you live? Surely your wives and children remember where you live? Go on, comrades! Angkar needs you. Don't think about your family any more, they will join you. Think about Angkar first.' There were no further arguments.

All in all, given the wild rumours and the nature of the operation, the exodus had been remarkably peaceful so far. It was not to last. The next morning, at the entrance to Koh Thom, seventy miles south of Phnom Penh, our convoy was stopped by four Khmer Rouge at the side of the road. They were standing by a mass of books and papers scattered on the sidewalk.

One of the soldiers ordered us to get out of the car. 'What do you have in your car, comrades?' he asked. 'Do you have printed matter?'

'What kind?'

'Any kind. Empty the car of all printed matter, all papers!' I could hardly believe what he was saying. 'Yes! Out with the books! Everything written!'

Perhaps he was looking for counter-revolutionary propaganda. That was understandable. I showed him my French–English dictionary and my technical books, explaining what they were and how useful they would be for the construction of dams, dykes, canals and roads.

But he was a peasant boy who knew nothing about books. 'These books contain imperialist thought!' he said. 'Leave them there, on the ground! Have you got other papers?'

I handed him the registration certificate of the Fiat, which was in French.

'Imperialist writing! Throw it away!'

'So we can keep these?' I asked, as my two teacher brothers, Theng and Thoeun, and my student sister Vuoch unpacked their Khmer books, holding them up uncertainly.

'No, no, no! It is all imperialist! All relics of feudal culture!'

Amazed, we got out all our printed matter – identity cards, driving licences, journals, books – and tossed them into a pile on the sidewalk. I was fearful for the three thousand dollars I had in my pocket. To my relief, they did not search me. Satisfied with what we had given them, they indicated that we could go. I stepped over the papers, books and journals strewn on the road, leaving them for the wind to scatter.

At this point, my cousin Oan paused. 'Thay,' he said. 'We have been talking. We have friends not far from here, over in Takeo. I think we could stay with them. Perhaps you could come as well?'

There were seven in his group, and he was quite able to take care of them. I looked at my father and my brothers. No, it would be better if we headed on south, just in case we wanted to slip over the border into Vietnam. It would certainly make things easier for us if we were fewer.

We all shook hands warmly, and wished each other luck. Oan and I looked into each other's eyes – a long, slow look – and then smiled, promising we would ring each other as soon as we all returned to Phnom Penh. Watched silently by the small bands of Khmer Rouge, he turned round and drove off, followed by his brother-in-law on the remaining motorcycle. The rest of us watched them until they vanished among the crowds of pedestrians and cyclists.

Slowly, without looking at each other, we moved on, now reduced to two cars and a bicycle. We didn't have far to go, and there was no chance of moving fast, so Sarun and Thoeun said they would walk, and Sim, promising he would ride carefully, volunteered to give Vuoch a ride on the carrier of his bicycle.

A mile down the road, in the centre of the village, we came upon a second checkpoint. A young soldier held up his hand.

'You must all get out, comrades,' he said through the open window.

'But we want to go south,' I replied. 'When can we drive on?'

I could see other cars standing empty, and already guessed the answer.

'You don't need your car, comrade,' the soldier explained. 'Angkar will look after it. Angkar will give you a receipt.' And indeed, he did so.

It seems extraordinary now, but I was so eager to believe him that I merely shrugged. A few days before I would never have given up the car without some sort of protest. Now I had no strong feelings about it. After all, we were all in the same predicament. And I had my receipt. I would simply pick up the car again on our return to Phnom Penh.

Avoiding my father's eye, I told everyone to get out and unload the suitcases and bundles of clothes, blankets and cooking utensils. Sim strapped a suitcase on the back of his bicycle, our only remaining means of transport.

I looked around. Through the slowly milling crowds, I could see soldiers sitting at a table. A Khmer Rouge boy was waving us towards them. Shouldering my way forwards, I saw that there was some sort of a survey in progress. One soldier was asking questions – 'Name? Profession? Age?' – while another took notes. Wary of Angkar's 'proposals', I put my watch and my ballpoint pen into a pocket, out of sight. My radio and cassette recorder were already wrapped up in clothes in one of the suitcases. Then I and the other men in our family found ourselves at the front of the crowd, with questions coming at us one after the other.

Between us we named the people who were left, and our

professions. We were quite open. I named myself, Any, our three children, and my parents; then there were my brother Theng and his wife Lao, with their three children and Lao's mother; Keng and her husband, the smiling Sarun, with their little girl Srey Rath; tough young Sim, my cousin; my other brother Thoeun, his two little children, his wife, and some of her family – a sister and her parents; and Vuoch. Twenty-five in all. I was becoming practised at listing them.

Then, after taking the names, the soldier asked: 'Do you have dollars?' He was not interested in riels, he said, but those who held dollars should give them to Angkar. Ahead of me I had seen a few refugees handing over their dollars, but I hesitated. I don't know what made me hold back. My dollars were just sitting in a pocket, but I was not searched. The soldiers seemed to assume no one would ever say 'no' to Angkar. It was not a question of lying – I simply didn't answer. There were too many questions coming all at once, and too many people answering, for the soldiers to take any special notice of me.

After we rejoined the family group, Thoeun suggested we did some exploring. His wife's family had relatives in the area, he said, and he wanted to see if he could find them. If he could, maybe, since Aeng was pregnant, it would be better if he and his family remained there. Eventually, asking around, his father-in-law tracked down his relatives, and Thoeun asked to stay. With five adults and only two children, they were a welcome addition to the workforce.

As for the rest of us – eighteen people, of whom three were old and seven were children – we would have to move on, southwards. I had two aims in mind – to settle my family in a rich region to assure a good supply of food for them, and, if possible, to keep the option of fleeing over the border into Vietnam. We would push on to the next village, Cheu Khmau, four miles beyond Koh Thom, and only eight miles from the border.

We couldn't walk that far, or at least not all of us could, especially with the amount of baggage we had. Sudath would have been all right, but not Nawath, or Keng's little girl, Srey, or Theng's four-year-old. It would also have been hard on my parents, and on Any and Lao, both of whom had babies to carry.

But there was a launch plying the Bassac River, a fifty-seater with a protective canopy. With any luck, we would be able to hitch a ride on it.

Around four p.m., word spread that the launch was leaving shortly for Cheu Khmau. With hasty goodbyes to Thoeun and his family, with hugs and forced smiles and promises about meeting up again soon back in Phnom Penh, I shepherded my flock on board, all of us passing suitcases and bundles to each other, and Sim wheeling his overladen bicycle. As the launch cast off, my mother and father stood at the railings watching Thoeun waving at us. Their faces were impassive, but their lips were moving. I wasn't sure if they were praying or suppressing tears.

As we approached Cheu Khmau, the sound of music came to us over the water, a revolutionary song blared through tinny loudspeakers. We looked at each other in surprise. Perhaps things were better organized here.

Indeed they were. After disembarking us, Khmer Rouge soldiers directed us two hundred yards down the riverside road to a pagoda, across the grassy compound, already crowded with people, and towards its central open-sided hall, which contained hundreds more people.

As we settled down in the compound, spreading our mats and blankets, I could see there was something going on inside. The Khmer Rouge were distributing food. That was good. It would be the first food we had actually been given since leaving Phnom Penh. I was about to tell everyone to get in line when I saw something else was happening as well. Before being allowed to eat, everyone was being searched.

This was no chaotic and noisy questioning, but a detailed and thorough examination of pockets and baggage, presumably for arms. In the process, however, the Khmer Rouge were confiscating foreign currency. It was all being done calmly and politely, and no one was being criticized for having dollars or francs. I was not frightened for our immediate safety, but for our future. My three thousand dollars, stuffed in a wad in my pocket was all the wealth we had. If we escaped, the money would be vital.

There was no time to make any elaborate scheme with the others. I glanced round, controlling my nervousness. We were all together, in a tight-knit group. Other families crowded us in front and behind. To one side, children were playing, apart from their families, and ignored by the Khmer Rouge. Suddenly, an idea came to me.

I squatted down behind my father, who shielded me from the Khmer Rouge ahead. 'Nawath,' I muttered, drawing him to me. 'Look at those children, having fun. Wouldn't you like to play with them?'

I glanced at Any, who smiled her agreement. As I spoke, I reached into my pocket and drew out the bundle of dollars. Nawath nodded.

'All right, then,' I said, 'But we can't have you looking like that.' I tucked his shirt in and adjusted his shorts, sliding the dollars into his pocket as I did so. 'Off you go. Just don't drop that packet, all right? Sudath, take Nawath over there to play with the others until we call you for food.'

Luckily, the Khmer Rouge were not interested in clothing, nor even in Any's jewellery. They merely made an inventory of it, and allowed her to go on her way. They would probably have taken my radio and cassette recorder, but by pure chance they did not unwrap the clothing into which they were bundled.

Then we had our food, and returned to our base. The children, delighted by their new-found freedom, were playing happily, forming new playmates instantly from amongst the other refugee families. 'Nawath! Sudath!' I called. 'Come and eat!' And as they ran up, I caught Nawath, tucked his shirt in yet again, and retrieved my money.

When the meal was over, the Khmer Rouge ordered us to sleep right there. Tomorrow, they said, they would find us somewhere to stay.

That evening – April 28th – while I was listening as usual to the Voice of America on my radio, keeping the radio carefully wrapped in clothing and lying on the bundle as if it were a pillow, I learned that the Americans had left Saigon. Just like that, without warning, a repeat of their hasty departure from Phnom Penh.

I gasped, and pressed my head down harder to catch the muffled voice. I knew the Americans to be unreliable allies, but after a decade of war this was astonishing.

'The Americans have left Vietnam!' I whispered urgently to

Any. 'We cannot go there after all!' I might have felt trapped, but no – in a strange way I was relieved. Now there was no need to go any further. Deprived of choice, a great burden lifted from me.

Any's reaction was the same as mine. 'It would have been a dangerous and difficult walk with the children and your parents,' she whispered back. 'At least there is no danger here.'

Next day, to a constant clangour of revolutionary music and songs over the village loudspeakers, the refugees were billeted on local families. Our family was one of the largest, and consequently it was one of the most difficult to accommodate. This time, however, our size was an advantage. The Khmer Rouge allocated us an abandoned hut that had belonged to a monk. It was of bamboo, raised on stilts, across the road from the pagoda. The thatched roof had been damaged, but otherwise it was in good condition.

We breakfasted on some of the rice we still had left from the Law Faculty and arranged the house, grateful that we were not under the eyes of any Ancients. It seemed a real privilege to live alone, in privacy.

In the afternoon, the distorted music on the loudspeakers was interrupted by a raucous voice. We were summoned to attend a political meeting in one hour's time in the hall of the pagoda. At the appointed hour, we all gathered up the children and walked across the road. Any carried baby Staud, while I held Nawath's hand, explaining that we had to listen to some men talking. My mother, with Vuoch by her side, gripped my father's hand, as we all eased our way silently into the pagoda.

Across the hall, half a dozen grim-faced Khmer Rouge officers were grouped beside a man I supposed was the village chief. Male and female, they wore the same black uniform, black rubber sandals and *kramars*, the red-and-white or black-and-white chequered scarves. There was a microphone on the table and loudspeakers attached to the pillars. We New People, very different, in our dilapidated coloured clothes, from the Khmer Rouge, huddled together in family groups, sad, weary, resigned. The eyes of some of the women were red and swollen from crying.

I saw Vuoch staring round wide-eyed, all her youthful joy

knocked out of her. Only Sim seemed unaffected, accepting anything that happened with child-like equanimity. Sarun had a scowl on his face, and Keng gave him apprehensive glances, afraid he might say something that would embarrass her, or, worse still, get him into trouble. We took our places submissively, without jostling and without making any noise. I looked around me. No one was smiling. Everyone looked like zombies. There was no conversation. Only a few young children broke the silence with their crying. A sort of religious calm settled on us as we waited for the speech to begin.

'Fathers, mothers, brothers, sisters, respected comrades and well beloved!' the speaker began, without saying who he was or what role he played in the Khmer Rouge hierarchy. 'You can count yourselves lucky to be received here by Angkar. During the time of the imperialists, you could not travel without identity papers. Now, you no longer need them. Those papers humiliated you, they were like dog-tags. You no longer need them. You no longer need to pay taxes in our new revolutionary society. . .'

Angkar might well exempt us from taxes, I thought, as the voice boomed on – it had stripped us of everything else. The man was clearly not educated, repeating his revolutionary clichés by rote, at random. But it wasn't much reassurance to discover that we were brighter than him. We had to endure him anyway. We listened, impassive, faces blank, shushing the children in whispers.

It was a long speech. Most of it I forgot at once, but I was to hear these phrases so frequently in the weeks to come that they became part of me. The litany, on that occasion as on many others, went something like this:

'You are free, liberated from the imperialists. You are free men. The imperialists are cowards. Those chicken-hearted people fled. Those who did not flee the country have been exterminated. The imperialists abandoned you, but Angkar is merciful. Despite your collaboration with the past regime, Angkar pardons you. Now that you have nothing, you have turned towards Angkar. Angkar is generous. It promises to feed you, to house you, if you abandon your old customs, your Western clothes. You must eliminate the traces of imperialism, of feudalism, of colonialism. The boys have hair that is as long as the girls. This is still an imperialist influence.

You must renounce all that and think of the political work that you will undertake in the coming days. If you have something to say to Angkar, say it. You should hide nothing from Angkar. Angkar says nothing, does not speak, but it has eyes and ears everywhere. The authority of Angkar watches over you . . . ' and on and on, repeating the same phrases in a different order ad infinitum.

After two hours he stopped, abruptly. 'We thank you for coming to listen to Angkar. Now go home.'

Back in our house, we agreed things could be worse. After what we had endured for eleven days, we were content. I assumed that the Khmer Rouge would call on me to help in the reconstruction of our devastated country. Hope and wilful self-delusion carried me along for a while yet.

At five-thirty the next morning, we were woken by the loudspeaker. 'Comrades! It's time to wake up! Come to the pagoda at six o'clock! Prepare yourselves for work!' Everyone was supposed to go, even the women. But I had children and my father was not feeling well. When I explained, the Khmer Rouge said that my mother should remain at home with Theng's old mother-in-law to take care of the children and my father.

The rest of us – including the other women and even nine-year-old Sudath – went across, joining the others who were standing waiting in the courtyard of the pagoda. To one side, I saw half a dozen Khmer Rouge handing out axes and machetes. After queuing up for tools, we were divided up. I found myself allotted to a group with Sim, Sarun, and Theng, in a group of two hundred men, while Any, Keng, Lao and Vuoch were in a women's group, and Sudath was told to stand with a crowd of children. Then, with a great shuffling of feet and murmured questioning about what we would be doing and calls to wives and husbands about meeting up again at the end of the day, the three groups separated.

We were all led off through fields and orchards to uncut bush, about a mile away from the village, where we were told that we had to clear a patch of undergrowth to make a cornfield. Later, Any told me the women were doing similar work not far away.

All day, I chopped and lifted. Soon, unused to such work, my hands were sore and my limbs ached. But I was not about to complain. I wasn't so badly off. I had seen children die, I had seen old people lying exhausted by roadsides. Compared to them, I was lucky. The family was intact. And besides, the presence of the Khmer Rouge was not oppressive or threatening. There were only a few of them and they joined us in our work, speaking to us as usual in quiet and polite tones. I counted my blessings.

So we began to live as labourers, according to the rhythm of night and day and the slowly changing season. Work was divided into two categories: field-work – clearing, irrigation, ploughing, planting – and larger-scale labour on canal digging, which involved joining up with workers from other villages. Life became harsh, but not brutal, a steady undifferentiated purgatory. I accepted it, and urged acceptance on the others (not that there was any choice) because I thought of it as a time of testing, and of limited duration. We were being reformed for some purpose, obscure perhaps, but real. In a way, I looked upon these days, even when the days became weeks, as a challenge. As usual, I responded. I wanted to look good in the eyes of Angkar to ensure a decent life for my family. I was, after all, a New Person. I was determined to achieve the status of an Ancient as soon as possible, and then return home. With that end in view, I – all of us – tolerated the drab austerity of our lives without complaint.

There was no relief from it. Cosmetics and fashionable clothing were all considered vestiges of capitalism, foreign imperialism, Western decadence. Our own clothing was despised. We were told we should become as much like the Ancients as possible, and advised to dye our clothing either by trampling it in the darkest mud we could find or by staining it with *macloeur*, the dark juice of a local fruit. Even spectacles, for some reason, were banished. The Khmer Rouge disapproved of sunglasses and seemed to equate prescription glasses with the evils symbolized by sunglasses. Friendship was subject to caprice, for work teams changed often. We could not travel, even to other villages. Our daily diet was rice and salt, with the occasional addition of dried fish. All the foreign food and drinks had disappeared. Anyway, there was nothing to buy it with. Money and markets had been abolished. Postal services, telephones and schools belonged to the past. Sport – all recreation – was forbidden. There were no medical facilities, though most city people had brought along enough to counteract the simple complaints, like headaches, diarrhoea and slight fevers.

It was, perhaps, toughest on the children, who had no toys, no books, and no schools to keep them occupied. Sim and Vuoch kept their spirits up, in their own different ways.

Most of the time, Sim played with them as if he were one of them, wrestling with them or playing hide-and-seek. But once, I remember, when he came home after work, he called Sudath and Nawath over and produced a paper aeroplane. I don't know where he found the paper, but the toy produced screams of delight. Then, of course, Visoth and Amap appeared and demanded turns at throwing it, at which point Sim produced three more paper planes, and for the rest of the day all four children were happy with these, their first and only toys.

Vuoch, to my surprise, developed hidden talents as a story-teller. She would have made a good teacher, for she had a natural authority. Whenever I saw them sitting round her, and heard her begin – 'This one is about Achey. You remember Achey, Sudath? Yes, the clever young man who always gets out of trouble. Well, once upon a time . . .' – I knew there would be no need to worry about the children for a while.

Political education sessions were held two or three times a week. At these meetings, as the tedious phrases rolled over us, we pretended a religious respect. Anyone who fell asleep was rudely awakened and sent for 're-education' – a dressing-down by an officer during which the offender was expected to confess his failures and promise to do better in future.

The few Khmer Rouge officers watched over all our activities. A chairman, a vice-chairman, and a secretary commanded assistants in charge of education, discipline and health.

The Khmer Rouge were informed about our doings by an official informer: the *chlop*, an Ancient appointed by the administration, who would hang about the houses to see what we were doing and overhear our conversation. We became wary, and learned to conceal our thoughts until we were isolated in the fields or having our evening baths in the river after work.

Through May and June, as I helped clear large enclaves in the forest, using a machete and a hatchet to cut bamboo, undergrowth, trees and thorny thickets, I was borne up by the thought that this could not last. Constantly, Theng and I and our colleagues at work reassured each other, with phrases that became almost as clichéd as those of Angkar. 'They want to put us to the test,' I would say, in response perhaps to one of Vuoch's barbed questions about the Khmer Rouge policy. 'They are trying to prove our capability. They will send us back to Phnom Penh when the time of penitence is over. One day Angkar will need engineers and instructors.'

There were, of course, numerous deaths. The dead were buried with the briefest of ceremonies. Husbands and wives were allowed to take time off for mourning, but they no longer had the help of monks. Though most monks, bowing to Khmer Rouge pressure, had abandoned their habits, there were ten who did not. Forced to work rather than depend on charity, and forbidden to take part in any rituals, or even say prayers for the dead, they obstinately refused to abandon their yellow robes, a decision that in Cheu Khmau at least was respected by the Khmer Rouge.

Our greatest strength was the family. Sometimes the children plagued their grandparents and earned themselves a scolding from me. But the eleven adults all got along together. My parents, who didn't work, organized daily life, distributing the food and dividing the rations. During the day they looked after the young children, while all the adults, even Sudath, went off to labour.

Any and the three other younger women supported each other marvellously. Lao, married to my younger brother Theng, was older than Any by two or three years, but showed her the respect traditionally due in our country to the wife of an elder brother. She might have found her position difficult, for she was more ambitious than Any, and always seemed eager for Theng to get on in the world. But Any's self-effacing manner actually pointed to her strength and discreet wisdom, and because of her tact there was never a hint of disagreement. Vuoch's assertiveness was always restricted to politics, and she was careful about giving that free expression, as we all were. Keng, sweet-tempered Keng, was the most submissive of all, except in defence of Sarun. She never criticized anyone, not even the Khmer Rouge. 'It is fate,' she would say, simply, a quietness of spirit that seemed to build a special bond between her and Any.

Given the feeling of unity that bound our family, we were able to retain something of our morale. We shared what we had equally and remained supportive, telling each other constantly that we would be going home soon. For a while we were protected from the worst effects of the Khmer Rouge regime by the goods we had with us. There was soap (though no toothpaste). We had a lot of clothes – I alone had eight pairs of trousers and a dozen shirts. We had our own food – a variety of canned products and a good deal of sugar. My mother and Any had brought along pans, woks, skillets and some metal bowls, so cooking was no problem.

But slowly, insidiously, the lack of food began to tell. Twelve hours of work a day reduced us to skinny shadows of our former selves. Staud, the two-year-old, began to suffer from lack of vitamins, his limbs becoming thin, his stomach swollen. Any's periods stopped. She discovered that many of the other women had stopped menstruating as well. It might have been something to do with the shock of the change when Phnom Penh fell, or perhaps with the lack of food and the debilitating labour.

As we used up our food, we found salvation of a different sort. The local peasants – the Ancients – had plenty of their own food. And we had goods that they desired. Within a couple of months, New People and Ancients had established the beginnings of a new form of economy, based on barter.

The outside world impinged on us hardly at all. Since most of the New People were billeted on Ancients, about twenty to a house, there was a good deal of contact between New People and Ancients. But the Khmer Rouge, both military and civil officials, lived apart in their own houses. Of the neighbouring villages, we knew practically nothing, and of the rest of the country, nothing at all. Occasionally we heard artillery and, at night, saw the distant flare of explosions, and guessed there was some sort of trouble at the Vietnamese border. From time to time a column of black-uniformed Khmer Rouge soldiers would march through the village heading southwards. But what exactly was happening, we had no idea.

* * *

During a political meeting one day in July, when we had been in Cheu Khmau for three months, and the rains had flooded the newly planted rice fields, the Khmer Rouge asked if any of those from Kompong Speu and Kampot provinces were willing to return to their village of origin. My parents had lived at Oudong in Kompong Speu. On the spur of the moment, thinking this was the beginning of the long-promised return to our homes, I raised my hand, and my parents, seeing me, copied me.

The next day, all the volunteers, about eighty people in all, gathered on the river-bank to get the boat back up river.

But there was not enough room in the boat for us all. Some of us, the Khmer Rouge said, would have to walk along the river. Don't worry, we were told, we would all meet up again at a pagoda two hours up river.

This was just the sort of thing we all feared, but there was no help for it. My parents had to ride in the boat, and we would not be able to carry the older children. I helped my parents find a place for themselves, for Nawath, and for Theng's two boys. My father said he could look after some of the baggage as well. The rest of us would go across the river in a smaller boat and then walk along the river-bank road.

Even before we set off, the ferry was pulling away. We waved anxiously, and set off, with Any and Lao carrying their babies, and the rest of us loaded down with our remaining bundles.

After an hour, we reached Koh Thom, where we had been stopped on the journey southwards. As I looked across the fields beyond the village, I saw a sight that shocked me and filled me with almost forgotten emotions.

There, stuck in an ungainly lurch, among dozens of other cars, sat my Fiat. The tyres had disappeared, the rims were rusty, the windscreen was broken, the seats torn out. I felt a sudden wave of nostalgia. The daily struggle to survive during the last three months had blotted out the past. Now, there, in my Fiat, I saw my previous existence and longed for it, with all its inadequacies. To think that I had once believed I would simply hand over my receipt and drive the family back to Phnom Penh, with the car still in perfect condition!

Any noticed my silence and remoteness. 'What is it Thay?'

These were thoughts and feelings I could not share.

'It is nothing, Any. I am tired.'

After another hour, we came to the pagoda in Prek Taduong. It was already crowded, for the boat had arrived some time before and my parents had already disembarked with the three children. 'There, you see?' Any said to Nawath. 'No need to worry. Here we are all together again.'

After establishing a base with our blankets and possessions under cover in the pagoda, I began to stroll around the village, listening to conversations and trying to get information about friends. By chance, I came across one of my students from Phnom Penh. He was with his parents, for Prek Taduong was his birthplace. He knew everyone and, being a generous boy, said he would get me some cassava.

When he arrived with it at the pagoda, we began discussing food. He suggested I exchange my watch for two fishing nets. He said he could make a deal for me with a Muslim. I hesitated. I didn't want to lose my watch. But Any talked sense to me: 'Come on! The Khmer Rouge can propose to take it at any time anyway. Better to have nets to get food for our children.' What could I say? I agreed, and went with the student to the river. He called out to a man sitting in a boat, fishing. The man hauled in his nets, and rowed over to us. Within a few minutes the deal was made. I handed over my watch, and received the two nets. They were good ones – lightweight, strong, newly made. It seemed strange that here, just up river from Cheu Khmau, Khmer Rouge authority was so much more relaxed.

When, back in the pagoda, I mentioned this to my father, he told me something else that gave me pause. In the boat, going up river, an old man had made some critical remark about Angkar. When being reprimanded, he was searched. The Khmer Rouge discovered that he was carrying dollars, pocket after pocket of them, perhaps ten thousand dollars altogether.

A young Khmer Rouge soldier had brandished the wad of notes and yelled at the old man, 'You're keeping imperialist money!'

Then, with a determined lunge, he had thrown the wad of dollars into the river. Stupefied, the passengers looked at each other. Why not keep the dollars? The young man could easily have confiscated them. Apparently, he had no idea of the meaning of foreign currency and how the Khmer Rouge regime could benefit from it.

How many Khmer Rouge officers across the country, I wondered, were currently repeating this ignorant and self-destructive gesture of empty defiance? Were all the Khmer Rouge simply arbitrary in their behaviour, with each man interpreting orders in his own way?

We stayed at Prek Taduong for one week, resting. The children were carefree, playing in and around the pagoda. My student brought food. I tried fishing, but without success. It didn't matter: life here was easier than at Cheu Khmau.

The locals, New People and Ancients alike, were engaged in building a dam. Their timetable was more flexible than ours had been, with work starting at nine and ending at three. There was nowhere near the same dedication to work, either from the Khmer Rouge or the workers themselves. My student told me how all the Khmer Rouge leaders here were from the area. Used to local habits, and knowing the locals personally, they were more indulgent.

This confirmed my general impression that there was no established rule for the whole country. In the absence of published laws, discipline varied at the whim of each village chief. For some, at least, that was good – life must still be acceptable in many areas, I told myself, despite the evacuation, the separations and the deaths.

At the end of one week, our little holiday came to an abrupt end. A convoy of five trucks, civilian trucks, covered with tarpaulins, roared into the compound. We were ordered to get in. After packing up our things as quickly as we could, Sarun, who was smiling beatifically that day, the sturdy Theng and I helped my parents, Any, Lao, Keng, Vuoch and the children into the vehicles. We threw up our bags, while Sim lifted his bicycle in. There were thirty or forty of us in each truck, all as excited as children, telling each other that now we really were returning to our native villages.

We set off north, towards Phnom Penh, along a road that had fallen into terrible condition. We were expecting to follow the route through the capital and beyond. But only about six miles up the road, the trucks turned off left into brushland, following a forest track. We looked at each other in surprise, holding on to each other as the truck bumped over the sun-baked mud, sending clouds of dust up behind us.

Where the devil were they taking us?

4 THE BEGINNING OF 'PURIFICATION'

As we bumped along through the forest, a terrible feeling came over me, an impression of plunging into the unknown, of losing my foothold, a repeat of the distress and the despondency I had felt on leaving Phnom Penh. Dust clogged our eyes and noses, but none of us felt inclined to complain about the discomfort. That was of secondary importance compared to our worries about an unknown fate and the deception of which we were the victims. On the faces of my family, and of all the others, I saw despair written. My father caught my eye, and stared blankly, as if to say, Didn't I try to warn you, my son? There was no denying now that all of us who had been herded so politely from our homes in the cities had been the victims of a colossal deception. We had been driven slowly but steadily into a nightmare from which it seemed we would never awaken. I caught Any's eye. She clasped Staud, protecting him from the jolts, and I felt a wave of gratitude for her strength.

After an hour or so, some ten miles into the forest, the trucks stopped in a village, beside a river. There was only a wooden footbridge. We were told to get out and walk across the bridge. On the other bank, our three Khmer Rouge guards told us – all one hundred and eighty or so of us – to continue walking for another mile, carrying our possessions.

We could not have carried our baggage without Sim's bicycle, our only means of transport. Piling it with as many bags as we could, we tied them on with a large cloth, leaving the willing, hard-working Sim to push it. The other men – the athletic Theng, myself and Sarun, who seemed to find amusement in Sim's task – shared the bundles as best we could. Any held Staud on her hip with one hand, and dragged a bag along with the other. When she was tired, she put him down and he had to totter along behind her. I carried two big parcels – clothing and kitchen utensils bundled up in tablecloths. Sudath was fit enough, and even five-year-old Nawath could keep up, but neither my parents nor Lao's mother were in any state for a long walk. Keng's little girl, Srey Rath, could manage, and so could Theng's two older children, but Lao had to carry her one-year-old daughter. We made a slow and miserable procession. Silent, morose, and apprehensive, we walked on with the other refugees. Nobody talked. The silence was broken only by the sighs of the older people.

At dusk, we reached a camp of sorts, another abandoned pagoda. In the distance we caught a glimpse of wood-fires. Khmer Rouge or refugees? We didn't know and it was useless to ask our three guards such questions.

The compound was a dirty, stinking place, strewn with cattle dung. Apparently our predecessors had been in ox-carts. We tried to clean up, until the gathering gloom forced us to spread out mats, light fires and console ourselves with the rice and fish left over from the pagoda.

The next morning, a new group of half a dozen Khmer Rouge arrived. One of them, his face expressionless, began to ask questions while another, more earnest and nervous-looking, laboriously noted down the answers. 'Who are you? Where do you come from? Do you have a large family? How many men? Women? Names? Professions?'

By now, I was wary of giving truthful answers. Better to be humble than truthful. I said, simply, that my name was Thay, not giving my full name, and that I was a technician in the Public Works Department. But neither my brother Theng nor Keng's husband, Sarun, attempted to disguise the fact that they were teachers. When the note-taker, a country boy unused to using a pen, had finished writing, the questioner said, 'Prepare to leave, comrades. The carts will be coming soon.'

Carts? This was a new development. Exchanging a few apprehensive glances, we gathered up our belongings, and settled down to wait. No one said anything much. Staud played around Any's feet, and then slept in her arms. My mother and father seemed to sink into themselves. Always ready to act the optimist, I remarked that perhaps we were going to Kampong Speu by some slow and roundabout route, but no one responded. Sim laid his bicycle on the ground and slept, as did Theng, with his second son Amap cradled in the crook of his arm. There was nothing else to do.

After a one-and-a-half-hour wait, bullock-carts, over twenty in all, pulled up outside the compound. None of them were large enough to take more than a few of us.

'Hurry up, hurry up!' I shouted, afraid the family would be separated. Everybody else had the same idea. It was a kind of race among the families to be first into an empty cart. Luckily, we managed to reserve three carts for ourselves halfway down the line – Any, Staud, my parents and my sister Keng with Srey in one cart, Sudath and Nawath with me, Sarun and Vuoch in another, and Theng and his family in the third – and the carts set off in single file, creaking and swaying. Sim followed on his bicycle. Clearly we were not going to be separated by much, but still every few minutes we would all find ourselves craning our necks, catching each other's eyes, waving and nodding to check that those in the other wagons were well. Sim, always cheerful, accelerated and dropped back, delivering messages between the carts.

With one noonday pause to eat, stopping hardly long enough for the stragglers to catch up, we came to a fork. The first ten carts were directed to the left. The rest veered to the right. By pure chance, we all found ourselves going in the same direction. Several families were not so lucky. Later, one man, accompanied by his two children, told me that he had lost his wife in this way. He had begged the Khmer Rouge soldier to grant him the right to follow her. The soldier turned a deaf ear, saying he didn't have the authority to make such a decision.

'Angkar,' he replied, 'is the only authority which can give you a reply.' But Angkar was always somewhere else, Angkar's authority always tomorrow, and meanwhile a family was divided for ever.

That evening, we reached Sramar Leav, in the province of Takeo, well-known as the strongest sanctuary of the Khmer Rouge movement. We were in a vast, irrigated plain, amidst rice fields scattered with sugar-palms. Winding past a few stilted, thatched houses, we came to the village, and turned in to the compound of an ancient pagoda.

We had hardly unloaded our bags when the local Khmer Rouge chief began to harangue us. 'Comrades! You will soon be returning to your villages, but it is July, right in the middle of the cultivation period. The rain will be coming soon. You must work here, cultivating rice, to produce our food. When this work is finished, you will leave again. Angkar requests that you stay here. Naturally, Angkar will accommodate you and feed you. It will take care of everything, do not worry. However, Angkar requires that you respect its orders and its discipline. You must try to purify yourselves.'

Purification: we were to hear that word many times in the sermons of the Khmer Rouge officers.

'Angkar wants to make real revolutionaries out of you,' he went on. 'You have worked in the fields in Cheu Khmau. You must have accomplished much.'

He paused, and someone raised a diffident hand. 'We did,' he said hesitantly. 'But we didn't have time to harvest the crops. We left too early.'

'I understand,' the official replied quietly but forcefully. It seemed to me the man was more educated than the rulers of Cheu Khmau. He spoke clearly and coherently without any of the wild promises we had become used to. 'Those fruits and vegetables will be harvested by Angkar to feed other refugees. Here you will feed yourselves from the vegetables which your predecessors planted. All production belongs to the whole population. We are masters in our home, and so are you. In Democratic Kampuchea we do not need external aid. Now it is Angkar who meets your needs. It is Angkar who fills your stomach. With Angkar, you will be responsible for your own destiny, by working hard, by producing what you need.'

Then the officials summoned all the refugees together for a formal meeting, moving to the edge of the open-sided hall, where there was a table with a microphone.

'Now,' came the chief's voice through the loudspeakers, 'who are the civil servants here?' I raised my hand and so did a few others. 'And the military?' After a few minutes it became clear he was classifying us into social categories, each group being allotted to one part of the village, the civil servants remaining in the pagoda, the ex-military being given houses in one area, workers and shop-keepers in another. Here, the New People were not to be housed with the Ancients.

As it happened, all the houses were occupied by locals and our family remained with another large one in the ransacked pagoda, being given a two-storey, brick-built structure formerly occupied by a monk. We were upstairs, the other family downstairs.

While Any and the other women swept the floors, laid out mats, and set up the cooking things, I discussed matters with my father. 'Look what they have done to the temple,' he said. 'Not a single monk left. They have no respect. What will happen to us?'

'Yes, father. But maybe this is just a step in our re-education. Maybe it's only temporary.'

Work started the next day. Any was to be part of the team that transplanted rice into the newly ploughed fields. I was to become a ploughman. An Ancient led several of us to the rice fields. There I was given a pair of oxen pulling a wooden plough with a metal blade. I had never ploughed before, but found it easy to guide the slow, placid and tireless oxen. It did, however, strike me as a fruitless exercise, for the fields were bone dry.

That evening, I discovered why, and at the same time learned something more of the peculiar society in which we had landed. As in every pagoda, there was a pool which acted as a focal point for village life. Since there was no river near by, the peasants used to come there to get water for drinking and washing. That evening, as I was collecting water for the evening meal, I noticed an old man beside me, a gnome of a fellow wearing very baggy shorts.

As I turned to leave, he said, 'Ah, you are the newcomer who lives in the pagoda house?'

I nodded warily.

'You see how they destroy everything? The temple, the monks,' I made no response, but he wasn't put off. 'What have you been doing?'

'Ploughing. But it is very hard.'

'Yes, it is very dry this year. The *pring*' – he was referring to the small blue cherries which are very popular in Cambodia – 'are not ripening at all. I have never known a year like it. You see,' he went on, giving me a shrewd glance, 'This is God's punishment for such sacrilege.'

Again, I made no comment. He might have been a spy, trying to set me up. We stood for a moment, but he made no move to go. He seemed to want to talk, so out of politeness I asked him his name. Ta Bun, he said, his wrinkled face breaking into a smile, and then was off again on the subject of the Khmer Rouge and how the village was being punished for its activities.

Then: 'If you have any spare trousers or shorts, you let me know.'

I still wasn't prepared to trust him. 'I will see. If I had, what could I get?'

'Sugar. Eggs. Fruit.'

I was to be grateful for that contact, for there was little enough for us at Sramar Leav. Even for that little we were supposed to be grateful. We had nothing when we arrived, we were told, now we had oxen and ploughs and land to till. In fact, the rice we were given made extra work for us. It was paddy rice, the complete rice grain with the shell intact, which had to be husked before it could be cooked – hammered in a pestle and then sieved to separate the husks and the grain. When we came back from ten or twelve hours' work, we had to spend another hour in this irksome task.

One month after the transplanting had finished, the rice fields dried up completely, and all the seedlings died. For a few days, we were set to building small-scale irrigation ditches. But clearly, as the Khmer Rouge realized, there was no point in building ditches if there was no water to flow in them. As the drought continued, the need for a long-term solution became ever more urgent. Several weeks after our arrival, Angkar mobilized us for the construction of a larger canal to lead water from a nearby lake.

Ordered to report to the site of the new canal, Theng and I found ourselves on the road that led past the village foundry. As we approached, we were drawn by the clang of hammers on metal. Clearly, there was something of some importance going on. We paused to look inside. An extraordinary sight met our eyes. A brand new Mercedes, up on bricks, its wheels off, was being torn apart by five blacksmiths. Half the body had already vanished. Two of the men were at work on one of the panels, and a couple of others were fashioning great wing-like blades from another section. Along one wall stood two tyres. Beside them were stacked little strips of rubber.

Theng and I stood watching, open-mouthed. Eventually, one of the men strolled over and asked what we wanted.

'Nothing. Nothing,' I replied, above the clangour of hammers and anvils. 'We just wanted to admire your beautiful work.'

His face lit up. 'Yes, it is beautiful, isn't it? Ploughshares and sandals. For the revolution.'

I was lost for words. Five men were labouring for days to turn an object once worth tens of thousands of dollars, rendered worthless by the Khmer Rouge's revolutionary economy, into objects that could previously have been bought for a few hundred dollars.

We turned to go.

'Creative initiative, comrades!' the foreman went on. 'That's what this is! Transforming an imperialist object into something useful for the revolution!' He turned, still beaming, and waved a hand proudly at his noisy enterprise.

'Wonderful,' I shouted.

We walked off, shaking our heads in silent astonishment. Hatred of imperialism was one thing. But where did this extraordinary hatred of imperialist objects come from? It was as if the Khmer Rouge regarded them as accursed, or plague-ridden, capable of magically undermining the purity of the revolution simply by their existence. It never seemed to occur to them that there were other practical uses to which 'imperialist' machinery could be put. Instead, they had to be seen as a symbol of the enemy – not for use against the enemy, but to be assaulted and destroyed.

It did not, therefore, come as a total surprise that the four-mile canal was to be dug without any machinery at all. Theng and I found ourselves part of a group responsible for making a 500-yard section, cutting into the earth with hoes, and carrying the earth to the edge in bamboo baskets, piling it up into levees on either side. It was an enormous operation which involved several villages, with a dozen different teams all in competition with each other, working from dawn until ten or eleven at night.

It was while I was working on the canal site that I had my first experience of an escape attempt.

I and my brother Theng met five former students who were living in a neighbouring village. As New People, there was no suspicion among us. At lunch break, we would form a little group, separate from the others. The students confided to us that they planned to escape. They had demonstrated against Lon Nol and felt bitterly deceived by life under the Khmer Rouge. They suggested that I join them. They said they had daggers, rations enough, and a map of Cambodia, but they wanted my advice on the best route to the Thai border.

Of course, I couldn't abandon the family, and just gave what advice I could. They were planning to go in September, the wettest month of the year. At that time, the route across the Cardamom mountain chain, hard at the best of times, would be almost impossible. I told them they would never be able to move or find their bearings, even if they succeeded in avoiding the villages and highways patrolled by the Khmer Rouge between Sramar Leav and the mountains. I suggested they wait until the next dry season. But they were young and impatient, and wouldn't entertain delay.

I could not contemplate escape right now, but their talk made me wonder if I might be able to engineer a move to a better area – such as Battambang, for instance, the richest of Cambodia's provinces, north-west of Phnom Penh, and nearer to Thailand. If an opportunity ever came to go there, it would be useful to know where we were. I proposed to deal with them. I would give them some dollars, which would be useful to them when they crossed the border, and in return they could give me the section of their map that they would not be using. It was a deal. In exchange for a hundred dollars, they gave me a piece of map that showed Battambang and part of the province of Pursat. On their section of the map, I drew a suggested route for them.

A few days later they slipped away together after work, planning to get a few days' start, for the village leader might think they were camping out at the work site.

Much later, in Thailand, I made inquiries about them. Nothing, absolutely nothing. I never knew what became of them.

Meanwhile, the rains had begun. We slept in the open on mats, near the work site, so urgent had it become that we complete our task. We had no tents. We just lay out on our mats beneath the trees, soaked. The place swarmed with mosquitoes. We shivered the nights away, huddling around fires built both for warmth and to keep away the insects.

I could see, moreover, that all our labour was going to waste. No one had surveyed the site, there were no plans, and no one kept records. The Khmer Rouge seemed to think that revolutionary fervour could replace the laws of physics. In each section thousands of men and women dug, obeying the orders of their local leaders, but without anybody even checking that the canal we were building ran downhill away from the lake. The banks were made up of loose earth, without any attempt to compact them. If water ever actually flowed along the canal, it would wash the banks away in no time.

Occasionally, at meetings, some particularly brave (or fool-hardy) technician would try to tell the Khmer Rouge how the work should be done. The reply was always the same: 'You don't know anything about the revolution. We do. Why do you try to tell us what to do?' Qualifications were declared to be useless. Diplomas were *saignabat*, 'the invisible signal'. What counted was physical work. That was *saignakhoeunh*, 'the visible signal'. That was tangible. Therein lay honour.

As time went on, I thought more and more about something old Ta Bun said to me one evening during one of our meetings at the pool. I had come to trust him now, and we made regular exchanges, my clothing for his sugar. 'The predictions of Puth are coming to pass,' he said, with a knowing nod and penetrating look from his wrinkled eyes.

Puth was a nineteenth-century sage who prophesied that the country would undergo a total reversal of traditional values, that the houses and the streets would be emptied, that the illiterate would condemn the educated, that infidels – *thmils* – would hold absolute power and persecute the priests. But people would be saved if they planted the kapok tree – *kor*, in Cambodian. *Kor* also means 'mute'. The usual interpretation of this enigmatic message was that only the deaf-mutes would be saved during this period of calamity. Remain deaf and mute. Therein, I now realized, lay the means of survival. Pretend to be deaf and dumb! Say nothing, hear nothing, understand nothing!

This canal will never carry water, I thought, and kept quiet.

There were, nevertheless, hints of better times to come.

Some time in August 1975, during a political meeting, the

Khmer Rouge chief announced that money was to be reintroduced towards the end of the year. He even posted the prices of some commodities – a kilo of beef, a dozen eggs, a kilo of rice.

This welcome news confirmed the rumours of political change. One of my neighbours was a teacher, Leang, who had arrived in the pagoda two months before us. Leang, a tall thin man with a wife and two children, had been a member of the central committee of the Democratic Party, the main opposition party under Lon Nol. His former eminence gave him certain privileges, and he was allowed to go fishing, not simply for himself but also for other residents in the pagoda. He used to borrow my nets, the ones I had acquired after leaving Cheu Khmau, and we often fell into conversation. From Leang I learned a little more about the Khmer Rouge.

He confirmed that there were two main factions, both of which had their own sanctuaries. The Khmer Rouge east of the Mekong were favourable to Sihanouk. These were the moderates, and they wore khaki. The other faction, the Maoists, the implacable puritans of the Khmer Rouge movement, who were hostile to Sihanouk, came from the south-west, where we were. They dressed in black. According to Leang, Sihanouk would act as arbitrator in this internal conflict. When he did so, we would all return home.

His confidence, born of years of lecturing, puzzled me. How could he be so certain? Where was Sihanouk? What did his power depend on? How could he exercise influence?

As it happened, Leang's information was correct. Sihanouk returned from Peking that September. We never knew it and his return changed nothing, but the rumours – true or not – conferred on Sihanouk the status of national saviour. We came to believe that he alone could overcome the ideological quarrels and restore some of our liberties.

Soon, I was sure, the schools and universities (at least) would reopen. They could do without engineers to build bridges, but how could a country live without schools and universities? What had happened to my educated friends who had joined the other side? I couldn't imagine all those who'd joined the Khmer Rouge being resigned to the denial of education. Logically, we would proceed to a more moderate and forward-looking society.

My confidence was boosted from another source, a Khmer Rouge officer I met through Chan, who worked on the canal in my group. Chan, a former trader of about forty, had been in Phnom Penh when the city fell and had been unable to return to his wife and children in Battambang. He had headed south to join his parents in the village a mile from the pagoda, but as a New Person had to live in the pagoda itself – the Khmer Rouge discouraged family sentiment since it undermined their ability to control New People. But while we were building the canal Chan often used to sneak away to visit his parents during lunch hour. Sometimes he invited me along, for the two of us got on well. He was a tough, stocky man, who had a habit of glancing about him as he talked, as if on the look-out for trouble; it was a habit that made me glad he trusted me. The two of us would slip away to his family's house, where we would gorge ourselves on pumpkin and palm-sugar, supplied by his elderly peasant parents.

There, Chan introduced me to the Khmer Rouge officer, Mith (Comrade) Pech, who was married to one of his cousins. Pech was a highly placed man in the provincial communist hierarchy. He had a motorcycle and the cut of his clothes showed his importance, as did the two pens which he proudly exhibited in his breast pocket. He was thirty-eight years old, and had completed his Baccalauréat before joining the underground. I was never sure whether he had joined the Khmer Rouge freely or had been forced into it against his will. Indeed, there was much about him that was mysterious. I never saw him smile. But Chan assured me that I could ask him anything I wanted.

One thing, of course, obsessed me. Were we going to return to Phnom Penh?

'Yes, I think that you'll be returning soon,' he said 'But I have no formal information on this subject. We must always, no matter what happens, respect the orders of Angkar.'

He appeared to be straightforward, but I dared not tell him the whole truth about myself. I was still a 'technician of a Public Works Department'. I told him that I hoped that one day they would make use of my skill.

He replied evasively, 'It's possible . . . but first you must be re-educated. This stage of your education is still not over. We think that we can make use of the technicians in a year's time. Don't worry. We are Cambodians like you. We will not abandon you.'

That was something. It was the first time that a fixed period for our penitence had been mentioned. Had the possible reintroduction of money any significance? No, that didn't mean that the New People had completed their ordeal. I said I thought that the engineers, doctors and teachers would be more useful in their real occupations than in the fields. 'No, no, you must all finish your re-education. You may be fully re-educated at the end of one year if you do not commit any errors, if there are no blots, no faults found by your leaders. Execute the missions which Angkar requests that you accomplish, correctly, without cheating.' We were clearly not on the same wavelength, but at least there was an end in sight.

Why the confusion over the return to our birthplace, I insisted, why did we have to stop at Sramar Leav?

My questions seemed to tax his patience. He scolded me for asking. 'Angkar is master of your destiny. It is important that you know it. Angkar has many detours. Angkar is not to be predicted. It might bypass different stages without prior notification. Do not believe that what Angkar says will be for ever. It may change at the next turn. It may proceed in leaps and bounds. But Angkar always has its reasons.' He spoke allusively, in parables, like a monk. I began to see that we could not be sure of anything. From one day to the next everything could change and expectations could be contradicted. The paradoxical nature of the organization troubled me.

There was one other question I wanted answered. While we were in Cheu Khmau, we had heard explosions from the frontier area. Were we at war with Vietnam? My question elicited the first good explanation of Khmer Rouge policy.

'You know, undoubtedly, that Vietnam is not totally revolutionary. It did not order the evacuation of the cities, as we did. We know that it is dangerous to leave the cities intact, inhabited. They are the centres of opposition, and contain little groups. In a city, it is difficult to track down the seeds of counter-revolution. If we do not change city life, an enemy organization can be established and conspire against us. It is truly impossible to control a city. We evacuated the city to destroy any resistance, to destroy the cradles of reactionary and mercantile capitalism. To expel the city people meant eliminating the germs of anti-Khmer Rouge resistance. This is but one of the aspects of our dissension with the Vietnamese.'

So now I knew for certain – there was no point in thinking of going to Vietnam.

But we had to get out. It was not so much the work on the canal that convinced me as what happened after work stopped. There came a time, after several weeks, when the canal was declared finished. There was to be a big political meeting and celebration, which sounded promising. We were all marched up along the levee to a huge field outside a village. There were thousands of people all walking in a huge column. At one point, there was water lying in the canal, and with a certain satisfaction I saw that here at least the canal must be sloping uphill. There would be no chance of water running anywhere from the lake unless there was a huge amount of it. And if there was that much water, if the rains were that heavy, then the canal would not be needed.

The meeting was presided over by the chief of the whole district. He was a powerfully built, grim-looking man with cold eyes, who had a reputation as a slave driver. Word had also spread about his origins. He had been a drunk, a thug, a small-time crook who had found respectability as a Khmer Rouge fighter and had proved his courage in the battle for Phnom Penh. The revolution had turned him into a leader.

Strangely, his oratorical qualities were undeniable. But instead of congratulating us, his speech was the same as all the others. 'You must work hard,' he said, 'Then Angkar will look after you.' All the old phrases. We sat and listened in stunned silence. A glance at my brother Theng and people near by was enough to show that we all felt the same. We had made a superhuman effort, but apparently Angkar couldn't care less about that. All Angkar wanted was yet more work.

How could we leave?

Angkar itself gave us our chance. One evening in early September, during a political meeting, an officer asked if there was anyone from Battambang, and if they wanted to return. Near by, I saw Chan and the head of another family raise their hands. Chan nodded at me. I raised my hand.

'From Battambang?' the officer said. 'I thought you were from Kompong Speu.'

'Well, my wife and her family are from there.'

That was good enough. We packed that very evening. The next morning, a convoy of thirty ox-wagons rolled up to the pagoda, ready to take us northwards. As we were getting ready to climb aboard, Leang came to wish us well.

'Maybe we'll meet again in Phnom Penh,' he said, wrapping an arm affectionately round my shoulder, 'When Sihanouk is properly in control.'

From anyone else, such optimism might have been mere empty ritual, but Leang seemed so well informed that his words turned our excitement into real hope. Asking someone to get a message of goodbye to Ta Bun, the old peasant who had been so eager to remind me of Puth's predictions, I settled our party of eighteen in two wagons. It was a tight squeeze. Sim still had his bicycle, however, and Sarun volunteered to ride on the carrier behind him. Reassuring ourselves with nods of encouragement, waved off by the lanky Leang, we set off. The sight of Sim and Sarun teetering along on the road beside us even raised a few laughs from the children.

'Will things really be better?' Any asked, placing my hand round her waist.

'They must,' I said. 'They couldn't be worse.' After all, in Battambang, I explained, we should get better food, and be near relations. Besides, if things didn't work out, I still had my piece of map, and we would be that much closer to Thailand.

For the moment, the warnings of the enigmatic Comrade Pech – 'Angkar should not be predicted! Nothing Angkar says is for ever!' – were forgotten.

5　THE GHOST TOWN

Soon after midday, clouds rolled in, and it began to rain. In the early afternoon, after about twelve miles, we were dropped off on Highway Two, which crossed the province of Takeo. As we stood huddled together in the rain, the Khmer Rouge explained to us that since we were leaving their region, we would have to abandon the carts and walk the last five miles to the Watt Ang Recar pagoda to wait for the trucks which were to transfer us to Battambang.

A miserable prospect. Dripping wet, without any protection, we unloaded the carts and watched them disappear back down the road, lumbering grey shapes fading away in the teeming rain.

Some people set off, plodding through the mud. Among them I saw the lone figure of Chan. We gave each other a wave, shouting that we would see each other in the pagoda the next day.

With our baggage, and encumbered by the children, we agreed there was no going anywhere in that weather. Covering our heads with blankets, we waited for the rain to stop, which it did after an hour or so. In the late afternoon sun, we spread out our things to dry. Sim laid his bicycle on the ground, and dozed. The mood lifted. Nawath, egged on by Sudath, woke Sim by tickling his nose until Sim tumbled them both into the still damp grass. The other children soon found playmates among the refugee families who had also chosen to remain overnight.

Just then, a strange caravan went past – some fifty carts and a few small Citroens being pulled and pushed by teams of men. They were collecting salt from the coast. This surreal vision – an army of men heaving along their burdens at a snail's pace – raised countless questions. Weren't there enough oxen for the wagons? Why should men replace oxen? Why push cars? How far had they been travelling? I supposed it was another strange indication of the country's collapse. Whole communities must be out of petrol and salt. Rather than organize supplies to be delivered from elsewhere by truck, the Khmer Rouge had forced each community to use some of its vital manpower in this exhausting task.

As we set up camp on the roadside, in a landscape of fields, scattered trees and a few houses, I noticed we were near a thatched hut, which gave me an idea. Staud had not been well for some time, and he had now developed badly swollen hands and feet. He in particular could do with shelter that night, in case it rained again. I persuaded Any to bring him to the house. Inside was an old peasant woman who, moved by the sight of Staud, agreed to take Any and the child for the night.

While I was preparing their bed, four Khmer Rouge suddenly entered. They stared at us, then went straight across to the old woman, who looked at them anxiously. Then without a word she took out a large earthenware jar containing palm-sugar. This was clearly a regular occurrence, for she scooped out a bowlful and held it out to the Khmer Rouge. Now, sugar had become an expensive and coveted product. We watched in envious silence as the soldiers ate the sugar, dipping coconut into it, talking quietly amongst themselves. When they had finished, the old woman hid the jar under the bamboo bed, and the Khmer Rouge left. No word had passed between them.

After a pause, I timidly asked for a small bowl of sugar for Staud. The woman pretended not to hear. I repeated the question. Now, embarrassed, she replied: 'The comrades told me to hide the sugar. I cannot give you any.' She seemed afraid, yet also ashamed. I didn't ask again.

In the morning, we and the dozens of other refugees who had camped beside the road prepared to set off. For the first time, we were confronted with the problem of carrying all our possessions for a considerable distance without any means of transport save Sim's bicycle. Neither Any, who had to carry Staud all the time now, nor Lao with her baby could take anything else. We would have to travel more lightly.

For half an hour or so, we fingered through our possessions, wondering what we could afford to leave and what we simply had to keep in order to survive. Clothing, blankets, mats, cooking pots – we needed almost everything, either for our immediate survival or to make exchanges. In the end, we decided to abandon our two cumbersome suitcases, wrapping up everything into more manageable bundles and sharing them out amongst us. The suitcases, containing a few odds and ends, we left with the old woman by way of thanks. I also gave her my cassette recorder, not that it was much use because I had taken the batteries to power my little radio.

Even then, when we actually came to leave, we discovered we were too weak to carry everything at once. After a brief discussion, we decided we could not afford to lose anything else. Those of us who were fit enough would have to make double journeys, leaving one load on the ground and returning for another load while the others waited for us.

As we walked, Any started to shiver. It began to drizzle again. Hour by hour, Any became worse, as did Staud, weeping softly in her arms. The two older children followed her, their hands clasped on their chests, their heads down. When I joined Sim, Theng and Sarun to return for another load of possessions, the two boys would squat down beside their mother, the very pictures of misery. My parents were too old and weak to do anything but plod on with Any, Lao, Keng and the other three children.

It took us until midday to cover the five miles to the pagoda. Like all the other pagodas, the place had been ransacked. It was already packed with refugees, who continued to arrive in dribs and drabs right through the day. But at least we were under cover.

As deportees continued to arrive, that afternoon and the following day, villagers turned up at the edge of the compound, wanting to barter their food for our goods. The few Khmer Rouge overseeing this way-station seemed to have no objections. I managed to obtain a couple of chickens in exchange for a pair of trousers and a sarong. There was a rumour that we would be able to carry no more than the minimum on to the trucks, so Any and I decided to kill and eat our chickens right then and there. In exchange for some more sarongs, I managed to obtain some sugar, cassava and even some medicine for Any and Staud. Fortunately, now that we were dry and resting, Any's fever disappeared after a couple of days, and Staud too improved.

In those conditions, where there was nothing to do but survive and talk, rumour thrived. Some people said they had heard news on Radio Peking that Sihanouk had returned. Everyone talked of 'five conditions' supposedly imposed by the Prince for his return.

Soon we knew them all by heart – religious tolerance and the repair of the pagodas, the reintroduction of money, the reopening of the universities and schools, the re-employment of officials and technicians, and freedom of movement. I tried to check the rumours by listening in to Voice of America's Cambodian service. There was not a word about Cambodia itself. Later, I learned why: the rumours were mostly fantasy. But I preferred to believe the Americans had simply lost interest in us – after all, I thought, why should they be interested in us when they had abandoned us? – and for a while longer, we lived in hope.

That wait lasted for two weeks, a long time when there is no hygiene, when families are piled in beside one another, and when rations are scarce. The only advantage in all this misery was that we were exempted from work and political instruction. Organization was minimal – the Khmer Rouge distributed rations only every other day.

On the day the trucks arrived, we were given rice for three days, told to pack, and ordered to meet the trucks on the highway, five hundred yards away. Soon there were more than two thousand of us lining the road. Once again, now that we were leaving and had some food, everyone found reason to be optimistic.

The trucks arrived, perhaps twenty or twenty-five in all, parking in a line parallel to the refugees. There were all sorts of vehicles – tip-up lorries belonging to the Public Works Ministry, Chinese trucks, American trucks, all without covers.

As they stopped, everyone began to pile in. For a few minutes, it was pure chaos, as families struggled to keep together. People overflowed from the back of the trucks on to the tops of the cabs and over on to the bonnets. I pushed Any, with Staud and Nawath, into the nearest vehicle. But by then, to my horror, the truck was already full. People were pushing and shoving to get places, desperate to find space, many leaving possessions behind them on the road. There was no way we could get Sim's bicycle aboard. It was just dumped by the roadside to be picked up by the Khmer Rouge. I helped my parents up into the second truck. Theng and his family – Lao, the three children and Lao's mother – were in the third, with my two sisters and Sarun. I found space, together with Sudath and Sim, in a fourth truck.

We were packed like sardines, sitting and standing tight against each other, a hundred people in a single truck. Sim and I were compressed side by side up against the back of the cab, with Sudath wedged between us. I felt I was going to suffocate, and tried to catch a glimpse of the rest of the family on the other trucks. Did the Khmer Rouge want us all dead? We were being treated worse than cattle, the victims of methodical, institutionalized contempt.

And even then not everyone had a place. Some old people and children were abandoned on the roadside. I heard one sick woman of about fifty imploring a Khmer Rouge soldier to allow her on to our truck to join her teenage children, who joined in the pleading. But the man had decided the truck was full, and refused to allow her aboard. 'Don't you worry about your mother!' he shouted to the children. 'Angkar knows where you are going!' The rest of us remained impassive, not daring to protest. The truck pulled away, leaving the woman weeping on the side of the road, crying 'May Buddha bless you!' after her vanishing children.

The convoy headed northwards through villages and small towns. Everywhere seemed deserted. Trucks were rare. Apart from our rumbling convoy, the country had become one of cyclists and pedestrians. An hour passed, two hours. Children wept, showers soaked us, the sun beat down. We had not been told when, if ever, we would stop. A few people urinated or defecated right there. Near me, two women fainted, lolling against their neighbours. After a while, when they did not recover, I realized they were dead. All the world's misery seemed crammed into that truck.

After two hours, we stopped. The Khmer Rouge driver and his co-driver noticed the corpses and ordered them to be lifted down. The bodies were lain by the roadside. There, apparently, they were to be left. When they saw what was happening, the families of the two dead women protested, weeping. Traditionally, the dead must either be buried or cremated. The idea of leaving them there by the roadside was unthinkable, sacrilegious.

I thought: Now I must not hope any longer. Now we are no longer human beings.

The realization cast all my recent optimism in a new light. The truth was that we were once again the victims of political machinations. First, Sihanouk's collapse into despotism; then Lon Nol's failure; then the Americans leaving us in the lurch; finally, the horror of the Khmer Rouge. Now I saw that there would be no relief from that horror. While the Sihanouk supporters had apparently proposed some sort of partial rehabilitation for deportees in preparation for Sihanouk's return, the puritan faction, to reassert their control, had intensified the process of 'purification'. In saying we wanted to leave Cheu Khmau to go to our native villages, we had been tricked into identifying ourselves as those with 'individualist leanings'. We had in effect denounced ourselves. This third deportation was nothing more than another step in our destruction as New People.

Since the evacuation of Phnom Penh, each transfer had served as a pretext for the Khmer Rouge to strip us of more of our property and more of our humanity. The abolition of money had cancelled at a stroke all our financial assets. Little by little, we had lost everything that was dear to us, and almost everything that would ensure our survival.

As the convoy set off again, we began to talk. Some people tried to keep their spirits up by betting on our chances of stopping in Phnom Penh. Indeed, we were nearing the city, and some of my neighbours in the truck were already sure we were genuinely on our way to Battambang. We looked around to find some encouraging sign.

There was none. The countryside still bore the marks of battle. Hundreds of cars had been abandoned, the ruined artefacts of a vanished civilization. I even spotted two rusting scrapers and three bulldozers that had once belonged to my own Public Works Department.

Then, as we passed the Chom Chau military post, which guarded the approach to the capital, we entered a new world. Everywhere, there were armed black-clad Khmer Rouge. Their automatic rifles – Chinese AK47's and American M16's – were in good condition. Here, there were Khmer Rouge soldiers in the rice fields, which were well irrigated. The corn and cassava fields were well kept. The nearer we got to the capital, the greener the countryside became.

We were heading towards Pochentong Airport. Craning my

neck to peer over the cab, I saw a red flag flying at the control tower. There was no emblem on it, although usually all flags, even the Khmer Rouge flag, sported the silhouette of the Angkor Watt Temple. The control tower was empty, the runway unused, dotted with skeletons of civil and military aircraft.

On then, through Pochentong itself. It was deserted. Not a single inhabitant, not a living soul in the markets or the villas. Doors were smashed open, furniture scattered, the gardens overgrown.

So we approached the area where the family had once lived.

'Look, Sudath,' said Sim, 'Phnom Penh.'

Sudath craned his neck and stood on tiptoe, straining to see through the crush of adults and over the cab. 'Phnom Penh!' he shouted up at me. 'Let me see, father, let me see.'

Together Sim and I levered him up between us until his eyes were level with ours. 'Are we going home now, father?'

'Home? No, not yet. We have to go right through, and on to another place first.'

All three of us stared around. On one side was the University, on the other the Monks' Hospital. I tried to catch a glimpse of my parents-in-law's house, but it was too far away. What had happened to them? It was as if they had fallen into a void, along with millions of others. Any never mentioned them now. It was too painful. They were part of a great unknown, an insoluble mystery.

'But, father,' Sudath asked, with a puzzled look, 'Why are there no people and no cars?'

I had no answer, and Sudath fell silent again, as awed as Sim and I by what we saw. All the houses seemed empty. Here and there, at road junctions, Khmer Rouge soldiers patrolled. Besides them, nothing moved. Weeds had taken over the roads and sidewalks. I didn't even see any cats and dogs. Our city had become a ghost town.

Yet, as I stared around, I saw there was life after all. Phnom Penh was still a city of gardens. All around, trees and flowers bloomed. Red blossoms shone from cushions of greenery, and in the trees and in the sky above, birds sang.

As the trucks rumbled on, travelling at hardly more than walking pace despite the lack of traffic, I found myself moved as I had never been since leaving Phnom Penh five months before. The contrast – joy above, desolation below – cut me like a knife. It was like passing through a graveyard, the buildings tombs surrounded by flowers. I wished that Sim, Sudath and I were with the others, to share the sense of loss. Then I looked around at the drawn and grimy faces of the neighbours, and saw I was not alone in my sorrow. I was not the only one blinking back tears.

Normally, to get to Battambang, we would have continued straight ahead, crossing the city centre. But instead the trucks veered left, taking a short cut through the Tuol Kauk residential area, empty now, and on past the television station, untouched but overgrown with vegetation, past the silent Lambert Stadium on the left, and the French Embassy on our right, deserted, its gates closed, then left at the Tonle Sap River.

Four miles north was a large market. It had undergone a strange transformation. All the stonework stalls and paving stones had disappeared. In their place were vegetables, as if to symbolize the Khmer Rouge revolution, as if to say 'We no longer have a market economy. Now we practise self-subsistence!' The few workers I saw on the road were peasants, Ancients, country people, from the Liberated Zones. To operate the small-scale factories demanded by the new economy, the Khmer Rouge had moved the peasants into town, and the factory workers from the town into the countryside.

Northwards, the trucks ground on through Oudong, my birthplace. We rumbled slowly through the market, lined with two-storey brick buildings, all deserted now, and on into the residential area of small houses, some of brick, some of wood, some thatched, some tiled. 'And look, Sudath,' I said, lifting him up again, 'Your grandparents' house!' The little earth-floored place was overtaken by weeds. Here I had spent my first ten years, happy, peaceful years. I remembered playing hide-and-seek in the darkness between these stilted houses. I remembered afternoons spent swimming in the lake. I was a good swimmer. I could hear my parents telling me: 'Eat your fish-tail, Thay, and you'll be able to swim like a fish!' I did as I was told, and swam well. I remembered once hiding under the bed in there for hours, to punish my parents for some terrible injustice committed against me. There was no sign of life in the village now.

As we left the village, I saw the rice fields I had known as a child. The floods that covered them ran over at the edges to join the waters of the river where I used to swim. I remembered those swims, and the sound of the blackbirds, and the sight of herons standing in the shallow waters waiting for fish. Some things had not changed: the flooded fields, the little shoots of green grass poking above the surface of the water, the blackbirds watching from the roadside trees, the distant stands of spindly sugar-palms fringing the floods – in these respects, Cambodia remained a place of timeless beauty. Somewhere, there would be a heron.

On then northwards, through Salalekpram and Kompong Chhnang, all deserted except for a few Khmer Rouge.

Dusk fell. The trucks stopped. I climbed down, and with relief brought the family together again. Everyone seemed well. I hugged Any, who said that Staud had been good, except for one spate of crying. We trooped to the side of the road and began as best we could to prepare a camp, spreading out mats and blankets, making a small fire to cook rice, and fetching water from a nearby stream.

As we waited for food, talk turned briefly back to the journey. I was muttering something about our cramped conditions and the removal of the corpses, when Vuoch broke in: 'And did you see what they had done to Phnom Penh? All those weeds! Buildings collapsing, the roads – '

'Hush, Vuoch,' my father interrupted quietly but firmly, 'Not here. We all know what these people are like. We all saw. We all felt the same. No need to say anything.'

After that, we ate in silence, and settled down to sleep.

At dawn, we rolled up our blankets and were ordered back into the trucks. With the new day spirits rose again. What were we afraid of, after all? Weren't we on the road to Battambang? The thought reassured me. Again, as we rumbled on, I allowed myself to believe in the possibility of a better life.

Another twenty miles further on, the trucks stopped. We were at Pursat, one hundred and fifteen miles from Phnom Penh. A barrier guarded the entry to the town. I saw the chief of the convoy go to talk to a group of Khmer Rouge near some small bungalows which served as offices. He was there for half an hour. The motors remained running, which was encouraging, but I didn't like the delay.

When the officer returned, the sentry made no move to raise the barrier. The trucks started – and instead of going straight ahead to Battambang, turned left into the province of Pursat.

So much for Battambang. A groan of dismay arose from us all. Once again, we were going to an unknown destination.

Pursat dropped away behind us. We passed a huge railway depot, where there were thousands of New People waiting alongside the rails, obviously New People from the colour of their clothes. For a moment, we asked each other if we were going to Battambang by train. But no. We went right past, on through flat agricultural regions of rice fields, corn fields and sugar-palms, then into forest, until, around midday, the trucks pulled up in a line at the Pursat River.

It was the end of the road.

Now we found ourselves part of some huge transit operation. All around, there were thousands of other deportees, waiting. Our convoy was not the first, and would not be the last. The sun hung over our heads from a clear sky. Warned not to wander off, we regrouped, and settled down on the river-bank. Any, Keng, Vuoch and Lao cooked rice while Theng and I improvised a shelter with some branches so that the children could sleep in shade. Later, I saw some groups leaving in ox-carts, heading into the forest. Others were crossing the river on barges. Clearly, we too were destined for the forest, to help tame one of Cambodia's wildest regions, Cardamom.

Cardamom was reputedly an unhealthy place, a forested, mountainous area where malaria was rampant. The land was hilly, the trees uncut, and the population sparse. The Khmer Loeu – Mountain Khmer – were almost tribal, living mainly from hunting and gathering. They had small rice fields, but their harvests were meagre, and they seldom visited the area's only established village, Leach.

Men in black – civilians, dark-skinned mountain people – moved about among us to register the names of families and the number of people in each family. We found ourselves included in a group of fifty families, with whom, later in the afternoon, we were told to break camp. Gloomy and resigned, we dragged ourselves to our feet, picked up our packages, and joined the crowd.

We must have made a dismal sight. Hemmed in by refugees behind and in front, Theng led our eighteen-strong group with his two boys on either side. Behind him came Lao, supporting her baby on her hip with one arm, and holding a bundle under the other. Then came Lao's mother, my mother, supported by Vuoch and my silent, stoical father, Sarun with little Srey, and Keng supporting a bundle on her head, as always near Sarun in case he said anything out of place and needed her support. I brought up the rear, accompanying Any with Staud on her hip, and Sim trying to keep Sudath and Nawath cheerful.

Sim was the only one of us unaffected by despondency. 'Come on, Sudath,' he said with a grin, as if he hadn't a care in the world. 'A walk in the forest! This will be fun!' I don't know what we would have done without him.

Instead of crossing the river, we were led through the slowly milling crowds and into the forest. As we walked, we passed small communities inhabited by New People like us. They stared at us with curiosity mixed with fear, keeping their distance, but eager to spot any relative or friend who might happen to pass. From time to time, a grimy face lined with exhaustion, hair plastered down by sweat, would light up with joy at the sight of a familiar face. But there was no time for more than a greeting. The delighted chatter was quickly interrupted as the column moved on. Every mile or so, we slowed or stopped to wait for the stragglers, for the line now stretched back well over half a mile, with the older people bringing up the rear.

Towards sunset, it began to rain, as usual in the rainy season. We were ordered to stop where we were. The downpour became heavier. There was no shelter. We covered the children with our jackets, and tried to rest on our soaked mats. Staud was crying, though Nawath and Sudath, toughened by months of hard living, squatted on their haunches silent and uncomplaining. Soon the ground was awash. Mud dribbled between our feet and soaked our bags. Water trickled down inside our clothes. Old and young alike huddled together, beaten and miserable.

I looked around. In the dying light and the rain, the mass of people around us were undifferentiated shadows, moving little, speaking little, eating the rice distributed at the Watt Ang Recar pagoda two days before. There was no service or community organization to take care of the sick. No one complained. We were all paralysed by fear of the Khmer Rouge, who stood around in groups of two or three, unmoving in the rain and the gloom.

Next morning, rations were distributed. The two Khmer Rouge in charge of the distribution stood under a thatched roof, one calling out names through a microphone, the other plunging a tin into a large sack of rice and measuring out the ration for each. As I received my ration – a half-measure of a condensed-milk tin, four ounces of rice per person per day – the soldier said, as he was saying to each of us in turn: 'Wait for Angkar's decisions! Don't go anywhere!'

And there we stayed for three days. Every day, the system was repeated – the tin of rice, the words, the interminable queue. It took up to four hours to get our half-measure of rice.

Then, on the fourth day, the words were different: 'Now we will allocate land to you.'

While we muttered to each other, wondering what was going to happen next, the heads of families were formed into columns, about fifty in a column. I lined up with my father and Theng. Where did they intend taking us, we asked each other. Close by? Or deep into the jungle?

With each column under the command of two soldiers, we marched off along a trail. After a mile or so, the Khmer Rouge began to allot plots of land in the forest, pointing out trees about twenty yards apart to act as markers. Here, in virgin forest, we were to construct huts. 'You have to stay here,' one of the black-uniformed young soldiers said, 'For ever.'

6 THE JUNGLE OF THE DYING

As I walked back to fetch the rest of the family and our baggage, the awfulness of our position struck me. Beneath a scattering of big trees, the jungle was a mass of saplings, thick undergrowth, tall grass, and thorns. There was no heavy canopy to protect us against the rain.

Without any clear idea of what I was doing, I began to clear the undergrowth with my tall young cousin, Sim, whom I had taken under my wing. Any spread leaves and mats on the damp earth as a base to take care of the children. Sim and I went off to cut poles, make holes to stick them into, and dig drains. Sim as usual worked as if he didn't have a care in the world, and even began cheerfully whistling a song that had been popular just before the revolution – 'I'm rowing a boat! Rowing a boat! Rowing a boat!'

'Be quiet, Sim!' I said, glancing round, 'You'll draw attention to yourself, silly boy.' He should have learned by now not to show any sign of happiness.

In the afternoon, we managed to tie a few poles together with vines and get the beginnings of a thatch on. There were no walls. Then I packed the floor of the hut with stones to make the ground as firm as possible, and covered this bumpy base with a carpet of leaves.

Towards the end of the afternoon, a loudspeaker called us for food. With the other men of the family, I went back down the trail. We gathered round a table, thousands of us, waiting for our names to be shouted out.

As dusk fell, I set about making a fire. The wood was as wet as the ground but I still had my two lighters left over from Phnom Penh, and, after scraping away the damp surface of the branches with my knife to reveal the dry wood within, we succeeded in burning a few branches to boil our rice.

We had never been in such a terrible situation as this. Before, we had always stayed in houses raised on piles, traditional houses protected from the damp. Our hut, set in the shade, would always be wet. It certainly was then. Even before dark, it began to rain again. Soon, the carpet of leaves and the mats over them were impregnated with water. We wallowed in a bog, freezing and worn out. Staud was now permanently sick. The other two children just stood or squatted sadly, watching us. As we huddled round the fire, Any and I looked at each other without speaking, and wept. No one spoke. Tears were the only words we needed, tears not so much for ourselves as for the children.

Those first three days were a nightmare. As soon as I stopped work on the hut, I fell silent, transfixed by our misfortune, numb with cold and fear, overwhelmed with gloomy thoughts. Only young Sim remained lively, indifferent to the discomfort. He was strong, with no responsibilities, and nothing seemed to bother him. It was Sim who was the driving force behind the building of the hut. He seemed to run everywhere, collecting wood and tie-vines.

While he worked, I checked up on my parents, who were with the other twelve members of our group three hundred yards up the trail. For the time being they all seemed well. Theng and Sarun, assisted by Vuoch and Keng, had started to build a house that was much more solid than ours. Their site was better as well – a clearing, shaded by two big trees, on a slope down to a stream. Srey Rath was outside playing with Theng's two boys, Visoth and Amap. My father was his usual stoical self, claiming in an off-hand way that he was fine. After all, he said, he had never expected anything better of the Khmer Rouge. But my mother, lying on a mat beneath a part of finished thatch, had been worn out by the journey. She forced a smile for me, and said she would be all right in a day or so. Only Lao, who had always been the most active of the women, seemed too downcast to do anything. She just sat beside her exhausted mother, hardly glancing up at me. Somewhat reassured, I walked back down the trail to see how Sim was getting on with the house.

Near our rudimentary home, another house was going up. Three sturdy men were working on it, tying roof poles together, and laying on thatch. To my amazement and delight, one of them was my old friend Chan. I had been wondering what had happened to him. I had last seen him walking off in the rain towards the Watt Ang Recar pagoda. Somehow, in that two-week wait in the pagoda, we had missed each other. Now, there he was again, slapping my shoulders in welcome, as delighted to see us as I was to see him. He introduced me to the two men he was sharing with – Keo, a former Customs officer, who had managed to send his wife and mother abroad before the fall of Phnom Penh, and Sun, a science graduate and a teacher about my age. They were clearly a resourceful trio, and were building a large hut, with a fine ridged roof.

Work started on the fourth day, by which time our houses were ready. The first task was to clear the forest, chopping trees and dragging them aside. Veal Vong, as our camp was called, was right in the middle of uncut jungle. There were no existing rice fields anywhere near by. We had to create our own. The pattern was much the same as before – wake up at six a.m., a break for food between noon and one p.m., work until six p.m. However, for the first time we were supervised by armed guards during our working hours. As we chopped trees, pulled up bushes, uprooted the stumps, and piled them into heaps beside the cleared land, the Khmer Rouge would suddenly appear to watch us, causing us to redouble our efforts.

As I discovered, wandering the trails and standing in line for food during those first few waterlogged weeks, there must have been five hundred or six hundred families in our camp, scattered over two or three miles of forest paths – nearly five thousand people in all.

Nor was the great exodus over yet. For several weeks after our arrival, thousands and thousands more, all city people in their tattered city clothes, all as distressed as we had been, filed past our hut, plunging deeper into the forest, to make new fields as we were doing. We watched them in silence, as we had been watched on our arrival. Always the same poignancy, the same drawn and mortified faces, the same tears, the same little dramas as friends and families met and parted, never to see each other again. So many people, so many wracked bodies, so many unsmiling faces. I began to wonder if we were part of some gigantic extermination programme, for the decrease in rations and the increase in forced labour could only lead to hundreds, perhaps thousands, of deaths. If this was purification, it was purification by the survival of the fittest.

As the days went by, I became ever more worried about the children. They had completely lost their carefree ways. They no longer played, not even with their cousins, Theng's two boys. They became silent and wary. Staud's condition worsened day by day. His feet were swollen, and he became weak. He no longer seemed to have the energy to cry. His state of health began to obsess us, and we fed him any little extra rations we could lay our hands on. At my heartfelt request, Any was exempted from work to look after him.

It was not long before the dying started. Even in the first week, I saw several people carrying corpses down the trail. It was hardly surprising, given the amount of people in the forest near us, and their state of health. The dead were buried in the forest, at the edge of our newly cut fields. I was told it was because the Khmer Rouge thought that the corpses should act as fertilizer for the future crops. Cremation, they said, was mere waste. You had to gather the wood, make a pyre, and attend the funeral – a waste of wood, labour and time. In Veal Vong, a corpse had its uses.

At first, these sights made little impact on me, obsessed as I was with my own problems. I hardly knew the families involved.

One evening, though, Staud's fever became worse. During that night it rained violently, so heavily that our roof of branches and leaves opened. Water cascaded on to us and ran over our mats, flooding the floor. The only way to avoid it was to squat, holding our clothes off the ground, or dangling them over branches and twigs leant against the uprights. But after a while, I gave up, and asked my three neighbours to give Any and the two younger children room for the night. They agreed readily enough.

When I returned home next day, Any was cooking the rice. Staud was all curled up, dozing on the mat.

'How is he?' I asked. 'Has he eaten?'

'He doesn't want anything. He just lies there,' replied Any sadly.

Indeed, the poor little boy looked terrible, like one of those children on famine relief posters we used to see in Phnom Penh. He was nothing more than skin and bone, his stomach bloated, his feet and legs swollen. The other two children were squatting near by, weeping softly, and shivering, waiting for their rice soup.

Suddenly, Staud called 'Mak! Mak!' (Mummy! Mummy!)

'What is it, Staud?' said Any, going across to him. 'What's the matter, darling?'

Silently, he moved his hand, beckoning her closer. She sat right beside him, and patted him. He closed his eyes again. After a few minutes, she took him up and cradled him. He said nothing, sleeping in her arms.

Half an hour later, he twitched, as if he was having a dream.

'Staud!' she said. 'Staud, wake up!'

He didn't respond. I shook him to wake him. Again, no response.

Any already knew the truth and was weeping bitterly, in silence.

'Yes,' I whispered, 'He's dead.'

For several minutes, I was too stunned to do anything, too battered by exhaustion and grief. Then I tried to take Staud from Any, and after a while she let me have him. I laid the poor emaciated little body down on a mat. Any sat beside him and cried.

Now I became aware of the two other children, shivering, not yet realizing the enormity of what had happened. I put my arms around them. It was as if I was in a coma, unable to move, unable to re-establish contact with life, fixed there between my two children, holding them to me, with my baby boy dead and my wife incapacitated with grief. At last, I thought, he is free. He no longer has to endure this infernal existence. At least he died quietly, in his sleep, without pain. I hoped we would be as lucky.

The thought brought me back to reality. I laid the two boys down on their mats and covered them with a blanket, then lay down beside Any and held her in my arms, feeling her body wracked by sobs. My mind began to wander. What would I do with the body? How would I be able to help Any and the children cope with their loss? Eventually, I drifted into an exhausted sleep.

Next morning, I told Any I would have to go to the village chief, to excuse myself from work, to get permission to bury Staud.

'No,' she said, and I knew her mind had been working over the same ground as mine the night before. 'No, he must be cremated. To bury him would be to abandon him in the forest. He would be lost for ever. I will collect the ashes and carry them with me wherever I go.' She looked up, haggard with grief and lack of sleep, her eyes red with tears.

'No one has been cremated here,' I said. Then, to console her: 'Don't cry. He is free. We will have other children. It is a relief for him.'

'Do something, my dearest Thay,' she begged, her voice breaking with sobs. 'I don't want him to be buried in the forest. We can't abandon him here. I want him to be warm . . . Staud was always too cold . . . let him be warm now . . . I don't want to leave him . . . I want to take him with me.'

'All right,' I said. 'All right.'

I was nervous of asking the village chief for permission to perform the cremation, but Chan, who got on well with the chief, volunteered to speak for me. Permission was granted, as an exceptional favour. The chief even came across to our hut to offer his condolences to Any, who was still weeping beside the body.

Leaving her to her grief, I walked up the trail to tell my parents what had happened. They both hurried back with me to offer Any consolation but, clearly, Staud's death came as no shock to either of them. 'Death will come to all of us if things go on like this,' said my father, his face set.

In the afternoon, Sim and I built a funeral pyre three feet high, forty yards back from our hut into the forest. I helped Any put Staud in the best clothes we had – shorts, T-shirt, even shoes. We laid him on the sticks and set fire to it.

The fire burned all afternoon, Any watched for a while, her face lined with grief, and then retired into the house. Sim just sat there, staring into the fire in silence. Later, in the evening, when the fire was burning low, the others came to watch the dying flames and sit for a while with Any. When they had gone, I collected the ashes in a small bag, which I laid gently by Any.

She had been right to insist on cremation. It helped to cope with grief.

A few days later, during lunch, my father came across to talk to us as he often did, bringing bad news – Theng's mother-in-law had died that day. It had been very quick. She had developed a fever the night before and died that morning. I had hardly addressed more than a few words to her through all the last months, but the suddenness of the death brought home to me how vulnerable we all were. One day, a child, the next an adult; when would it be my parents' turn, or Any's, or the other children, or my own?

Now, death came with increasing frequency in the forest around us. The bodies were buried all around the edge of the clearings by grave-diggers appointed by the village chief. Grave-diggers became necessary because the families had become too weak to dig the graves themselves. It was not a bad job, for it meant being exempted from work for a day.

There was no relief from the unrelenting labour, except for the tedious political meetings and a day off every ten days. Time was measured now by the numbers of deaths per day in the people round about us – four deaths, five deaths, sometimes as many as ten deaths a day.

Hope died, and was buried along with the corpses. Mourning became part of our slavery.

As conditions worsened – the rice ration after several weeks was dropped to one can for six people each day – a new economic system, barter, ensured survival of a sort.

It appeared that three or four miles away, there were villages occupied by Ancients, as well as many other camps established by newcomers like us. We had frequent contact with both Ancients and New People, for New People, supervised by Ancients, were often sent into the forest to cut bamboo. Columns of people would stream past our hut in the morning carrying cooking pots, with small bags of food at their waists, returning in the evening laden with bamboo. Often, a casual greeting would lead on to conversation, and thus contacts and friendships developed. The Ancients received rather more rice than we did, and in addition were allowed to grow their own food. And we, the city people, had possessions – mainly clothes, but also jewellery, watches, the occasional radio – that were of interest to the peasants, who were willing to exchange their rice for our goods. Regular contacts with passers-by ensured that everyone knew the relative value of their goods.

Strangely, it became clear that the Khmer Rouge were also feeding rice into this black market system, and profiting from it to acquire goods for themselves and their families. Where did all this rice come from?

Eventually, the explanation got around. The amount of rice to be distributed was calculated on the basis of the census carried out on our arrival. But the only people who knew the actual number of survivors were the Khmer Rouge themselves. They simply never reported many of the dead. Rice for those who had died kept on arriving. Thus, the worse we were treated, the more deaths there were, and the more rice the Khmer Rouge had for themselves.

These embezzlements institutionalized the black market in which the Khmer Rouge themselves played a vital role. A sort of exchange rate was established – the equivalent of 10 cans of rice (rice was always measured in terms of condensed-milk cans) for a pair of trousers, 4 cans for a shirt, 6 cans for a cotton sarong, 15 cans for a silk sarong. A *tael* of gold – just over one and a quarter ounces – bought 30 to 40 cans' worth. Automatic watches were much in demand, both by the Khmer Rouge and by the Ancients. A good wristwatch could fetch 60 to 80 cans' worth of rice. My radio was now out of batteries, and I didn't think it worthwhile to buy more on the black market, so I offered to exchange it. I received 25 cans' worth of rice for it.

A few city deportees acted as brokers, among them a contact of mine who had been one of my subordinates in the Public Works Department. He took the risk of meeting the relatives of the Khmer Rouge (for the Khmer Rouge themselves could not be seen to be playing a part in the system). He would negotiate the deal and, as his profit, take a share of the rice. If, for instance, I parted with jewellery to the value of one *tael* of gold, in exchange for which he received from the Khmer Rouge 40 cans' worth of rice, he would pass on 35 cans. The system actually worked fairly well. The local Khmer Rouge, or, rather, their wives and their parents, respected their promises on the whole. They recognized that this illegal exchange could only work on the basis of confidence and discretion.

All of us resorted to bartering: my father, Theng, and Keng (acting on behalf of poor Sarun) as well as myself. Thus both households held together, and I was able to feed not only my wife and children, but also my cousin Sim.

Sim was drafted into a youth brigade a couple of weeks after our arrival at Veal Vong, and was based in a camp elsewhere, two or three miles away. But every evening, he sneaked back to have dinner with us. He wasn't meant to do it, and would have been severely punished if he had been found out, but that didn't bother him. He was quite happy to take the risk. 'Anything for a little extra food!' he used to say, with a carefree smile. Though his rice ration was larger than ours, because he worked correspondingly harder, he could always do with more. We were happy to oblige. He had always been a willing worker, never showing a sign of unhappiness. His arrivals in the evening brought a little joy into our bleak lives. It was about the only thing that made Sudath and Nawath smile.

Having brought considerable quantities of clothing and jewellery with us, we were amongst the lucky ones. Some people at Veal Vong had nothing at all – no medicine, no clothing, no jewellery, no dollars. You would think, therefore, that they were outside the system. But even they found a niche to supplement their rations. The best way was to specialize in the search for food. On our day off – once every ten days – we were allowed to gather what we could from the forest. Those who wished therefore, could turn themselves into expert gatherers. Some tracked down land crabs, some caught fish with lines or traps, some collected mushrooms. They then exchanged their delicacies for rice.

Yet still the people died. First malnutrition and exhaustion undermined them. Strangely, the men succumbed more easily than the women. Perhaps it was to do with the amount of work; or perhaps they were not so able to withstand the shock of having their world destroyed, of no longer being in control of life; or perhaps, in these gruelling circumstances, the women possessed some deep-seated strength that was normally hidden.

And among the men it was the harder workers, the apparently stronger ones, who tended to succumb more quickly. Often, they were the once well-off, over-eager to prove they had set their old ways behind them. Weakened by their efforts, they fell an easy prey to any one of a number of illnesses – diarrhoea, dysentery, beri-beri, malaria.

Secondly, food-poisoning was a common cause of death. Rice

soup was mixed with polluted stream water, or unknown wild plants, or mushrooms. Especially mushrooms. There were a number of different species, and we didn't know much about them, learning from hearsay how to differentiate the edible ones from the poisonous ones. For those who chose wrongly, death arrived quickly – vomiting and stomach pains were quickly followed by diarrhoea and death. Before eating any mushrooms, I made sure that other families had already eaten some of them before us. I wasn't about to risk the children's lives for the sake of mushrooms.

Then I began to notice the disappearances.

The first one I noticed was Ming, a Vietnamese neighbour. There were several Vietnamese families in the village, all of whom had been told they would be able to go home soon. Somehow, the time never came.

Ming was a tall, strong character with a wife and four-year-old child. I liked him. His wide smile and broad shoulders always seemed to carry some comfort. One day he confided to me that he had found a crafty way to make his ration grow. In the evening, during the rice distribution, he went up to the bags, and, as people pressed around awaiting their turn, he stuck a special craftsman's knife – a long hollow tube with a sharpened end – into one of the bags. Out flowed the rice into his waiting scarf. By the time he told me of his trick he had got an extra six cans' worth of rice. But the next time he tried it, one of the Khmer Rouge spotted him. He was seized and led away for 're-education', and his wife was left anxiously awaiting his return.

Day after day she waited. Days turned into weeks, and still he didn't reappear.

Then I noticed that a number of former Republican officers who had tried to conceal their identity had vanished. A couple of times, a worried wife asked me, 'Have you seen my husband? He went off to cut bamboo and I haven't seen him for two days.' I thought perhaps they had escaped.

When Sim failed to appear one evening, my uneasiness increased. We were expecting him as usual, and he just didn't come. We shrugged, and told the children he would be along as usual the following evening. 'Yes, he's probably got some extra work, silly fellow,' I said. But he didn't come the next day either, or the next. No one had seen him. I wondered if perhaps he had fallen ill. A week passed, then two weeks, then a month.

I suppose I suspected what had happened, but didn't like to admit it to myself. There came a day, however, when I saw the truth, and could no longer deny what had happened to Sim and the rest.

I was with my neighbours cutting bamboo shoots, perhaps two miles from my house, deep in the jungle. Ahead of me I saw an ideal bamboo tree – a dozen separate stems, with a number of tender little shoots growing up between them. As I approached it, I noticed a strange smell. Then, almost at my feet, I saw a shape and a patch of dark blue. I looked closer.

It was the body of a man in a dark blue shirt, face down, and badly decomposed.

I stood back, feeling shocked, but not surprised. It was like the confirmation of something I had known for a long time. I thought: it's too close to the village. It's been put there on purpose to frighten us. That thought was even more frightening than finding the corpse.

Later, an acquaintance told me about Sim. He had been spotted by Khmer Rouge on his way to our house, and taken away into the forest for 're-education'.

'What harm am I doing?' he had protested. 'I'm just going to my cousin's to eat, the way I always do. What harm is there in that? No one has ever stopped me before, I didn't know I was doing anything wrong. Please comrades, now I know it's wrong, I'll never. . .'

'No, no comrade, you are an anarchist, you do not obey orders. You must come with us.'

He had simply vanished. I was told he must have been cudgelled to death like so many others, to save bullets and prevent anyone hearing anything.

Poor naive Sim. An anarchist, the brigade leader told the rest of his group, an anarchist who loved his freedom too much. We never told the children. He simply disappeared from their lives.

It must have been in October, when we'd been in Veal Vong for just over a month, that people began to speak openly about running away. There was no need for secrecy among the New People. Family after family told me that they couldn't stand it any longer, that they had nothing to lose, and planned to flee across the mountains and into Thailand, seventy miles away. Families would organize themselves into small groups, and the next day they were gone, without any real preparation.

They were acts of the purest desperation, for there was little chance of reaching safety. The Cardamom mountain chain towards which they plunged through the jungle rose to peaks of five thousand feet. There was still torrential rain, and the rivers in the mountains would be rising and falling dramatically within a matter of hours. If the problems were bad for the students who fled from Sramar Leav, how much worse would they be for families with women and children, weakened by lack of food and hard work? At the time I wanted to believe that some of these families were successful. Now I think it's more likely that most, if not all, fell prey to Khmer Rouge patrols, or simply died.

But with nothing to lose, it seemed better to risk death in the jungle than drift into certain death here. I too planned to escape, infected by the enthusiasm of the others.

Any and I began to hoard food, and formed our own little group of conspirators. I brought the adult members of my family in on the scheme, though none of the others wanted to join us. I kept it from the children, who might unwittingly have betrayed us. Our three neighbours, Keo, Chan and Sun, said they would join us, as did another family group, the Chreans. Chrean was a stocky little man, much smaller than me, of about forty, with a much younger wife and her twenty-year-old sister. Although my three neighbours tried to persuade me to leave the children with my parents, arguing (rightly) that they would slow us down, Any and I refused to consider it. It seemed to us that a successful escape would involve no more than having enough food and knowing how to avoid the Khmer Rouge in the forest between our camp and the river. Once across the river, we would head west over the mountains.

One day, when we judged ourselves to be ready, I went with another escaping family along the path to the river, three miles away, as a reconnaissance. In order not to attract the attention of the Khmer Rouge, I followed them at a distance, pretending to be looking for bamboo shoots. From the river bank vegetation, I saw them cross the river. It was a broad stream, eighty yards across, but shallow. The men, the women and the children all held hands, making enough of a chain to stand up against the current. Slowly they forded their way across, the water swirling around their waists. It looked easy enough. I planned our escape for the next day.

I went to see my parents and the rest of the family to inform them of our impending departure. They were all for it. 'Yes, Thay, you must leave,' my mother said. 'If you stay here you will die. If you leave, you will have a chance of being free again. It will be better for Any, better for the children, if you make the attempt. Even if you fail, it is better to die in the mountains, free, than to stay here. I will pray for you. Above all, do not worry about your father and me.' She gave me one of her quick little smiles. 'We are already too old.'

My father, too, gave his approval. 'Make sure your children remember their grandparents. Tell them that Chhor and Loan will be with them in spirit.'

'I will, father.'

As I embraced the others, my father was still talking, saying he had nothing to give me but his good wishes and his prayers. 'But,' he added, as an afterthought, just before I left, 'Perhaps this will be of help, my son. It is an old Sanskrit prayer that may be of some protection against the dangers of the forest.'

He then muttered some syllables which meant nothing to me. It sounded like some sort of a chant, a mantra. Out of respect for him, I asked him to repeat them. Again and again, he repeated the words, until I had them by heart: *Neak mo puthir yak, meak a-uk, meak a-uk, meak a-uk.* Say that, he said, whenever you feel yourself to be in danger, and repeat it seven times. He had no idea what it meant either, but I learned it dutifully. *Neak mo puthir yak . . . Neak mo puthir yak* – as I repeated my sevenfold mantra, the sound of it gave me confidence. . . *meak a-uk, meak a-uk, meak a-uk.*

'But,' my father warned, as I embraced them with tears in my eyes for what I thought was the last time, 'Don't allow it to make you too audacious. It will help you only if you help yourself.'

* * *

The following day was one of those on which we were exempted from work to gather extra food in the forest. We left that morning, like ordinary villagers going off to hunt for fruits, mushrooms and bamboo shoots, but with extra clothes, cans, utensils, my one remaining fishing-net, the little bag of Staud's ashes, and other things wrapped up with the rice in our clothes. Keeping apart in order not to raise any suspicion, urging Sudath and Nawath along as fast as we could, we wound our way along the trail through the forest to the river-bank. We were the first to reach the meeting point, three hundred yards from the path, back from the river.

After a few minutes of anxious waiting, the others – our three neighbours and the Chreans – joined us. We edged forwards to the river itself. To our disappointment, it was higher and wider than it had been the day before. There must have been heavy rains up in the mountains. There was no way to make a human chain and ford across those surging waters.

But no one was willing to consider retreat yet. We decided to try to build a raft. There was bamboo enough in the area. We had knives and axes, and, after all, a hundred yards was not far. The adults could swim, and the women and children could sit on the raft beside the baggage. In fact, it didn't seem to me as if we had any choice. I had the feeling that we were being pushed by some invisible force. Our commitment, the simple fact of having left the village, and of standing there by the river, made us believe that we were already halfway to freedom.

Chrean kept watch, with his wife and sister-in-law. Making as little noise as possible, Keo, Chan, Sun, Any and I began to cut and prune bamboo canes.

Time passed. Noon. One o'clock. Two o'clock – and at five we had to be back in our house. After that, our absence would be noticed. At around three we had enough bamboo. But there was no rope. I decided to sacrifice my fishing-net.

We had just begun to tie the bamboo together when Chrean hurried up to us. He said there were many people foraging near us. They were all New People, but he admitted he was nervous. Looking at him closely, I saw that he was not simply nervous, but terrified – trembling, glancing round, and covered in a cold sweat.

'I must go back!' he stuttered. 'I can't go on! There's still enough time for me to return to the village by five o'clock. Don't worry! I won't talk. I won't say anything.' I have never seen a man so panic-stricken. And it was so unexpected. There had been nothing in his behaviour before to indicate that he would crack up under pressure. 'Please excuse me, Thay, but I don't have the courage to cross.'

We were all stunned. Here was one of our leaders, imperilling us all just when we might have been able to seize freedom. We all began talking in indignant, urgent voices: 'You can't give in like this – it's impossible – you are our neighbour – the Khmer Rouge are going to wonder about us – if you return, they'll see we've tricked them – they'll get you, then they'll come after us.' I repeated the arguments for going. An escape now, in mid-October, was a risky enterprise at the best of times, but it was a risk we'd all accepted. Better to die in the forest than rot in the village.

He wouldn't listen. Instead of replying, he just turned round and led his wife and sister-in-law away.

His fear proved contagious. I heard Chan mutter, 'Maybe he's right. Maybe we should all go back.'

No, I said, how could we return to Veal Vong without being spotted? I began to improvise a new plan, not simple, but possible. There were still hundreds of families coming past us every day to set up new camps deeper in the forest. If we could pass ourselves off as a family of newly arrived deportees and follow them on down the trail to a regular crossing point, we might at least be able to cross the river, and once we were there, break away and continue on through the forest. After all, there were no identity cards any more. We were safe as long as no one recognized us.

It was agreed.

Before leaving, we had to cover all traces of our work. The raft was broken up and the bamboo thrown in the river along with the torn fishing-net. Later, I realized what a waste it was, but at the time I didn't give it another thought. I still thought we would be across the river and into the mountains before nightfall.

By now, however, Keo, Sun and Chan had also lost their composure. They urged Any and I to hurry up, but with the two children and our baggage, we couldn't. I told them not to panic, but they wouldn't wait, hurrying on ahead to the spot where the Khmer Rouge were ferrying new arrivals across the river.

We weren't far from the place when the three of them came running back down the trail. 'They asked us which group we belonged to and the number of the group,' Chan said, his eyes wide with fear. 'We didn't know anything about any group numbers! We couldn't reply!'

Now we had no choice but to go back.

We arrived towards dusk, at about five-thirty. I told Any and the children to hold back in case of trouble. Apparently my three neighbours had not been missed, and simply set about making an evening meal, but with me it was different. Peering in, I saw that a number of the things – clothing and mats – had been moved. The place had been searched.

My other neighbour, who lived across the trail, saw us arriving and called out, 'Hey, Thay! The Khmer Rouge came to visit your house this afternoon. You're for it! I heard them say that you were running away.'

'Running away?' I said innocently. 'I went out this morning like everyone else to pick mushrooms and tubers.'

'Where are your children, then? They didn't see your children or your wife.'

'Any wanted to go along and we couldn't leave the children alone. What's so odd about that?'

'But where are your things, Thay? There didn't seem to be many of your things in the shack.'

As the man retreated back to his house, Any joined us.

'What is it, Thay?' she asked anxiously.

'The Khmer Rouge were here,' I replied. 'Don't worry. I'll think of something.'

Strangely, the danger seemed to calm me. I found I was able to plan my next move carefully.

Not far along the trail there lived a man who had been a truck driver in the Department of Public Works. His name was Saly. We had worked together for three years or more in the old days, and I trusted him.

'My friend, you must help me,' I said, as I came into his house. 'There's no one else I can trust around here.'

'What can I do, sir?' he asked. He always called me sir, although I told him not to. I explained to him what had happened, and then: 'Will you keep my extra clothes here, the baggage I took on my escape attempt? Then, if the Khmer Rouge ask you, tell them I left my things with you this morning for safety when we all went off to look for food in the forest.'

He agreed readily enough. I fetched my pack and borrowed from him some tubers to back up my story, leaving him two cans' worth of rice and some salt in exchange.

By now, the news of my return had spread. A few minutes later, two Khmer Rouge had arrived: the village chief – a tall man who, it was said, had once been a fervent Buddhist – and a soldier. The chief seemed impatient.

'We know that you tried to run away, Thay. You returned because you couldn't cross the river. Right?'

'No. Who told you that?' I said, feigning surprise. 'I went to gather tubers. Look, my wife's got them over there.'

He didn't want to believe me. 'Why did you take your family into the forest?'

'My wife wanted to come along and bring the children, that's all. The younger one wasn't well, and the elder one wanted the trip.'

'Well then, where are your things?'

'My things? I left them with a friend up the trail. That reminds me, I ought to go and get them back. Why don't you come along? You know you can't leave things in an unguarded house. Even under Angkar's rule, not everyone is to be trusted. We've lost quite a few things lately.'

I didn't for a moment doubt Saly's loyalty.

'Back again!' I said cheerily, as I walked in. 'I came to get the things I left with you this morning.'

Saly, as calm as I could have wished, said 'Fine,' and then, with a look at the chief, added, 'Anything wrong, comrade? Comrade Thay asked me to keep his things for the day. My wife and son were going to be home all day. He can take his things, can't he?'

The chief nodded. There was no reason any more not to believe us.

With that, I temporarily renounced escape, at least in a large

97

group, for I now had learned another lesson of survival: not to trust appearances. Apparently reliable people could change in the face of danger. But I was still determined to leave Cambodia. My parents too were adamant that I shouldn't give up. When I told them the story of how the escape had failed, tears came to their eyes, and my father told me not to despair, other opportunities would arise.

From now on, however, I would act alone. I analysed my past and my character, seeking some confirmation that my decision was the right one. I had always tried to assert my individuality, developing my talents, taking whatever opportunities offered themselves. I thought I was reasonably flexible. I knew how to be humble and had also had some experience in leadership. I would organize our flight, taking as much of the family as I could, on my own terms.

Time passed. Life once again became a round of work and political meetings, the burden made easier only by the regular small additions to our diet that I managed to obtain by making exchanges. My main concern was to keep a low profile until another chance to escape presented itself.

It was the unfortunate Sarun, Keng's husband, who showed me how vital it was to remain inconspicuous. One day, I was working near him as usual, for whenever we could we arranged to be as near each other as possible, especially since little Staud's death and the disappearance of Sim. Sarun was in one of his moods. Because of his accident, he was an unpredictable fellow, often charming, and usually amenable, but on some occasions capable of being extremely irritating. With Keng's uncritical support and our understanding, however, we had so far managed to prevent him causing offence to the Khmer Rouge.

On this day, as we were clearing new ground together, he began to cut at the undergrowth, more and more viciously, working himself up into a rage.

'What kind of revolution is this?' I heard him mutter. 'We have to work too hard.'

'Sarun, keep your voice down,' I warned. There were guards not too far away. But Sarun took no notice and just shouted angrily, more loudly this time, 'No, Thay, you tell me! I'm hungry and tired! What sort of a revolution is this?'

Out of the corner of my eye, I saw the guards look up. I moved away, hoping they wouldn't associate me with this outburst.

'What sort of a revolution is this?' Sarun shouted again, to no one in particular, wielding his machete like a madman. 'Hard work! Hunger! Nothing else!'

The two guards came up to him. 'What did you say, comrade?' asked one.

Sarun stopped cutting, turned to him and looked him in the eye. 'I said: What sort of a revolution is this? We have to work too hard and we don't get enough to eat! There! That's what I said!'

My heart sank.

'Very well. If that's what you say, follow me.'

The guards led him off into the forest.

Silence.

I waited, my heart racing.

Nothing.

Not willing to take any risks, I returned to my work, hoping against hope that Sarun would reappear.

An hour passed, two hours.

Eventually, I could not deceive myself any longer. I knew I would never see Sarun again.

That evening, after work, instead of going home, I went straight to my parents' house. As I entered, Keng glanced up with a smile, as everyone else did, expecting to see Sarun. I just looked at her. The smile left her face.

'Sarun?' she asked, pulling Srey Rath to her. I nodded, and sat down heavily.

There was so little to tell. I had no memorial of words I could conjure up for him.

As I finished, Keng burst into tears, holding Srey Rath tightly to her. 'I knew something like this would happen,' she wept. 'I knew it, I knew it, I knew it,' and then could speak no more.

I placed my hand on her shoulder, feeling at a loss, and caught my father's eye. 'Well, perhaps – ' I began. My father shook his head, as if to say: Don't say anything. There is no hope. We all know that.

I nodded slowly, kissed my mother, and left.

* * *

Now, after four deaths, we were down to fourteen – my family of four, my parents, Theng, his wife Lao and three children, Keng and her little daughter, and Vuoch – and still there was no sign that our 'purification' would ever end.

All we had left was the vague hope that the Khmer Rouge had accepted the five conditions imposed by Sihanouk. That seemed the only way that we would ever find our way back to the cities and resume a decent life.

At a political meeting soon after Sarun's disappearance, the chief seemed to add weight to the rumours by confirming Sihanouk's return and saying that a new chapter was opening in the reconstruction of the country. Sihanouk, he said, was about to set up a new administration. He then asked for any specialists, graduates, officers of the former government, doctors, engineers and students to register themselves on a special list.

Some forty people raised their hands, even some senior officers who had until then carefully concealed their identity. After a few moments of indecision, I kept my hand firmly in my lap. I remembered that incident in the pagoda when, just after leaving Phnom Penh, the Khmer Rouge called for power workers to return to the capital, and then sent them off alone, without their families. No, I thought, if I go, we will be separated. Best remain quiet. If asked, I would repeat what I had always claimed – that I was a mere technician.

We never heard any more about those who left. We never knew what really happened. The rumour was that they had been executed, but there was no evidence. They vanished, that is all I know.

Now – towards the end of 1975 – the rations dropped again, to one can of rice among eight people each day. Once, in November, for two days, we had nothing at all. The Khmer Rouge said the trucks had not arrived. On already empty stomachs, this was quite literally more than many of us could bear, especially as rumours spread that the rations had been misappropriated by the Khmer Rouge officers. That way, we told each other, they could raise the price of rice on the black market and acquire jewellery and clothing more cheaply.

Normally, no one would dream of protesting, but this was too much. The second day, there occurred an unbelievable event. A few hundred New People held a peaceful demonstration in the village with five teachers as their leaders to protest at the lack of food. I kept well clear, and I warned my brother, Theng, the teacher, to do the same. But I was told afterwards what happened.

In a slow and dignified procession, the protesters moved towards the guardhouse, the wood-and-thatch place where rice was distributed every evening. There were three Khmer Rouge officers present at the time.

In front of the guardhouse, the leaders came forward. One of them improvised a short speech, pouring out grievances to the village chief. As his speech went on, his tone became ever more earnest. The food system had no sense. The rations were pathetic. The work was too hard. There was no medicine, and no hospital.

When he had finished, the chief replied, speaking at first in a gentle and reassuring tone. Angkar had done everything possible. We weren't to forget we were not working for Angkar, but for ourselves. The harvest was yet to come. If we worked hard, our harvest would be more than adequate. No fish? Angkar did not eat fish either. The delays in food deliveries were independent of Angkar's will.

But as he spoke, his voice rose, and each phrase became a threat: 'You provoke trouble. You disturb the peace of the village. You sow doubts in the minds of the people. You say Angkar is not concerned about your health, and yet Angkar has done everything to help you. What did you bring here? Nothing! Angkar had to transport you, supply you with rice, give you land, and still you have produced nothing. Yet you now protest, because of a slight delay. Is that the action of a good revolutionary? Is this the elimination of individualist leanings? No!'

The rations came the next day. But a week later, the five teachers and some other villagers involved in the protest disappeared. Armed Khmer Rouge, who constantly patrolled the village, had removed their victims one by one during the night. The distressed families appealed to the village chief for information, but he knew nothing about it.

There was never any news.

But then the Khmer Rouge intentionally wrapped repression in mystery. All their sinister tasks were accomplished in secret, while in public they always spoke politely, even at the worst of times, preparing death with unfailing courtesy.

The disappearance of the five teachers intensified our anger. Amongst ourselves, we railed against the tyrannical system by which we were enslaved. Supposedly, there was no more corruption. Of course, we who survived only because of it knew better. Even suppose it were true, what did we have to eat? Better to be fed under injustice than starved by equality. In opposing past vices, the Khmer Rouge had disposed of all virtue. Claiming to offer life, all they provided was death in the name of ideology.

Yet there was no way to transform our anger into action. There was no possibility of an uprising. I constantly talked about the idea with my brother and father. But we were so vulnerable, how could we revolt? The villages were constantly patrolled. Contact between many people was made impossible by the *chlops*. There was certainly no way of building up any sort of an underground between the different communities.

Besides, we had no arms and no food. Even if we'd been able to procure arms and kill the fifty Khmer Rouge in the village, what would happen to us? We didn't have enough food to build up any reserves to sustain a guerrilla army. In our state of weakness, after a few days of wandering in the jungle, death would have been inevitable.

By the end of November, one-third of the population of Veal Vong had died. Under such atrocious conditions, we had only one duty, one aspiration – to stay alive. This could be done only on the basis of the surreptitious bartering of our remaining wealth and the preservation of family solidarity.

For us, it was easier than for others. Our bartering had cost us half our jewellery and a good part of our clothing, but there was still a lot left. I still had my three thousand dollars. Theng, Keng, and my parents contributed equitably, each of us willingly offering our share (Vuoch, being a student had no possessions of her own and still relied on my parents). We didn't eat to our hearts' content, but we managed to keep our health. That was the essential thing.

Besides that, our family was a strong one. We had all been touched by death, and we had grown to accept it. Keng had grown closer to my mother after Sarun's disappearance.

And Any slowly came to terms with Staud's death. There came a time when she decided that Staud should belong to the forest. Together, we took the precious little bag of ashes, waded out into the stream below my parents' house, and scattered the ashes on the water, watching them as they drifted slowly away out of sight beneath the overhanging bushes. 'Goodbye, my little Staud,' whispered Any. 'May Buddha's blessings go with you. Goodbye.'

Our occasional disputes were always centred on the rations, and usually on Nawath. Sudath, who was nearly ten now, was self-sacrificing. Nawath, though, aged five, was always eager to find any food that Any tried to store away. He was an active child and, even at that age, seemed a determined survivor. He was the one who put us under pressure. Any often smacked him, though never hard enough to risk outright rebellion on his part. Besides, with Staud's death, he was the youngest. We found it hard to punish him.

In this sense, we were a good revolutionary family, for Angkar had banished disharmony within households. Husbands were forbidden to beat their wives. Insults were barred. Children were not meant to be scolded.

Well and good, except that the tension now emerged in other ways. Children were encouraged by the Khmer Rouge to denounce parents whose behaviour fell short of this ideal, and I had already heard of cases of children complaining to the Khmer Rouge about their parents. Family squabbles merely became clandestine.

The punishment for arguing in public was there for all to see. In Veal Vong, there was an old soldier of about fifty, who constantly used to argue with his wife. Twice, he was officially warned that his behaviour was in violation of Angkar's egalitarian principles. The squabbles continued, until finally the man lost his temper a third time, and slapped his wife. The next day, he was taken into the forest. He never returned.

Our survival and our emotional well-being depended on food,

and food could only be bought. The goods we had to exchange were limited. But I had with me a huge dollar reserve which in these circumstances was largely worthless, until it occurred to me that I ought to try to use my commercial skills to give these dollars some value.

Logically, the dollars should have been worth something, for I knew that many people had them. The problem was that there were not enough in circulation for them to acquire a fixed value. It was better to spend gold. But gold varied in value according to the aesthetic appeal of the object in question. Necklaces, for example, fetched one-third again as much as bracelets. For anyone who worked these things out, as I did, it was clear that the system was full of holes. For example, I could theoretically buy a *tael* of gold for 200 dollars, and with that *tael* of gold buy 40 cans' worth of rice. Yet, with the same 200 dollars, if I traded it directly, I could only buy 20 cans' worth of rice. What I had to do, therefore, was to create a stable market for dollars.

First of all, I built up a stock of about fifty cans' worth of rice by exchanging clothing and jewellery. This gave me a margin of safety to put my plan into operation.

Then, I went to see a broker, a Chinese who was branded as a New Person along with the rest of us, and who had a reputation for making deals extremely quickly.

'My friend, you have dollars?' I asked, 'Someone asked me for some.'

My question perplexed him. 'Why dollars?'

'Don't ask me, it's for a friend. But if you can find some for me, I'll give you rice in exchange.'

'But why? Can't you explain?'

'I suppose because dollars will be important if we return to Phnom Penh,' I said. 'The embassy personnel there use dollars. It's a strong currency. That's what you would need to travel abroad. Overseas only dollars count. When the day comes, the dollar will have a high value in relation to our new currency. And it's stable, not like gold. The value of jewellery varies with taste. But a hundred dollars is always a hundred dollars. Anyway, if you can find any, I'll exchange them with you, for my friend.'

The Chinaman, knowing there were plenty of dollars around, and having good contacts, soon bought me two hundred dollars, for which I duly gave him twenty cans' worth of rice.

The rumour of our exchange spread quickly through the camp and to two or three neighbouring villages. Suddenly, people began to think their dollars might be of immediate, rather than long-term value.

Naturally, my broker was among the first to cash in on this new market. After a few days, he reappeared at my house. He seemed unhappy. 'You cheated me, Thay,' he said. 'The others give me fifteen cans of rice for a hundred dollars but you, you only gave me ten.'

So already, dollars had risen 50 per cent in value. I calmed him by giving him 15 cans of rice in exchange for another 100 dollars. Everything seemed to be working out perfectly. My stock of rice had gone down, but in this tiny, enclosed, artificial economy, my dollars had acquired value.

I was soon able to put this development to good use. Over the next few weeks, working through the same broker, I spent a thousand of my dollars buying one hundred and fifty cans' worth of rice. Those purchases, which not only enabled us to live reasonably healthily, also had other repercussions far beyond anything I could have planned.

This had nothing to do with me, deriving entirely from a growing belief that the Khmer Rouge regime would fall, a belief which united New People and Ancients alike. This belief was suggested, in part, by the inefficiency of the Khmer Rouge administration, in part by wishful thinking, but in a large measure by the growing faith in the predictions of the great sage, Puth.

There were indeed strange coincidences between Puth's words and the calamities we were suffering. Puth said: 'Black crows will scatter *lovea* fruits throughout the land.' The *lovea* fruit is green, spherical in shape, smaller than a plum, shiny, and looks appetizing, but when it is opened to be eaten, it is always full of lice. When people analysed Puth's predictions in the light of recent events, the 'black crows' were seen as the men of Angkar, all dressed in black, the *lovea* as the Utopian ideas of communist ideology, and the lice as the contents of that ideology – murder, famine and misery.

Puth said: 'During this accursed era, the people will be so hungry and deprived that they will run after a dog to wrangle over a grain of rice stuck to its tail.' Before, nobody believed in these predictions. When the elders talked about them, we would sneer and tease them. Who could imagine that famine would befall a country that exported rice? Puth had proclaimed, 'Blood will flow as high as the elephant's belly before peace returns.' Who would believe that of such a peaceful, unified country? Now, those terrible predictions were becoming truer every day. All values had been reversed and desecrators reigned.

Fortunately, this time of horror was to be of a limited duration. The reign of the *thmils*, the impious men, would last only seven years, seven months, and seven days. Then the *thmils* would be executed.

This became almost an article of faith between New People and Ancients, for now even the original inhabitants had begun to tire of the Khmer Rouge. Previously, the peasants had lived peacefully with their families, owning one or two pairs of oxen, buffaloes, rice fields, a plough, banana trees and coconut trees. Half a year's work provided enough food for the whole year. Now, everything belonged to the community. Private property was abolished. The peasants had to pool their carts, ploughs and oxen for communal use. Even fruit trees belonged to the community. Nobody any longer felt responsible for anything. The economy declined, and the peasants became increasingly bitter.

Consequently, since, in the long term, everybody counted on the defeat of the Khmer Rouge, everyone was eager to acquire wealth. Peasants coveted city goods, New People coveted food, and now everyone began to value dollars as the medium by which food, jewellery, gold, and medicine could all be exchanged.

During December 1975, the rumour spread that we would all be moved on soon. A happy thought – at that time of year it was wet and cold. Our blankets were not thick enough and at night we had to keep the fire burning if we wanted to sleep. Eventually, the rumour reached the chief, who denied it categorically – 'You will stay here all your life!'

But at the end of December, we were called to a rather special political meeting. The speaker was unfamiliar to us. Without beating around the bush, he asked, 'Are there any volunteers to leave?' He didn't say where to. 'If so, prepare yourselves to leave today!'

Some of my friends looked at each other, their eyes wide. 'Why did Angkar change its mind?' they asked each other. The question didn't bother me. I had long since ceased to query Angkar's plans. Angkar did not change its mind. That implied a firm direction. In fact there was none. Angkar was not to be predicted, but was also infallible. Its unpredictability was part of its infallibility. The error was ours for thinking Angkar had a mind to change. All we could do was accept, and in this case act, or not, as we chose.

It became clear that there was some rivalry involved. The village leaders wanted us to stay, while the new arrival ordered the volunteers to one side to have their names taken. 'Angkar needs you to work in another place,' he said. 'It is a better work site. It is not located in the middle of a forest. The conditions there are more pleasant.'

Some of the villagers feared new disasters if they moved. I was not so sure. As volunteers began to move to one side, I discussed the matter with Any, Theng, Vuoch, Keng and my parents. Our situation at Veal Vong was not good. The rations were meagre and the region damp. True, no one was promising better rations, and no one had told us our destination. But I had other good reasons to leave. I risked being recognized by a Khmer Rouge as a former high official of the Republican government. If that happened, I didn't give much for my chances. And I still wanted to get closer to the frontier. Another village might offer a better chance of escape.

Besides, I knew that the Khmer Rouge of Veal Vong did not care a jot about us when they urged us to stay. They were only concerned about our value. The rations were still being allocated according to the number of inhabitants. More people meant more rations, more deaths, and more spare food for the local Khmer Rouge. Our departure would undermine this paradoxical, parasitical economy. If we left, how would they obtain gold and jewellery?

Within minutes we had decided: we would join the volunteers.

That afternoon, the thousand volunteers – slightly less than half the survivors – were marched off. Carrying what possessions we had left, the two children walking between us, and the rest of the family close behind, we returned towards the main road.

Three miles along the trail, we reached a pagoda which was a refugee centre. There we were told to wait for trucks.

To our astonishment, life improved as if by magic. Rations were doubled: one can of rice to every four people per day. Perhaps the harvest had been better there, or perhaps the Khmer Rouge wanted to encourage us to believe in their promises. If so, it worked. Despite myself, I felt a flicker of hope.

By bartering one of Any's skirts with locals, I obtained some sugar, a cylinder of brown palm-sugar packed in discs two inchs across and half an inch thick. It was a delicacy that seemed to come straight from paradise. None of us had had sugar for several months. Delighted, I broke off pieces and handed them out. I will always remember the first piece melting on my tongue – bliss, unbelievable bliss. Prolonging the joy as long as possible, we all slowly sucked our sugar, heads back so as not to lose a drop of saliva.

I was also able to exchange two 100-dollar bills for two chickens. A hundred dollars for a chicken – what a bargain! We made the most of them. I killed them on the spot, plucked them, and grilled them on our fire. The remnants we turned into soup. There was enough that evening for the whole family to have a feast, all fourteen of us. We really ate our fill, offering each other tasty morsels, picking each bone clean, laughing as if celebrating the rightness of our decision to leave. It is hard for anyone who has not been really hungry to know the sweetness, the euphoria of eating well. Suddenly the pain of the last months seemed to fall away. It was a strange feeling to be reborn so quickly, and so simply. We told ourselves how very, very lucky we were.

After two weeks, the trucks arrived. On seeing them, all our remaining apprehensions disappeared. There was enough room for everybody. We were not packed in like sardines as we had been on the previous trip. There were thirty of us in each truck, which was not too bad. And of course we had less baggage.

We had hardly travelled ten miles towards Pursat, back the way we had come so many months before, when the trucks suddenly turned left through sparsely scattered trees, the countryside where woods and rice fields alternated.

THE JUNGLE OF THE DYING

Then, in the distance, we saw a river and village, rich in cassava plots and fruit trees, a region untouched by the war, with trees intact and no shell holes.

Paradise indeed, compared to the hell of Veal Vong.

7   THE SCOURGE
OF ANGKAR

On the evening of our arrival in the village – Chamcar Trassak, one of a line of seven villages along the Pursat River – we were assembled for an introduction to our new community. We were to camp there that night, and the following day we would be divided among the villages. 'You will be comfortable here,' the Khmer Rouge officer addressing us said. 'You will no longer need cooking utensils, because you don't need to cook any more. Angkar will take care of you. Those who have cooking utensils should give them to Angkar. Keep only your spoons. We will no longer distribute rations. From now on we are going to eat communally.'

A gong rang. We were directed to tables laden with food. Rice, real rice, hard rice – *bay* – and lots of it. Fish. Fruit. Vegetables. At last, we decided as we talked, Angkar was treating us as we deserved. We congratulated ourselves for deciding to come, and pitied those who had remained behind. Imagine the emotion of some families who had had nothing to exchange and who, for months, had had nothing but rice soup and wild plants. Now, suddenly, real rice and fish! Sitting down together for the first time since leaving Phnom Penh, we smiled at each other. I realized looking round how changed we were – my mother a shrunken and frail old lady, my father now walking with a permanent stoop, Any, Vuoch, Lao and Keng scrawny, the children emaciated. I supposed I must look as terrible as Theng. Now, perhaps, we would regain our health. Enchanted, the children rubbed their tummies in satisfaction.

The Khmer Rouge even served us. Unheard of! Young girls and boys, all dressed in black, passed round dishes, while the Ancients – the locals – did the cooking. The Khmer Rouge watched us good-naturedly and chided us paternally: 'Eat slowly! Think about your health to serve Angkar better! Don't quarrel over the food!'

No one took any notice. We just lunged at the food and started to stuff it into our mouths. I gobbled everything I could lay my hands on – rice, fish soup, vegetables, anything.

After several minutes, two men at the next table keeled over, groaning. They were carried off by the Khmer Rouge. We heard later that one of them had died in terrible agony. It was the first time that I had seen what food could do to a really empty stomach. None of the rest of us were deterred. There seemed to be no limit to the food. Everyone could eat his fill. We were so busy eating that we had no time to talk, let alone find words to express our joy and gratitude to the Khmer Rouge. All we knew was that we could breathe again, and the time of misfortune was over.

After a final night under the trees, my parents, Vuoch, Theng, Keng and their families were told they were to go to another village a mile or so away. For a moment, we all felt panic-stricken. Separation now, after all we had endured, after months of sustaining each other, would have been too much to bear.

But we were reassured by those around us. It appeared that the area along the Pursat River which we were occupying had formerly belonged to Vietnamese, all of whom had been repatriated. Hence the initial surplus of food. Originally there had been two villages. Now, those villages were mostly occupied by Ancients, and New People had built five more. In our new relaxed regime, we would be able to see each other regularly. Any, I and the children waved the others off as they marched away, with hundreds of others, along the mud track by the side of the river, waving until they disappeared among the sugar-palms.

After the departure of the others, I was set to building houses, not the fragile shacks of Veal Vong, but houses built on piles, solid and well sheltered. The houses were built communally, by groups specialized in different parts of the construction. We were allotted one already built. While Any looked after the children, I became part of one of the teams. That first day, my group of six was appointed to cut tree trunks for poles. While we were working, one of the men saw a cat and its kittens in an abandoned hut not far from the village. In Phnom Penh, people used to say Vietnamese ate dog and cat meat. I did not know if it was true or not, but the idea of such barbaric practices made us laugh. There was nothing funny about the idea now. Without the slightest hesitation, the man seized the animals and drowned them in the river. We were all delighted, and divided the catch between us. We needn't have bothered – food remained plentiful, and we all thrived.

After a week – at the end of the first week of January 1976 – we learned over the village chief's radio what lay behind the introduction of communal feeding. The country had a new constitution. Now any means of production belonged to the State, to the collective. Only the 'usual personal objects' remained as individual possessions. We spent a long time discussing the phrase 'usual personal objects'. We had our clothes. What else counted as personal? Kitchen utensils? We no longer had them since the meals were communal. Vegetables? But if we harvested the vegetables we had to give them to the commune. Same thing for poultry. In the language of the Khmer Rouge, we were subject not simply to communal meals but to 'unity of feeding' – an odd revolutionary expression signifying that everybody should eat the same thing.

After another three weeks, we learned a little more about the nature of the vast social experiment of which we were a tiny part. An enormous meeting was called some ten miles from Chamcar Trassak. Everyone in the area had to attend. The chief of the region was going to address us. I went with Any and the two children, thinking we might meet up with the rest of the family. No such luck. The field where the meeting was held presented an unimaginable spectacle. There were thousands of men and women there, and columns were streaming in from all the surrounding villages. Each village had a place which had been allocated in advance.

When everyone was settled, the speaker began to develop Angkar's favourite themes – the ideology of the classless society and the horrors of the defunct capitalist system. Then: 'You have already successfully crossed two large deserts – the People's Revolution and the Democratic Revolution.' By the 'two large deserts' and the two revolutions I understood him to mean the civil war against Lon Nol and the evacuation of the towns. 'Now,' his voice boomed from the loudspeakers, 'We have to begin the Socialist Revolution.' At the time, my health and my family's health restored by good food, I had no idea what was meant by the term 'Socialist Revolution' – no apprehension that it would entail crossing a third desert far more deadly than anything that had gone before.

In the crowd, Any happened to spot a distant cousin of hers – Neary, a woman in her late twenties who came from Pursat. Neary lived at Don Ey, the village at the end of our line of seven communities, four miles from where we were. She was alone, her husband having been taken away for 're-education', and suggested that we join her. She said life was even better at Don Ey. She said she would arrange permission for the move.

She was as good as her word. Two weeks later, Neary returned for us.

The path along which she led us linked the seven villages, running along the top of the river-bank through agricultural land – rice fields with scattered palm-trees, coconuts, mangoes and stands of cassava – and on the way we were able to make brief contact again with my parents and the rest of the family, who lived in a village in the centre of the line.

The move looked as if it would be a good one. Neary lived in a large house, but she only had two children, a daughter the same age as Sudath and a son a little older than Nawath. We were still only a couple of miles from my parents.

My first job at Don Ey was threshing rice. I had to lead the oxen that trampled the paddy from the stalks. I then gathered up the straw and swept up the paddy, while the women collected the grains. Once, I would have been slipping rice grains into my clothing all the time. Now there was no thought of stealing.

With good food, it was even possible to accept the endless political meetings, which were of two kinds. There were mass meetings of several hundreds held every ten days, at which a Khmer Rouge official would harangue us about the benefits of communal life. But the most frequent type, held every three days or so, with no more than twenty people in each group, was the self-criticism session. A Khmer Rouge would remind us of our duties to Angkar and invite us to admit our shortcomings.

As a New Person, I was by definition inferior to the Ancients and to the Khmer Rouge, and I soon learned the formulae of self-criticism: 'I humble myself before the supreme Angkar. I humble myself before those gathered here so that they can see me.

Before me I see the mud that stains me, but only my comrades can see the mud that stains my back. Comrades, I need your help to become aware of my faults and my errors. I humble myself before Angkar. I must be a good revolutionary. I thank Angkar. . .' and on and on in the same humble tone of voice, eyes lowered. We were supposed to reveal everything: what work had been done, how well it had been done, how hard we had worked, how much rest had been taken, even how many times we had crapped, concluding with a ritual formula: 'I humble myself so that Angkar can purify me, criticize me, and educate me to be even more submissive.'

It was a strain and humiliating, but it seemed a small price to pay for a full stomach.

At the end of February 1976, I was detailed to join a contingent fishing at Tonle Sap, the great lake that is a natural reservoir of the waters flowing south of Phnom Penh, where they join the Mekong. Tonle Sap lay the other side of Pursat, some forty miles away.

For the first time since the evacuation, I was to be separated from the family. Yet so contented were we now, so completely had Don Ey's good conditions overlain the memory of Veal Vong, that there was nothing disturbing in the prospect. As I kissed Any and the children goodbye, I reminded them that we were all well-fed, that they had Neary to help look after them, and that I would only be away for two or three weeks. I had often been away that long in Phnom Penh. This was just like another business trip.

To reach the fishing site, we walked along the river to Pursat, about twelve miles away, carrying our baggage – a hammock made from jute sacking, a carrying bag made of a trouser-leg, a blanket, a scarf, a pair of trousers and a change of shirt. Military trucks took us on to Krakor, twenty miles from Pursat.

On the way I saw a curious sight – thousands of young people working in dried-up rice fields, making one-foot-high embankments to keep the water in during planting. They were well established rice fields, but now their shapes were being changed. Apparently, now that the Khmer Rouge had abolished even the peasants' private property, the differences in the size of the rice fields was unacceptable. Since everything belonged to everyone, all the rice fields had to be the same size. The old embankments, the symbols of personal property, had been knocked down and now new ones were being made.

The trucks took us on the final six miles to the lake shore, a vast flat area of reeds that floods annually, almost doubling the lake's area. We found ourselves in Kompong Luong, an old fishing village of stilted houses which stood a few feet above the surrounding reed-banks. Here we were shown into a large isolated building made of wood and roofed with reeds, open at the sides.

Our very first meal in Kompong Luong brought us down a peg. That evening, we were served only rice soup, a watery mixture of rice boiled in water. We looked at each other, bewildered. Why rice soup at the work site, when we ate proper rice at Don Ey? The team leader saw our shock. 'Comrades, be quiet. Back at Don Ey they won't be eating hard rice either. This is unity of feeding. You must understand. We are having difficulty with our transport.' Those of us from Veal Vong had heard that excuse before. We fell into an uneasy silence.

Over the next few days, we worked hard, casting the nets from the shore, dragging them in, and picking out the catch, often working until late into the night, cleaning the fish by firelight. But we still only had rice soup. As the days passed, we became hungrier and hungrier. Furtively, we began to sneak fish away from the nets and hide them in our clothing, drying them over the fire at night time. That couldn't be tolerated, of course. We were soon made to count out all the large fish caught during the day. Fortunately, it was impossible to count every single fish, and we still managed to filch tiddlers.

During the first week, as hunger was beginning to take its toll, I acquired an additional insight into the extraordinary world of the Khmer Rouge. I was at the well, collecting water (for the water of Tonle Sap was not considered healthy) when one of the Ancients, a local, started to chat to me. As a New Person, and not from the area, I was wary of him – he might have been a *chlop* eager to report me for 'individualist leanings'. But he wasn't put off.

'You don't like us Ancients, do you?' he said, but without any resentment. 'It shows. But listen, comrade, the Ancients are not all alike. In the beginning it was different. We accepted them then. They speak gently, but they are harsh. In our village, we think the Khmer Rouge have tricked us. All we do is struggle to stay alive.'

I still refused to be drawn into conversation. But the more I thought about it afterwards, the more I believed what he said. It was my first real indication that my feelings were shared, not only by the New People, but the Ancients, in whose name the revolution had occurred.

Almost at once, within days, there came other evidence of unrest. Rumours began to circulate about guerrillas fighting for Buddhism and liberty across the other side of the great lakes. Once or twice, we heard shots. At one of the lakeside villages, it was said, there were hundreds of boats, which belonged to people who lived around the lake who no longer felt safe because of guerrilla activity. Was there really an active underground? There was no real evidence, but the thought was an inspiring one.

A week or so after we arrived at Tonle Sap, in early March, I heard that a medical team had arrived in the camp. In nearly a year under the Khmer Rouge, it was the first time I had heard of any health inspection. The word spread. People suffering from any illness could consult the team.

Immediately, everyone declared themselves sick in order to receive some medicine, for by now we were all again beginning to suffer from fatigue and malnutrition. 'Why don't you go?' a friend of mine said, 'Everybody else is. They're giving a serum, a mixture of medicinal plants and coconut milk. It can't do any harm.'

The medical attendants were all very young, boys and girls in black, without anything to distinguish them as doctors. From the treatment being given to those in front of me in the queue, it seemed there were only two remedies in the Khmer Rouge medical kit. The first, which was a rather repugnant brown liquid, was dabbed on to ease localized pain. The second medicine was a clear whitish tonic, which was injected.

When I came to the desk, a girl asked. 'Do you have pain anywhere?'

'No,' I said, 'I'm just exhausted.'

On the table in front of the girl were twenty soft-drink bottles – Coca-Cola bottles, Pepsi-Cola bottles, 7-Up bottles – ten with the brown liquid and ten with the transparent liquid. There were also four syringes lying in swab trays. Without even bothering to disinfect the needle or my arm, the girl plunged a syringe into a Pepsi-Cola bottle. The needle had already been used a dozen times, under my very eyes. All the medics were using all the syringes indiscriminately to inject anyone. I had a sudden fear that maybe I would be better off without this 'tonic', but it was too late now to change my mind.

Two days later, I awoke with a high temperature, sweating profusely. Later, at work, I began to shiver. Strangely, a friend who had received the same injection was fine. The third day was just as bad. My friend said I had malaria. Possibly he was right, for there had been several cases of malaria at Veal Vong, but it was a strange coincidence. One thing was certain – I couldn't possibly claim I had been made ill by the injection. That would have been a criticism of Angkar.

My illness worsened day by day. For better or worse, I managed to work for a week. But at the beginning of the second week, when I tried to work, I collapsed several times. I was useless, and asked for permission to return home. 'Rest and we will make a decision,' my chief said. For the next two days, I lay sweating and shivering, until the chief had to admit that I would be of no further use. I could go home the next day. How? By walking. When I asked for a friend from Don Ey to accompany me in case I fainted on the road, the chief said 'No! Out of the question! You're sick, and you will leave alone. It is a great privilege to leave alone. I'm doing you a favour. Don't test my patience!'

For another night, I shivered and sweated, wondering if I would have the strength to walk, thinking there was nothing else I would rather do than die. It was only the thought of Any and the children that gave me the strength to make the effort.

In the morning, I struggled up and prepared my baggage. I was six miles from the main highway, twenty from Pursat, and forty from home. The only way to travel was to hitch a lift. That would not be easy. All I had was permission to return to my village. I had no authority to arrange transport.

I set off around midday, with uncertain steps. I hadn't covered much more than a quarter of a mile when I had to stop. I found myself in front of a house which stood on piles beside the lake. It was unusually large, I noticed, as I leaned heavily against one of the supporting posts.

Above me, an old man appeared. 'What are you doing there?' he asked, staring down at me warily.

'I have malaria,' I gasped.

'Where do you live?'

'The other side of Pursat. I'm going home to convalesce. I'd like to find a truck to give me a lift.'

'You can't travel in that condition. You look like death.' I certainly felt like it. 'You must eat if you want to reach home. Come in.'

It took me an age to climb up to him. 'Quick!' he urged. 'You mustn't be seen!'

Inside, there were three other people – his wife, one of his sons, and a young girl. On the old man's instructions, the son opened a cupboard and took out an ampoule of medicine and a syringe. I could tell he knew what he was about by the way he handled the syringe and then cleaned my arm with alcohol. While he injected me, I looked around. I saw the family was, by the standards of Ancients, rather well-off. They were what the Khmer Rouge called 'little capitalists'. After the injection the man's wife offered me a bowl of dry rice – rice, not soup – and some dried fish. I could hardly believe it. I mumbled my thanks, and began to eat, finding difficulty swallowing.

Suddenly the young girl spoke up: 'I know a way for you to get to Pursat. My uncle drives one of Angkar's trucks and he's going that way. I'll ask him to give you a lift.' She seemed really eager to help, and slipped away after giving me a description of her uncle's truck.

A few minutes after she disappeared, I saw the truck pass by in front of the house. It didn't stop. Immediately sensing there was something wrong, I began to wonder what Angkar would make of my presence in the house. I had an order to return to my village, not stop when it pleased me and chat to whom I liked.

After another few minutes, I realized that the injection and the food had had some effect. I felt energy and strength returning.

The fever was still there, but at least I felt able to walk. 'It's better I leave,' I said. The others nodded. With heartfelt thanks, still clasping some of the dried fish, I clambered back down the ladder.

Luckily, a few yards further on, I saw a Khmer Rouge military truck parked. The driver, seeing me approach, asked me where I was going, and offered me a lift.

Later, back at Don Ey, on the return of our fishing group, I was to learn from the others on the fishing team what happened to the family who had helped me. The young girl had found her uncle in the company of a Khmer Rouge soldier and asked him outright whether he would give me a lift. Of course, such friendliness towards a New Person, expressed by someone not in a position of authority, was entirely unacceptable to the Khmer Rouge. The uncle, frightened, reproached the girl. When the details came out, the young girl and her family were accused of counter-revolutionary attitudes – showing humanitarian feelings to a stranger. To the Khmer Rouge, it was bad enough to feel generosity towards a family member or a neighbour, let alone towards a stranger, and a New Person at that. It was an act that smacked of rebellion. The whole family had been arrested and deported to another province. I never knew what became of them.

My truck driver dropped me at Pursat. It took me two more days to walk home. Villages were set at regular intervals, and whenever it rained, or I was hungry, I would stop and show my pass. Since I was travelling officially, I was allowed the regular ration, which was no more than a bowl of rice soup, so I knew that things were going to be bad back in Don Ey, just as the Khmer Rouge had said. I wondered how my family had been faring in my absence.

In all the villages, I asked for medicine. I was looking for quinine or some medicine containing quinine, to control the malaria. In the second village I was assured I could get some if I had something to give in exchange. All I had was some dried fish left over from my hour with the peasant family in Tonle Sap, which I had been saving for Any and the children. Apparently fish was good enough. In exchange for half of it, I received two tablets of Flavoquine, which seemed to control the malaria enough to get me home.

As I approached my house, I became more and more apprehensive. There seemed to be fewer people about, and those I saw looked terrible, hollow-cheeked and ghostly. It was like Veal Vong all over again. People avoided my eye, and no one spoke.

I hurried to my house, calling for the children. There was no response. Fearing the worst, I climbed the ladder and peered inside. To my relief, both Sudath and Nawath were there, along with Neary's two children. But as they came to me with smiles on their faces, I saw they were very changed. They were depressed shadows of their former selves. Hugging them, I noticed Sudath had a sore on his foot.

'Oh, it's nothing, father,' he said with an attempt at a smile, 'I fell on a stone when I was out trying to find some fruit.' Nawath had small swellings on his hands and feet.

How was their mother, I asked. Any was fine, they said. She was out in the fields, and would be back at dusk.

Later, when I saw her coming with Neary, I was shocked, unwilling to accept that the skinny figure dressed in black carrying a sickle was really Any. I waved, and the two women looked up, puzzled. Then Any's face lit up, and she broke into a run. 'Thay! Thay, dearest! You're back! You're back!' she shouted.

'Yes, but slow down!' I called back with a grin, as she forced her spindly limbs up the ladder. 'Be careful, or you'll fall.'

That was all the emotion we dared express outside. But in the house, she fell into my arms, pressing her face against my chest and her hair against my cheek, gripping me with a strength that surprised me. We stood for a moment, locked together in relief and delight.

Then she pulled back, and stared at me, her eyes wide and serious.

'You look terrible,' she said. 'You're so thin and pale. What happened?'

'You look terrible, too, my little Any.' We both laughed. 'But it's good to see you. I missed you.'

Then I told them all of my work, and the malaria, and my return trip.

As I finished, she smiled again. 'We should be thankful for the malaria,' she said, with a giggle.

'What?'

'It's thanks to the malaria you came back to us.'

And for the first time in weeks, I laughed, and just as quickly clapped a hand over my mouth. It would never do for one of the Khmer Rouge to hear laughter coming from the house of a New Person. The sight of me sitting there suppressing laughter set the children off, and for a few glorious minutes we sat giggling like children in class, our hands clasped over our aching mouths.

Later, when we had calmed down, Any confirmed how bad things were in Don Ey. All around, people showed signs of debilitation due to malnutrition and overwork. But it was more than that: the area had been stricken by all the diseases we'd been used to in Veal Vong, and more – diarrhoea, dysentery, various types of fevers and malaria, all aggravated by exhaustion. The most common complaint, however, was oedema, a direct consequence of starvation in which the blood begins to break down and exudes a liquid which collects in the feet and hands. It is a strange disease. The swellings increase, like balloons, until the bloated skin becomes translucent and smooth. There is no pain, but you are overwhelmed by a general debilitating weakness, as if your limbs are too heavy to move. Eventually, every movement becomes such an effort that you don't want to do anything else but lie there. Already, the dying had started.

The following morning, I explained my condition to the village chief. Seeing I couldn't work, he suggested I go to hospital, but I said I would rather convalesce at home.

Day by day, conditions worsened. The rice soup became ever more watery. Since we ate communally, we were no longer allowed to have rice at home, a rule enforced by the lack of utensils with which to eat and cook. Even from this Angkar sought to make political capital. At the self-criticism sessions, from which I was not excluded during my convalescence, our professions of faith had to take account of the lack of food: 'I do not eat very well. Angkar does not have enough supplies, but this allows me to get used to hunger and become more resistant. Angkar helps to harden me, and I thank Angkar.'

Over the next three weeks, Any tried to exchange some of our jewellery for food. But food was scarcer now, and more expensive. One *tael* of gold – valued at 200 dollars in Veal Vong, and equivalent to 40 cans of rice – now bought only 3 cans' worth of rice. Moreover, it was hard to find brokers. The system established so successfully in Veal Vong simply didn't exist in Don Ey. Some families just starved, unable to make exchanges, or unwilling to pay the prices. An entire Chinese family, in whose house was stored quantities of jewellery, all died of malnutrition.

Shortly after my return, I heard from friends that my parents had fallen sick, and that my mother was actually in hospital. Fearing that nobody at the hospital would take care of her, I asked for permission to go there to get some medicine, which would give me the opportunity to see her and discover the exact nature of her illness. If I played my cards right, it would also give me a chance to see my father.

The hospital was in the village next door to Don Ey, while my parents' village was a mile or so beyond that. Instead of going straight to the hospital, therefore, I walked past, and on to visit my father, whom I had not seen in over a month.

A little nervous that I would be spotted, I climbed the stairs to his hut. He was lying on a mat on the bamboo floor. Seeing me, his shrunken face lit up. 'No, don't move,' I said, and told him what had happened to me and how the family was. Despite his own illness, he was concerned. He showed me three mangoes he'd been able to gather the previous night. 'Eat,' he said, offering me one of the mangoes. 'You must be hungry, Thay.'

I was run down and in desperate need of vitamins, and fell on the ripe fruit. As I ate, he began to talk. Keng, Vuoch and Theng had often been able to visit while I was away. 'But I thought I was going to die without seeing you again,' he said, weakly. 'I am going to die, you know. When I die, if it is true that my soul endures, I will help you.'

Tears came to my eyes. He took my hand. 'I knew from the beginning that this regime would be bad, but I couldn't convince you,' he said, with a ghost of a smile.

'Father, you were right,' I replied. 'I rationalize too much. You know that. That is my fault.'

'Too much thinking obscures wisdom,' he whispered, stroking my hand. 'You must keep your feelings pure. Don't worry about me. My death is a deliverance. But you, you must get out. Act ignorant, do not speak, do not grouse, do not argue. Stay alive, my son. Stay alive to escape. Escape, to stay alive.'

'Yes.' I brushed my tears away, and took his hand again, knowing as I did so that I might never see him again. But time was short, and I still had to get to the hospital. 'Father,' I faltered, 'I . . . I must visit mother.'

'Yes.' There were tears in his eyes as well, but he seemed at peace. 'Be careful. Go now. Stay alive, my son. Stay alive.'

I left him in a daze, telling myself he was wrong, he couldn't be dying, because I was not ready for his death, not ready for life without the knowledge that he was there. Yet at the same time I knew I ought to accept that what he said was true. Death will come to us all sooner or later, he used to say in Veal Vong. Death is a release. I heard his words in my mind; I had long accepted that they would apply to me; but somehow I could not accept that they would apply to him.

Suddenly, a terrible thought occurred to me. That mango! If he really was dying, I should never have touched it. At the thought of my selfishness, tears sprang to my eyes. He was weaker than I was, and had no one to make exchanges for him. Perhaps that mango would be the difference between life and death for him. How brutal, how thoughtless of me to have accepted it.

And so, still wrestling with my emotions, almost unaware of my surroundings, I came to the hospital.

The hospital consisted of five buildings – an administrative section and four others for patients – all wood and bamboo structures with woven reed walls, and surrounded by mango trees. The patients slept on wooden or iron beds, but had to bring their own blankets. Nursing care was almost non-existent. It was as if the sick were considered parasites. Since they didn't work, they deserved nothing but harsh treatment. Good treatment would only encourage malingering. Here you could expect only a bit of clear water with some grains of rice in it twice a day. In their lunatic determination to ensure that people were really sick, the Khmer Rouge made them sicker.

I wandered through two of the buildings, and was halfway through the third, slowly scanning the lines of patients when, to my surprise, I heard a voice: 'Thay!' It was my sister Keng. Beside her, playing on the floor, was her six-year-old daughter, Srey.

'Keng! what are you doing here? Are you sick?'

'No, I'm here because of mother.'

Mother lay in the next door bed, asleep. Keng had pretended to be sick to take care of her. She was running a number of risks. For one thing, she might have been denounced as a malingerer; for another, even being in the hospital was dangerous, for there was even less to eat there than back in the villages.

'It's diarrhoea,' said Keng. 'She's been here for five days.' Then she put her mouth to mother's ear. 'Mother! Mother! Wake up, Thay's here!'

There wasn't much I could do for her, except talk, telling her of my stay at Tonle Sap and about my conversation with my father. Keng told me about Theng and his family. There had already been another death in the family – Theng and Lao's baby girl had died of diarrhoea the week before I got back. When I said how sorry I was, Keng shrugged philosophically. 'Like Staud, she is one of the lucky ones.' Theng was now working on dyke-building a day's march away, leaving Lao to look after the two boys.

After an hour or so, I picked up some tablets for oedema – sweet things that seemed to be entirely innocuous – and left.

Three days later, when I came to see my mother again, she said in a voice that was little more than a whisper, 'Thay, your father died last night.'

So: he had been right, after all.

I held mother's hand, and Keng's, and we were silent. Srey watched us, wide-eyed. My mind became an intense mixture of emotions. Relief that his suffering was over combined with gratitude for what he had tried to pass on to me – strength, stoicism, wisdom – and overwhelming sadness that I had not been able to see him again.

I wept, in silence, but as I sat there, trying to control my emotions, I noticed my mother's face was set. 'I didn't expect him to die before me,' she said, after a minute. 'The Khmer Rouge discovered him this morning. He died in his sleep.'

'He said his death would be a deliverance,' I said, trying to be philosophical, insisting to myself that death was rapidly becoming something to be welcomed rather than feared. 'Don't be sad. Death will come to all of us.'

'Yes, Thay,' said Keng, from her bed, 'To us all.' I saw from her eyes that she too was not well. I touched her forehead. She was feverish. I told her she was young and strong, but I wondered how long she – how long any of us – would last. The sickness seemed to have struck down men, women and children, without distinction.

Keng's illness created new difficulties. I didn't want to leave the two women on their own. Whatever the risk, I had to make up a story to get myself to the hospital on a regular basis.

By the time I got home, I had my story ready.

I went to the chief to request that I be hospitalized. He, of course, couldn't understand why I had refused to do so a few days earlier. 'It's just that I can't be hospitalized overnight,' I explained. 'There are too many sick people there. It's better I sleep at home, and spend the morning there for treatment.' The chief, a fat man who might in different circumstances have been jovial, accepted that without demur.

After a day of commuting between my home and hospital, I discovered I received soup at the hospital, at mid-morning, and returned in time for the midday meal at the village. If I was careful, if I got the timing right, I could receive double rations. Officially, as far as the village chief and my work supervisor were concerned, I was hospitalized. As far as the hospital was concerned, I slept at home. The only risk was that if any of the Khmer Rouge or Ancients from my village saw me eating at the hospital, they might realize I was taking meals in two places and report me.

Every day, then, I carefully made my way to visit my mother, Keng, and Srey Rath, leaving after I had checked up on them and gulped down my rice soup. Every day, the hospital became less a hospital and more of a morgue. Every day, I counted some fifteen bodies, and every day there were more sick, until, even with the deaths, there were no more beds, and the sick and dying were relegated to the floors and to the courtyard outside, exposed to the sun and showers.

Day by day, Keng worsened.

A week later, I found her lying, panting, her eyes wide with fear. Still for some reason I kept up the pretence she would soon be well.

'Have you had your soup?' I asked with as much cheerfulness as I could muster.

She whispered something I could not hear.

'Don't ask, Thay,' my mother replied for her. 'She cannot speak any more.'

I looked at Keng again, and heard her mutter, 'Thay . . . Thay.' I put my head down to her mouth. 'Burning,' she whispered, 'Burning.' And then spoke only with her eyes, glancing at me, at our mother, at little Srey beside her holding her hand.

'Mother,' Srey said, plaintively, 'Why don't you speak to me?'

Keng tried to say something, and failed. Tears sprang to her eyes.

I knew then that she could not survive. Hope for her, for myself, for all of us drained away. We were all destined to follow her. Seeing her, seeing that she too knew the truth, I forgot my father's words. In this hell, death was preferable to life. For Keng, for us all, death was not an enemy to fight, but a friend who brought relief from suffering.

I found that my tears had ceased. It was as if, expecting my own death, I had allowed a part of me to die already.

The next time I arrived at the hospital, Srey was in Keng's bed. My mother was asleep.

Already knowing the answer, I asked Srey where Keng was.

'They took mother away,' she replied. 'Grandmother says my mother died. Grandmother says she will die too. Am I going to die, uncle?'

I held her hand, my face unmoving. I felt relief that Keng's suffering was over. The only surprise to me was that she had gone before my mother. That was the only uncertainty now – not whether death would come, but when it would come, and how.

'Am I going to die, uncle?' Srey's question interrupted my thoughts.

I held her hand, and felt that it was hot. I guessed she had the beginnings of fever already. 'Don't worry about death, my child. Dying is just sleeping, for ever. If you die, you will be with your mother again. There is nothing bad about it. Death is peace.'

At this point, my mother woke up. She was resigned to death, though somewhat to my surprise she was not yet resigned to the business of dying. 'You have to do something, Thay,' she said, with sudden urgency. 'I am so hungry. I have to eat. Listen, I have some things you can exchange for food.'

She kept her jewellery wrapped in the clothing in her bag at the foot of her bed. Feeling inside, I found her diamond earrings, a diamond brooch, a diamond pendant, and a gold necklace. 'If anything happens to me,' she said, 'You take the rest of my jewellery. You will need it to look after Any and Sudath and Nawath. Any is a good girl, a sweet girl, Thay. She loves you, and she loves Sudath as if he were her own. You must look after them all. Remember what your father told you. Live for them.'

At home that evening, I told Any what had happened. She had been expecting the news, but she was still unprepared. She sat on the floor of the hut, held her head in her hands, and muttered Keng's name over and over again through her tears. I sat beside her, with my arm around her shoulder. Keng had been a good friend to her, more like an older sister than a sister-in-law. The two of them had shared so much suffering and labour, looking after the children and our parents. It was through Keng that Any had grown so close to my mother. Sudath and Nawath had loved playing with Srey Rath. As Any wept in my arms, I knew there was nothing I could say to comfort her.

The next day, I found Vuoch lying in bed with Srey alongside her.

'I'm not ill, Thay,' she explained when she saw my expression. 'But I have to look after mother.' She was not ill yet, perhaps, but she was as weak as the rest of us, and knew the risks, knew she was probably giving up her chance of life. She had been in a work team, and received her due rations. Now she had renounced that dubious advantage in exchange for half-rations, as well as running the risk of being denounced as a malingerer and picking up a fatal infection. She had claimed she had a stomach ache, because there was no way to check that. To sleep in the same bed as her sick niece, Srey, seemed suicidal, but mother and daughter were very close, and nothing would have kept her away.

For the next week, I kept my routine, taking my two meals and my medicine, returning home in the late morning, reporting back to Any, making discreet inquiries about sources of food for my mother. In fact, diamonds had almost no value locally, and all exchanges were as difficult as ever. No one had heard of dollars here. Gold remained the only true security.

Every day, while Srey's fever became worse, Vuoch and I would talk. It was all I could do to make her keep her voice down, for she was full of bitterness. 'You see, Thay, our father was right about these people,' she complained time after time, her despair tinged with more than a trace of her old passion for political discussion. 'Look around. These fanatics have destroyed our country.'

It took a whole week for the fever to strike Vuoch. When I arrived that day, I saw that her shrunken features were sallow. She looked as ill as Srey, who was now only semi-conscious in the bed beside her. I touched her forehead. It was burning. But she was still determined to talk.

'The ideology sounded so good,' she said, though her voice was hardly more than a whisper, 'But it just became an excuse for destruction and oppression. These fanatics. . .'

'Rest, Vuoch,' I said, glancing round nervously. 'Don't talk. You'll be better soon.'

'I like to talk.' She pulled me down to her, and went on in a whisper. 'Thay, I know I'm dying. We're all dying. But listen: you used to say father and mother didn't understand the Khmer Rouge. I believed you. I had so many hopes, like you. Patriots, indeed! Now we know what they are. Communists.' She paused. 'Some people say that this is not true communism.'

'Maybe,' I said, weakly.

'Well, let me ask you this. Do you really believe that if Marx, Lenin and Mao had not been born, we would be in this hell?'

I looked round again, nervous of being overheard. 'Hush, Vuoch,' I muttered.

'Well?' she asked severely, raising her voice. 'If those Communists had not been born, would we be – '

'Yes, yes, you're right,' I said hastily, and saw her nod in satisfaction, as if, having established the truth, she felt she could die in peace.

*　*　*

Three days later, when I came, Vuoch was gone. Only Srey remained in the bed, too weak to speak.

A few days after that, Srey too had gone.

'They took her away this morning,' said my mother, without emotion, when I sat down beside her. 'She was a good little girl. She was not frightened. She said she was going to sleep, to find her mother. A good little girl. I don't know why she went before me, though.'

My mother, her cheeks sunken, waited for death impassively. I thought she was going to die without anything to lighten the burden of her last hours, but to my joy, I managed over the next few days to exchange her necklace for three-quarters of a can of sugar, a soggy brown mass like molasses.

'Mother, look!' I said as I arrived for my morning visit.

'Ah!' She sniffed, and opened her eyes. 'Sugar!' she said, and smiled, as if she had won a prize. I helped her to sit up and handed her a spoon. She began to eat right then and there.

'Mother, don't eat too much too quickly. It will be bad for you.'

'I don't care. I will die anyway. Now I will die happy. Here, you have some, too.'

I had to admit she had a point, and smiled. She was still eating when I went off to receive my rice soup.

When I came back the next day, her bed was empty.

I stared. Even now, even though I had known for days she would die, even though I had wished her suffering over many times, I was not prepared. I stood in silence, tears flowing, looking foolishly at the empty bed, until I noticed the sugar can. It was empty. She had eaten a whole pound of sugar! The shock to her poor wasted body must have been more than it could take. The realization made me want to laugh through my tears, an intense combination of sadness and relief and admiration. By hastening her own death, my old mother had, in a small way, seized control of her own destiny and died not in misery, as her persecutors had prescribed, but as she wished to die – happy.

I remembered her smile at the taste of that heavenly sugar, and hoped that when my turn came I would have such luck.

I remained there long enough to gather up the possessions of my mother and my two sisters. In each bag, there were several changes of clothing, and wrapped in the clothes some jewellery, watches, rings, and necklaces. All would be useful in the struggle for my family's survival, and, I hoped, for our escape.

For another week, I followed my routine, commuting between village and hospital. All around me, every day, death struck, and the dead were carried out to make way for the dying. It was so routine that I hardly noticed the changes any more, until one day, while I was dragging myself out of the hospital after receiving my medicine and drinking my meagre soup, I heard a familiar voice: 'Thay!'

There, sitting on a bed, was my sister-in-law Lao, Theng's wife, whom I had not seen for weeks. If she had not spoken, I would not have recognized her. She looked like a living corpse. I could see from her expression that I looked the same. I limped over to her. There beside her, lying silent in the same bed, were her two boys, Visoth and Amap.

'We came in yesterday,' she whispered. 'I was told mother, Keng and Srey Rath were here. But I can't find them.'

I sat down on the bed and took her hand, and told her about the deaths.

She sighed, as if she had known the truth already, and stared impassively at the wall, stroking Amap's head.

'How is Theng?' I asked. He at least, with his athletic build, would be strong enough to endure a while longer.

But for an answer, she just turned and looked at me.

There was no need for her to say anything. Eventually, my voice shaking, I asked: 'When?'

'Last week. He collapsed at work, and died so quickly he never even had a chance to get to hospital.'

We fell silent, weeping. There was nothing more to say, nothing further we could suffer. Tears were the only expression of what we felt, and they expressed nothing of our agony. It astonished me that I still had tears to shed. My child, my mother, my father, my sisters, my brother, all gone, all except Thoeun, whom I had last seen in Koh Thom before this descent into hell. Suddenly I felt a desperate need to know that he and his family were all right, that I and Any and Lao were not the only survivors.

We were silent for a while. At last, I stood to go, saying I would see her whenever I came to the hospital.

A few days later, I found her alone in her bed. She was lying, staring with unseeing eyes at the ceiling. I sat down on the bed and took her hand. Slowly, she turned her head.

'Thay,' she said, struggling to sit up, then collapsing back. 'They died yesterday – both of them – Visoth in the morning, Amap in the evening.' Her voice sounded as if it were coming from a long way away, her skin was drawn tight across her skull, and her hand was icy. There was nothing I could say, nothing I could do except look at her. Her eyes moved, but there was no life in them.

'My only wish now is to die,' she muttered, when I stood up to leave. 'I just want to join my children and my husband as quickly as possible.'

Two days later, her bed was occupied by someone else, and I knew her wish had been fulfilled.

What could we do? Nothing. When would it be our turn? Next, perhaps. So Any and I told each other every night.

Every night, death was closer. Eventually, he visited our house. Neary, Any's cousin, lost her son. On the verge of breakdown, she was ordered to go to cook for a mobile team ploughing in a field some miles away. She took her ten-year-old daughter with her, leaving us alone in her house. What happened to her in the end I never discovered.

One day, as I was collecting my soup at the hospital, a crowd gathered at the edge of the room, staring out under the thatch. From the next door building, I saw patients streaming, about forty of them, a silent and submissive column of suffering humanity, watched over by half a dozen Khmer Rouge. There were people among them who could hardly walk. Others were weakened by oedema, and moved as if in a bad dream. The strongest had to support the weakest. 'What's happening? What's happening?' everyone asked each other.

One man in the crowd seemed to know. 'They found a dead body in that room. A young boy. They say it had been eaten by a dozen of those people.'

So it had come to this. My reaction was more curiosity than

horror. I could understand why they had done it. The reaction of the Khmer Rouge was no surprise either, nor was it a surprise that all forty of the patients should be treated as guilty. We were used to injustice. What appalled me was the emotional response of the Khmer Rouge themselves. I heard the hospital staff, all dressed in Khmer Rouge black, shouting 'They are ogres! They are ogres!' In Cambodian mythology, flesh-eating ogres were the principal evil figures. The revolutionaries despised what they called our 'superstitions' but they knew how to use them to their benefit for propaganda purposes.

Ogres! You have full bellies, I thought. You do not know what it is like. It is you who have driven us to this. It is you who are the true ogres.

Someone asked the medics with more than a hint of irony, 'Where will these *ogres* go?'

'The ogres will not last long,' came the reply. 'We have a special camp for them. They will not live more than a month. This is only justice.'

And so steadily, inevitably, we lost the semblance of humanity. Day by day, we watched our own destruction. Sometimes in the evening, Any and I would look at each other and our tears would begin to flow, without either of us saying anything. Any was exhausted. During my long illness, it was she who did all the domestic work. After returning in the evening, she had to make several journeys to the river three hundred yards away for water. She would boil water on the fire for washing and the laundry.

The only relief from illness and exhaustion lay in sleep. Sleep allowed us to forget our misfortune and our hunger. Strangely, it was a real release, and not only for us – most people, as if escaping from the day-time nightmare, reported astonishingly beautiful dreams. I found it somehow reassuring. If I had been frightened of the nights as well as the days, I think I would have given up.

Day by day, I became more of an animal. Once, on my way back from hospital, I saw some small frogs hunting insects beside some ox droppings.

I thought: food.

I hunted around for a stick, and then, with a few swift strokes, killed half a dozen frogs. When I brought them home to Any, she was delighted. We grilled the frogs over our fire and ate them, taking care not to be surprised by the Khmer Rouge. Thereafter, whenever I smelled ox droppings, I looked around for a suitable stick, and frog became a regular part of our illegal diet.

Not only frogs. Grasshoppers, crickets, tadpoles, snails, lizards (although they were very difficult to catch), and even three snakes. All of them we grilled.

Although I was suffering from oedema, at least I was getting three rather than two bowls of soup a day. My children were in far more need than I. Sudath, who had an infected cut on his leg that simply refused to heal, remained stoical. He was a great help. In spite of his leg wound, he helped me on my scavenging expeditions. Sometimes, I would be able to sneak fruit – mangoes, oranges, guavas, limes, pomegranates – using a stick to knock them from trees reserved for the Khmer Rouge. He would keep watch, throwing pebbles or whistling if he heard anyone coming. Then, later, after dark, we would share the fruits out, creating delicious moments of ephemeral sweetness in the bitter wasteland of our lives.

Such moments – indeed, our very survival – depended on sharing what we had. But Nawath, now six, and always at home, was too young to be anything but demanding. He could never accept the idea of sharing. If, for instance, I gave the active, larger Sudath a little more – an extra fruit that I had scavenged or a larger frog – Nawath would complain and cry.

Once I managed to obtain some illicit cooked rice by barter. I said that we'd eat it that evening and took Sudath off to see if we could find some small animals to go with the rice. When Any returned home from work, I went to get out the rice, and found the pot empty.

My heart sank, my face fell, I felt like weeping. I looked at Nawath, for he had been the only one in the house in our absence.

'Yes, father,' he said, his expression begging forgiveness. 'I couldn't bear it. I tried not to . . . then I tried only to eat a little. . .'

All at once, I was overtaken by a terrible anger. I hauled him from his corner, took up a stick, and began to thrash him. I have never felt such wildness in me. I beat him, and beat him, and beat him, with Nawath crying, 'I'm sorry, father! I'm sorry!' until I felt Any pulling at my arm. Only then did I realize what I was doing, and stopped.

In an agony of remorse, I took Nawath into my arms, and rocked him, and wept with him. That is what hunger can do to you.

One evening, I found a toad. You have to be careful with toads, for their bile contains a dangerous poison. I took out the bile with great care, being careful not to let it break. Inside, the toad was full of black and white eggs. Having cleaned it to my satisfaction, I grilled it. Any didn't want any. She said she'd heard that toad's eggs were as dangerous as the bile. 'And don't give any to the children!' she said. I refused to believe her, and cheerfully ate the lot. It was very good.

That night, I was gripped by a terrible pain in the stomach. I just had time to clamber down the ladder and stagger into the bushes when I was seized with a fearsome attack of diarrhoea. I was already sick and skinny, and my body was distended by oedema. All it needed was diarrhoea to crush me completely.

When I got back in, Any was surprisingly unsympathetic. 'I told you,' she said crossly. 'You see what happens if you don't listen to me.' But the pains and the diarrhoea continued, and gradually her petulance gave way to concern – 'If it goes on like this, you'll be dead in three days.' It was nothing less than the truth, for we had seen countless people succumb to much lesser afflictions. Nor did it seem such a terrible idea. It had become commonplace to die like that, like a dog.

Well, death wasn't so bad. But like my mother, I became desperate for something sweet.

That insatiable urge inspired in me a wild idea. Not far from our home, there was a sugar-palm tree. I had noticed that every morning one of the Ancients climbed the palm tree to collect the sweet palm-juice in bamboo cylinders.

The next morning, I told Any I wanted to taste sugar-palm juice again, and asked for her last bracelet to see if I could make an exchange. She handed it to me, and then, on the point of leaving for work, she hesitated.

'I don't want to leave you alone,' she said, caressing my brow and wiping the sweat from my face.

'No, Any. You can't stay, you know that. If they found you here, they would punish you, and me as well probably. That would really be the end of me.'

I would not normally have dared approach the peasant, being afraid that he would denounce me, but desperation stifled caution. When I saw him beginning to return from his collecting trip, I positioned myself in the bushes, and stepped out in front of him as if by coincidence.

'Comrade, I would like some of that juice,' I said, boldly.

He looked at me suspiciously. 'No, I am sorry, the palm juice belongs to Angkar, and to my workers at the blacksmith's.'

There was nothing else for it but to stake everything on one card. But as I really believed I had only a few days to live I felt I had nothing to lose.

'I have gold,' I said.

'Really?' He sounded astonished. 'Gold?'

'Yes, here it is!' I showed him the bracelet.

'How much do you want for that, then?'

Clearly, he had never exchanged anything in his life and his reply made me fairly certain that he wasn't about to denounce me. I even had a chance to set my own rate, if I trod carefully.

'How much will you give me?' I asked.

He shook his head. 'I don't know. What do you want?'

On the village black market, the bracelet was worth only about one-and-a-half cans of rice – half a *tael* of gold. That was the equivalent of about three cylinders of palm juice. 'I'll let you have it for twenty-five cylinders,' I said coolly.

'Twenty-five? That's a bit much, isn't it?'

Well, at least he had accepted the principle of the exchange.

'OK. Twenty, then.'

'All right. But you have to give me the bracelet first.'

It was a deal. Twenty cylinders, the first one right then and there, the rest delivered one at a time over the next nineteen days. He poured the first instalment into two large condensed-milk cans. I went back home happy, certain he would not denounce me. After all, he was now as guilty as I.

My blacksmith was as good as his word. Every morning, he brought another cylinder of palm juice. For almost three weeks, I awoke at dawn and had palm juice for breakfast, sharing it with

Any and the children. For some reason, people said that palm juice was not good for oedema. Apparently, they were wrong. Day by day I felt better and looked better. My diarrhoea cleared up. My oedema improved. That palm-juice put me back on my feet.

One day in early May, when Any was out working, a Khmer Rouge suddenly entered the house. Sudath, frightened, ran to the back of the house and hid. I don't know what the man wanted, but Sudath's action gave a focus to his suspicions. Hauling the boy out, the Khmer Rouge began to question him, asking what he was doing running away like that. I interrupted: 'He was running to go to the toilet.'

The man ignored me. 'Where do you work?' he asked Sudath.

Sudath looked at me with frightened eyes. Again I replied for him: 'My son has a leg wound, he – '

'If he has a leg wound,' the Khmer Rouge officer interrupted, 'Why does he run so fast? He should be working. I see you still have individualist leanings. You are sick, and you keep your son at your side. If you're sick, you should stay by yourself. Your son must join the children's brigade.'

I urged Sudath forward, and showed the sore on his leg. 'Look,' I said, 'See for yourself. He could do with a few more days' rest. Couldn't you grant him that?'

'No! No! You must purify yourself, liberate yourself from feelings. The child belongs to Angkar. You should not wish to keep him for yourself. He is strong. He can work. Don't tell me he can't. I saw him run.'

I didn't know what to say, but Sudath bowed to the inevitable. 'Father, I will work,' he said. 'I must go. Anyway, perhaps I'll get better rations this way.'

For Any, the news was a terrible blow, for she loved Sudath as her own. He was a solemn child, and had been since his mother died, but he was uncomplaining and hard-working, a support both practically and emotionally. How could we get along without him?

That night, we prepared him as best we could. I gave him my pack, the one made out of a trouser-leg which I had taken to Tonle Sap, and Any made him a hammock out of a rectangle of cloth and a couple of pieces of rope. I told him to work hard, but only when the Khmer Rouge were watching. He was to rest whenever possible. Be careful, I said, don't trust people easily. We wouldn't see each other for several weeks, and who knew what would happen in the meantime?

He left the next day. I watched him go apprehensively. He was so skinny, with the skin pulled taut over his skull, and he had that wound on his leg. He looked much older than his ten years. He was a brave boy, I thought, as Any and I waved him goodbye. 'We'll see you in a week!' Any shouted, stifling her tears, as he disappeared with a final wave behind the next house.

Five days after his departure, when I was alone with Nawath and Any was at work, a boy came by whom I recognized as one of those who worked in the children's brigade.

'Uncle Thay,' he said simply, 'Sudath is dead.'

I felt as if I'd been struck.

The child just stood there and watched me.

'You mean . . . he's *dead*?' I asked stupidly. It was impossible. I refused to believe that I had heard him properly. How could Sudath be dead, when only a few days before he had been caught running about the house?

'Yes. He didn't wake up this morning and he is dead. He is at the camp.'

I could not doubt him, and felt a terrible void inside me, as if I had been stunned.

I went to Nawath and held him, repeating quietly, 'Your brother is dead! Your brother is dead!'

Then, for the second time in my life, I was overcome by anger. My child was dead. Someone, something, had killed Sudath, and I didn't know who or what. I had to discover the truth, take revenge, do something, anything to resolve the mass of conflicting emotions within me. My own need was great enough; but what would I tell Any when she came home that evening? How could I face her with such news, without even knowing what had happened?

I began to hobble frantically all over the village, until I found the village chief. 'My son! My son!' I shouted, not caring how distraught I appeared. 'I want to see my son's body!'

The chief must have been used to seeing people in this sort of state, because he hardly reacted at all. 'But you are sick. How could you go and see your son if you are sick?'

'By walking slowly. I want to go and see my son's body. You must understand. I am sick. I am going to die anyway. I am not depriving Angkar of my energy.'

He nodded, and wrote something on a piece of paper, authorizing me to see Sudath's body at the camp, two miles or so from the village.

I walked there slowly, resting my swollen legs frequently. In the camp, scores of children were milling about beneath their thatched dormitory building. I limped in amongst them, asking for those who had known Sudath, and then asking how he had died. They didn't want to reply, remaining stubbornly silent.

The camp chief came across to me and again I demanded, How did my son die, how did my son die? In a cold and detached tone, the chief gave me the official version. Sudath had fainted at work. His comrades had put him to bed, and he simply had not woken up in the morning. That was all. I couldn't even see his body. He had been buried already. I never learned the truth. I only knew that Sudath died five days after he left our house.

The chief put Sudath's clothes, his shoulder-bag, and new hammock on a table. 'Take them if you like,' he said, without a flicker of emotion.

I picked them up, and limped away.

8 ESCAPE FROM DON EY

For the next six months, from May to October 1976, Any, Nawath and I managed to survive, emaciated and ill as we were. Any slowly came to terms with the shock of Sudath's death. I knew in my heart of hearts that I would have to go back to work sometime, and so it turned out. Against the background of unrelieved toil and never-ending hunger, the scavenging for extra food, the few exchanges we could make for an additional can's worth of rice, a few incidents stand out in my memory, because of some risk taken, because of another few days' survival guaranteed, because the experience seemed to offer some new insight into the Khmer Rouge system. And through it all, I remained watchful, gathering whatever information I could, hoping always to find some way of arranging escape.

One afternoon in May, a Khmer Rouge officer came to see me. 'Thay!' he said. 'There's a woman dead over there!' He pointed to a house two hundred yards away. 'Go now and bury her! You'll meet another comrade there.'

Since the only people in the village during the day were the sick, it had become their task to bury the dead. Now it was my turn. I knew the house well. Once there had been six people in that family. Three had already died. Until the night before, three remained: two women – a teacher and her sister – and the teacher's little girl. Now the sister was dead, leaving the teacher alone with her four-year-old daughter.

When I got to the house and climbed the ladder, I looked in and saw the teacher with her child, sitting silent and withdrawn. The corpse was lying on the floor, enveloped in rags and old clothing, like a mummy. Only the head was showing. Not a scrap of skin was visible from the rest of the body. That struck me as odd, but I and my companion asked no questions. We just wanted to finish our task as quickly as possible and return home. We lifted the corpse down, and carried it about a quarter of a mile away from the village into a copse, where we found a patch of clear earth between other mounds, and dug a hole and buried the body.

139

I thought that was that. The next day, after hurrying back from the hospital, I went to collect the midday ration from the village communal dining area. It was drizzling rain. As I reached the canteen, I saw that something was up. Usually people were sitting at the tables, waiting for their soup. That day, everyone was gathering in silence to the side of the canteen hut. I went closer and peered through the crowd.

There I saw a lamentable sight. The teacher – the sister of the woman whom I had buried the day before – was crying, lying with one cheek on the muddy ground. She was almost naked, and her face was badly bruised. Her arms and legs too were black and blue. Her daughter was sitting beside her, her face a blank, staring round in shock.

'What happened?' I asked.

The story came from many mouths, whispered in low voices, for the Khmer Rouge were already waving us towards the tables. The woman had eaten the flesh of her dead sister. She'd been caught with a piece of human flesh in her pot. That explained, of course, why the corpse had been covered up so carefully. The Khmer Rouge had beaten and kicked the woman all morning, until she lost consciousness.

Transfixed with horror, not at the woman's action, but at what had led to it, I stared at this awful sight, a woman driven to cannibalism, and the frightened child beside her. Meanwhile, the Khmer Rouge were telling us: 'Move on! Do not pity this ogress!'

By evening, when I went past for the evening bowl of soup, the woman was still lying there in the mud. She was dead. I never knew what became of the little girl.

For some time, it had been a fear of mine that the Khmer Rouge, seeing me move around, would order me back to work, despite my horribly swollen feet and hands, and my laborious movements. After all, I was really no sicker than anybody else. There was no one who was healthy and strong. Labour was done by the sick, or not at all.

A few days after the death of the 'ogress', a working party was ordered into the forest to look for *prang* – a large forest root which was normally poisonous but could be cut into strips, soaked for a week to remove the poisons, and then added to rice soup. It had become vital to find extra rations, such as *prang*, banana tree roots and the shoots of sugar-palm trees. Our need was officially recognized. I was told that I would be part of the foraging party.

I accepted my bad luck philosophically, and did my best to reassure Any and Nawath that everything would be all right. I doubt if she believed me – I did not believe it myself – for any separation increased the chance of catastrophe. Still, we were surviving. If nothing untoward happened, as long as we both did enough work to avoid drawing attention to ourselves, we could go on like this for many months. That at least was what I told Any as I hugged her goodbye.

The area of forest in which the *prang* grew was about ten miles from the village, towards the mountains. There were not enough carts to carry all forty of us, so we would have to walk.

For our two weeks in the jungle, our rations were the equivalent of 400 cans of rice, in a large 224-pound jute bag. Since we had no cart with us, we would have to split the contents of the bag into 40 small portions. Everyone had the equivalent of 10 cans of rice in their shoulder-bags.

Ten miles is a long way for sick men to travel on foot. There were frequent stops. Here was the sort of opportunity I had longed for. At each stop, I went into the jungle, as if to answer the call of nature, and then, once out of sight of the supervisors, I plunged my hand into my bag and took out a small quantity of rice, which I transferred to my scarf. I hid the scarf in the leg of a pair of trousers I had brought along as a change of clothing. I hoped that once we arrived no one would bother to measure the rice we had been given. I figured it would waste too much time. 'Nothing ventured, nothing gained,' as I constantly told myself.

It took all day to get into the forest. Towards dusk, upon our arrival, we were asked to return to Angkar the rice we had carried. We lined up, and each man poured his load into the large bag that the Khmer Rouge had brought along. At first they checked the amounts by decanting the rice into a bag with a condensed-milk tin. Ten cans of rice; another ten; and another. I was getting perilously close to the front of the queue, and was wondering how on earth I could manage to transfer my rice back into my pack when one of the Khmer Rouge interrupted his comrade: 'Why are you counting? Who would dare steal from

Angkar? We're wasting time.' When my turn came, I simply tipped my bag into the sack, and no one paid any attention.

At once, I slipped off into the forest again, and hid my little bundle of rice in the hollow of a tree trunk, and covered it with leaves. If anybody discovered it, there would be nothing to connect it to me. If it wasn't discovered, I would have a good chance of retrieving it at the end of our two weeks' work.

Which was exactly what happened.

When I got home, I was delighted to find that nothing had changed. Any fell into my arms and the terrible apprehensions we had endured vanished. And when I showed her the extra rice, she was doubly happy to see me. She scolded me, smiling, for taking such a risk, but we both knew it had been worth it. Every day for a week, Any, Nawath and I were able to share an extra half-can of rice, moving us all a little further from the line that separated life from death.

I knew a man, a former Customs official, Sem, who was quite highly placed in Phnom Penh under Sihanouk. He was an educated man, who often liked to mix French in with his Cambodian. Long since separated from his family, he lived alone. Sem – tall, strong, always willing – had ensured his survival by working well. He was well known and liked because he worked in the kitchen, a coveted job. A year had passed since the fall of Phnom Penh, and the new constitution promulgated by which small items of personal property were allowed. This article of the constitution had been widely discussed during political meetings, and the Khmer Rouge had begun to sport watches. That had encouraged Sem to bring out his own watch, a fine gold Omega. A New Person with a watch! His gesture was quickly remarked in the village.

During one mealtime, a group of Khmer Rouge 'proposed' to 'borrow' his watch, for Angkar. Sem bristled and refused: 'Comrades, I cannot lend it to you, I need it for work, to go to work on time.'

Naturally the Khmer Rouge were angry at his refusal. The leader stepped forward: 'Look at me, comrade Sem,' he said, 'I am the group chief and I don't have a watch. I have to tell the time for hundreds of workers. You've been wearing your watch for years; surely you can lend it to me for a while.'

Sem stood his ground, but cleverly changed his tactics. 'Excuse me, comrade, you must advise me – I think I'm allowed to keep it under the new constitution. Tell me – am I right or not?'

Since the conversation was taking place in public, and since the Khmer Rouge themselves had made such an issue of this matter, there was nothing they could do about it then and there.

Ten days after the incident, however, Sem was removed from the kitchen and sent to the forest to cut wood.

A week passed. Sem did not reappear.

Then, during the midday meal, I overheard a group of Khmer Rouge talking outside the canteen. 'Ah, comrade,' I heard one man say, 'I see you have a new watch.'

'Yes.' The other held up his hand proudly. 'It's Sem's watch,' he went on, making no attempt to lower his voice. 'You remember, that traitor who always used imperialist French words. When we took Sem for re-education, he tried to run away. I shot him.'

'You're a lucky man,' his friend said, enviously. 'That's really a nice watch!'

In the last week of May, my long convalescence came to a sudden but not unexpected end. For a week, I had been working in the kitchen. In one way, the assignment was a stroke of luck. Cleaning the tables, sweeping the floor and scraping off the plates, I could grab the occasional finger-lick of food or spoonful of soup. But in another way, it worked against me. I was noticed. After that final week of supposed convalescence, a Khmer Rouge officer arrived at my house and said, 'Comrade Thay, you have been resting too long. I think you must be better now.'

'I'm still sick, comrade. You can see my legs,' I said, knowing at the same time that I could no longer risk antagonizing the Khmer Rouge. 'But you are right, comrade. I am always ready to follow the orders of Angkar.'

'Good. Angkar needs you to go to Lolok Sar to till rice fields.' Lolok Sar was on the outskirts of Pursat, not far away. 'You leave tomorrow morning.'

Any was horrified at the news, but, as I told her, I had no choice. Best put a brave face on it, and hope that this separation would be as easy as the previous one.

'Don't worry,' I said. 'I won't be far away, and I'll come back as soon as I can.'

Anyway, it was vital to avoid giving any offence, for they were clearly wary of me. All I could do was work hard, taking every precaution not to be denounced as a bourgeois. I certainly didn't want to risk my true status being known. I determined to remain as cool as possible, to keep myself to myself, not get excited even when provoked. You had to be made of stone, to stay deaf and mute, and blindly obey orders, if you wanted to survive.

In Lolok Sar, we worked from six in the morning until noon, with a fifteen-minute break at about nine. Our rations were a bowl of rice soup twice a day.

The mornings were tough. Splashing barefoot through mud behind the untiring oxen for six hours, there was no chance to rest. But the afternoons were better, for they were spent watching over the oxen while they grazed. A conscientious revolutionary allowed his oxen to graze at liberty, following them so that they didn't get lost and didn't eat the shoots of young rice plants. The oxen could feed better when they were free.

I, however, made use of these moments to rest. I led the oxen far away from the rice fields and tied them to a post. While they grazed, I took a nap, sleeping lightly, keeping an eye on the oxen, and checking from time to time to see if their bellies were swelling nicely. If they remained flat, I had to change position quickly and find a spot with more grass.

One afternoon, on waking up, I found that one of the oxen had slipped its cord. Disaster: I was a double criminal. I had fallen asleep, and lost my ox. It was the end of the day, and I would never find it before dusk. The Khmer Rouge would never forgive such a fault, which was bound to be revealed during the meeting after supper. I searched frantically, fearing the animal was devastating the local community's gardens. No luck.

Evening fell. I was in utter consternation. What could I do to avoid the wrath of Angkar? Nothing. I returned with my one ox, not daring to tell the chief of my loss. Paralysed with fear, I ate in silence.

During the political meeting, as was usual, the Khmer Rouge repeated their favourite ideological themes, then we were divided into small groups, and invited one by one to make self-criticism. Everyone was supposed to judge his own actions and his day's work, while one of the Khmer Rouge guided us with questions: 'How do you conceive your work? Are you satisfied with it? Did you make any mistakes? Did you see any comrades making mistakes, or doing anything forbidden?'

My turn came. There was no escape. 'I worked hard,' I said, 'but I inadvertently fell asleep while tending the oxen. It was only for five minutes, but I found that the ox had gone.' I didn't admit that I had tied the oxen up in the first place: 'I looked for the ox all evening and couldn't find it. I have made a mistake. I ask Angkar and all of you to judge me. I will accept my sentence from Angkar and you.'

The leader who led the discussion replied, 'Comrade, it is good that you admit your mistake. But you should have done it before. If you had, I could have sent people out to look for the ox. Now it's too late.' He was right, of course. I just stood there, my head lowered like a naughty child. 'Why did you wait to tell us? Why did you even take time to eat? Tell us – did you intend to sabotage our work?'

I trembled inwardly. That criticism could well lead to an accusation that I was a counter-revolutionary. People were led away into the forest for that sort of thing. I had no good answer. 'I acknowledge my fault,' I said. 'I admit my stupidity for having kept quiet.' Humility was, as always, the only possible policy. 'I am willing to accept any useful punishment.'

All the men, a dozen or so, now had to criticize me. One by one they repeated what had been said. They were obliged to do it, or risk being accused of complicity with me.

That over, the men went away, leaving just three people behind, New People like myself, but selected for qualities not yet apparent to me. The chief pronounced sentence, quietly, with a chilling finality. 'Until now, Angkar has used gentle words – revolutionary words – to reform you in your work, in your acts and your daily behaviour. Angkar has tried to help you for one whole year, and you are still not reformed! You still have bourgeois attitudes! Your behaviour strikes a blow against the revolution. Angkar has tried to forge a new character for you through gentle persuasion. But you remain rebellious. You force us to use the hard way – "hot education". I am going to ask your three comrades to correct you.'

The leader withdrew, leaving me alone with my three torturers, who began discussing what they were going to do to me. I could see they were serious. There are always people in such circumstances who, not satisfied with singing the praises of the victors, are also eager to lend a hand in torturing their compatriots.

The three men began to shower me with kicks, slaps and punches. I fell, and lay unmoving on the ground, knowing that I must not respond. When the leader returned to see how his orders were being carried out, the blows began to land harder. I was picked up, slapped, punched in the stomach, allowed to fall, kicked, and all the time I knew I must not defend myself or even scream. That would have been to express opposition to Angkar's decision. If I cried out in pain, if I fought back, if I shouted at my torturers, I was liable to a more severe punishment. To be too soft or too hard, to be a coward or a rebel, were equal crimes. I simply had to endure to stay alive.

While the blows landed, I told myself that it could have been worse. You must always think that the offence deserves more than the punishment that it incurs. I made no sound, I did not flinch, I said nothing. Eventually, after perhaps fifteen or twenty minutes, they stopped, leaving me bloody, but with no bones broken.

The next day, I obtained leave for the day in order to find my ox. I discovered it without much difficulty, near a house. The inhabitants of the house had found it destroying a vegetable patch, and tied it up. The ox followed me docilely.

As I walked, a thought occurred to me. There I was, my mission accomplished, alone in the countryside. And it was still early.

I tied the ox to a tree and slept until noon.

Towards mid-June, my limbs began to swell up again. This time the oedema was worse than before. First came the swelling of the hands, feet and face; then, as the liquid built up, my legs became heavy. As the days went by, I moved more and more slowly. My lower back and legs – the buttocks and thighs – seemed like dead weights. My legs no longer responded. It was an effort to lift my behind up a ladder. This time I knew it was serious. This time, I thought, I'm dying.

Obviously my ploughing days were over, for a while at least. In early July, I was sent back to Don Ey, with a few other victims. I arrived home after five weeks' absence. To my surprise, Don Ey was full of people, though most of them looked terrible. Again, I found myself approaching the house with trepidation. In five weeks, anything could have happened. Any and Nawath could both have died, and I would have been none the wiser.

To my relief, as I climbed the ladder to the house, I saw Nawath. 'Father!' he shouted when he saw me, and came across to greet me. Delight at finding him alive was replaced by shock at the sight of him. He had developed oedema. His arms and legs were swollen, and he moved painfully slowly. He looked like a little, serious old man. Anxiously, I asked after Any. She was still working, out transplanting rice. I breathed a sigh of relief.

But she too had suffered dreadfully. When I saw her that evening, limping towards the hut and dragging herself painfully up the ladder to me, she was very different from the Any I knew. Her face was bloated with oedema, and so was her lower body. She smiled at the sight of me, but by the time she had climbed to the hut, she was incapable of saying more than 'Thay, dearest. You're back. You're back.' We just held each other, gently – for we no longer had the strength to grip each other with any passion – and stood stock-still in each others' arms for several minutes.

Then she told me what had happened in my absence. In the seven villages scattered along the river from Don Ey southwards, so many people had died that there were only enough now to populate two. The five villages set up by New People before we arrived had been abandoned, most of the survivors joining the two older villages, of which Don Ey was one. Apparently, these two villages, which had been there originally, and had more Ancients in them, had survived the famine better.

Now, there was a second way to tell black-clad Ancients from the New People in their ragged city clothes. The New People were the ones with swollen limbs.

Through the third quarter of 1976, nothing changed. People

continued to die. The Ancients said that rice was not all that scarce, but that Angkar wanted to starve us to death. Indeed, the policy was made quite explicit. I remember an officer at one political meeting coming out with some particularly chilling words: 'In the new Kampuchea, one million is all we need to continue the revolution. We don't need the rest. We prefer to kill ten friends rather than keep one enemy alive.'

We died, the desire for life dying before our bodies. Babies were born in Khmer Rouge families and among the Ancients, but there were no births among the New People. When the stomach is empty, desire is no more. Any and I had not made love since we left Phnom Penh. Once, love-making had been one of our greatest pleasures. But that was just a happy memory now. In Don Ey everyone was chaste. Our bodies were wasted and there was nothing to stimulate them. Female beauty was a thing of the past.

Strangely, in emotional terms, that didn't matter at all. As our bodies wasted away, as the rest of the family died, so we became increasingly all in all to each other. Once, I had taken such pleasure in the way her hair brushed her neck, the feel of her slim body, the depths of her dark brown eyes. Now the hair was lank, the body bloated, the eyes dimmed with disease. Physically, there was nothing left on which to base love. Yet we were more in love than ever. As our bodies weakened, our love grew – a strange irony, given that by destroying our bodies the Khmer Rouge sought to destroy our souls – expressing itself in the ways we touched and spoke and helped each other. When we shared our illicit fruit with Nawath in the darkness, we found strength in the sharing, and the touching, and the wordless tears at what had become of us both.

In all other respects, we had nothing. Patriotism, intellectual life of any kind, conversation, humour, all these were things of the past, eradicated by our hellish persecution. Our only preoccupation was to survive, our only consolation the predictions of Puth: 'Salvation comes from the West, and when peace reigns again, after the disappearance of the *thmils*, a new era will begin.'

Salvation from the West? We would have welcomed anybody – Japanese, American, French, Chinese, Russians, even the

Vietnamese. Does a drowning man question his rescuer?

Without help, however, we were doomed. We could not help ourselves. Conspiracy was hard, an uprising unthinkable. Travel was banned, whispering was prohibited, and there were informers everywhere. Acts of heroism were suicidal. I heard of two young people in a neighbouring village who seized a rifle from a Khmer Rouge and fled into the jungle. One was shot, the other vanished.

If there were guerrillas, we knew nothing of them. How could you feed guerrillas in a country where all food was in the hands of Angkar? With rations doled out in driblets, communally, it was impossible to establish stocks. Anyone living in the jungle would die of hunger. I could see no way of organizing any resistance.

Yet the spirit of resistance survived, even grew stronger, for the *thmils*, the atheists, by destroying, created that by which they in their turn would be destroyed: hatred.

I never stopped dreaming of escape. In fact, I had already raised the possibility with two men I had met in the hospital – a lecturer called Roeun, and a former army major. They too had had enough. Roeun had lost his wife and three children, and the major had lost three of his five children.

As it turned out, it all came to nothing. A couple of weeks after we started planning – devising ways of getting information about the terrain to the west, wondering how we should collect provisions – both of them were sent off on work missions, and I never saw them again. But the thought of escape continued to obsess me. It was either that or accept the near certainty of death for myself and my family, either through denunciation or disease.

One day, in early November 1976, my greatest fear was realized.

We were eating all together at the tables by the canteen hut, when I noticed a Khmer Rouge standing with three others, glancing over at me repeatedly. His face meant nothing to me, and I thought nothing of it until he came across and said, 'Hey! Don't I know you? What's your name?'

'Thay. My name is Thay.' I still suspected no danger.

'Aren't you Pin Yathay?'

I looked at Any and my neighbours. Many of them knew my full name. It would be foolish to deny it. I tried to dismiss my mild deception as of no importance. 'Yes, Thay and Pin Yathay. It's all the same, I just shortened my name.'

At once he went on the attack. 'You were a director of public works. You're an engineer trained by imperialist America.'

Now fear gripped me. 'How do you know me?' I asked, my pulse beginning to race.

'I know you well, comrade. Don't you know me? I worked on the Pursat–Leach road, under Sun Yi.'

The project was one of many I had visited in my capacity as director before the war, and I remembered Sun Yi well, for he was an efficient supervisor, if something of a disciplinarian.

The Khmer Rouge continued sarcastically, 'You don't know me, eh? Well, of course, your workers knew you, but you didn't know them. You were too high for that, and I was too low.'

'I cannot know everybody, comrade. Anyway, I always treated my staff well. You remember that, surely?'

But the Khmer Rouge was not to be appeased. 'I didn't say that you had committed any mistakes,' he said bitterly, 'but you were supervising Sun Yi, who expelled me from the work site. He dismissed me just because I had stolen a can of diesel fuel. I couldn't feed my family on the minute salary the government paid me. I was arrested, and Sun Yi, *your* subordinate, testified against me. And how many cans of diesel fuel had he stolen? That's the sort of justice we got under your regime!'

I told him I had known nothing of all this.

'But you were his superior, and he expelled me, and I was forced to join the underground! And then you hid your identity. You concealed your former position from Angkar!'

The whole table was silent. The other Khmer Rouge were staring across at me. I was desperately trying to force down the panic inside me, and display confidence.

'Comrade, I didn't conceal my identity. Thay is part of my name. I humbled myself because we are all equal in the revolution and I was eager to do Angkar's will. I have always done my work conscientiously. I have fulfilled all my duties as a revolutionary –'

He cut me off with a gesture of disgust, as if he had heard enough, and moved away. All my neighbours had their noses in their soup, pretending to be invisible and whispering furtively. Any gave me a long look. I could see she was as frightened as I.

Two days later, a New Person with whom I had worked in the kitchen, came to look for me in my hut. The kitchen staff, who served everybody, overheard much. He was scared. 'Thay, you're in danger. I heard the one who recognized you talking about you with his comrades. He said: Why not take you into the forest? The others said not to bother, because you were sick and would die anyway. They decided to wait a week. If you're not dead by then, they'll take you into the forest, that's for sure.'

When he left, I sat unmoving. My first reaction was to give way to despair, to give up, to surrender to my fate. Everything was lost, I was going to die anyway, I knew that. There was no escape. We swelled up and died. It was the law of nature, unalterable. We all died one after another. There was nothing to be done. What did it matter? I would die, and the sooner the better, there in the house with my wife and son.

Then the true enormity of my situation struck me. There would be no such choice. Even that tiny freedom would be taken from me. There would be no gentle, natural passing with my family beside me. They were going to slaughter me, like an animal, away in the forest.

At that thought, I felt another sensation, a surge of raw energy that drove out all other feelings. The instinct for self-preservation took over, and I suddenly, desperately, wanted to stay alive. I told myself: 'Pull yourself together! Sharpen up! Get out of this! You've always succeeded before! This is your last chance! Do something!'

I began to think. What was to be done? Leave alone? But there was Nawath across the hut, lying prostrate, his limbs swollen. I could hardly bear the thought of leaving him and Any. But neither could I imagine escaping with them. Better they should have a chance to live here than die with me. Better that I should get away, and give myself a chance to live, or at least die on my own terms.

It was all very simple. My mind was made up. I had to tell Any of my decision, that very evening.

After we had eaten, as we sat on the floor opposite each other, with Nawath sleeping behind his cloth partition across the hut, I prepared myself to speak. I was certain of my course, but that did not make me any less nervous. It was a terrible thing to do to us as a family, a terrible thing to impose on Any. But as I glanced up at her, and saw her sweet and wasted features lit dimly by the flickering flames of the cooking fire, I knew there was no other course. It was purposeless to stay on there merely to face death. They would be alone all too soon, anyway.

'Any, my dearest,' I said, 'I have something to tell you.' She looked up, without surprise, and I realized she had been expecting a decision of some kind. She too must have known that I could not stay. Speaking softly in order not to wake Nawath – I could see his little bloated face round the edge of the partition – I began to explain. I was doomed, I said. All the former high officials had disappeared. I was trained in the West. I was irredeemable in the eyes of the Khmer Rouge. They would come for me in a week, and that would be that. 'But you're a woman, Any, if you were alone with Nawath I don't think they would harm you.'

She said nothing, but I saw her gaze turn to one of horror.

'You can live on here with Nawath,' I went on. 'It's the only answer. I'll take my chances in the forest. If I succeed, we'll meet again. But I have to go soon. In one week, it'll be too late.'

'You'll leave?' she said. 'Leave me here with Nawath?' And suddenly she began to sob as if she were being torn apart.

'Yes, my dearest. It's the only way,' I said, desperately. For the first time, I began to realize that she had not come to the same conclusion as me. 'What did you think?'

'Not that. Not that.'

I said nothing, for there was only one other course open, the one that was impossible to contemplate. She would see that in a few minutes, I thought, and accept my decision.

But no. With hesitations and bitter sobs, she went on, 'It's impossible, my dearest Thay . . . I don't want to be separated from you . . . I prefer to die with you rather than to stay here. . .' As I listened to her in silence, unable to say anything to stem the slow, whispered outpouring of words and sobs and tears, I couldn't believe that she understood what she was saying. Soon, soon, she would see, and know why I had to go alone. 'I cannot live without you!' she sobbed. 'I prefer to die quickly and cleanly, with you.'

She paused, wracked by sobs. I waited for her to say: But if you think it is for the best, of course that is how it must be.

Silence.

To my astonishment, I began to realize she meant what she said. For the first time in our lives, she was refusing to accept my judgment of what was best.

The silence dragged on, broken only by her gasps. She was looking at me. I could see the highlights cast by the fire on her cheeks and in her eyes. Still she said nothing further. I knew then she had understood all along what she was saying.

I felt the strength of her, as well. Once, she had asked my opinion even before buying a dress. Now she had been hardened by experience. She knew what she was doing, knew that in any event she and Nawath would die, knew that we were in the process not of choosing life over death, but of choosing different ways of dying.

And she knew that, having chosen, there was one more fearful choice still to make. There seemed nothing I could do or say to help her through it. It was too awful for me to put into words. If I spoke the words, it would turn something that was merely a nightmarish fear into dreadful reality. I could not say them.

'But,' she said at last. 'But what shall we do with Nawath?'

Yes: those were the words I had refused to utter.

'Tell me, Thay dearest. What shall we do with Nawath?' She broke down again as she struggled to express the thought. 'He can't come with us. We can't carry him, and he can't walk far. They would catch us and kill us before. . .' She paused, her face working to control her emotion. 'We . . . we have to leave him behind. But . . . what are we going to do with him if we leave him?' She broke off again, overcome by sobs.

Could she really contemplate leaving Nawath? It seemed an extraordinary thing for a mother to do. I realize now that she had made a mother's supreme sacrifice. People say that for a mother the supreme sacrifice is to die with her child. No – if death is inevitable, the mother's supreme sacrifice is to abandon her child, if thereby she can prolong her own life.

I did not understand all that right then and there. But I felt her resolve, and knew there was nothing I could say to make her change her mind. After what we had been through, after being made one body with her by what we had endured together, it never even occurred to me to argue her out of her decision. I don't think I could have done so. I simply had to accept that things were different now.

Any was still sobbing. 'What do we do with Nawath?' she asked again, and fell silent. I knew from her tone of voice, and the silence, that she already knew the answer, for there was only one. Knowing it, again neither of us could bring ourselves to express it. Again, expressing it would make it irrevocable.

I glanced at Nawath, still asleep. I felt I wanted to go to him, stroke his head, provide some comfort for him, or myself. But I did not move. I couldn't risk waking him. I glanced back at Any. Her eyes were lowered, as if waiting for me to pronounce sentence.

After another eternal minute, the burden of silence became intolerable. I felt it as an accusation against me for evading responsibility.

'You know there is only one thing to do,' I whispered. 'We must take him to the hospital.'

The hospital, where people went only to die.

I looked into the shadows of her eyes. 'We must,' I said.

She knew that this time I was right. Nawath's chances were better in that morgue of a place than in the forest, while ours were better in the forest than there in the village. We would all die anyway; but to ensure we all lived as long as possible we had to leave him. While we would at least die together, he would die alone, abandoned by the only ones who cared for him.

The next morning, I asked for permission from the village chief to take Nawath to the hospital. He was very ill – his feet, hands and cheeks all bloated – and my sincerity couldn't be doubted.

Back home, I explained to Nawath what I was going to do.

He made no protest. Together, we walked laboriously, slowed by the weight of liquid in our limbs.

At the hospital I put him to bed. I had brought him all sorts of blankets and clothing so that he could live on alone in the hospital. Still he didn't say anything except, 'Father, will you give me food?' I promised to bring him some dried fish, and sat beside him to arrange his clothing and blankets.

Suddenly, a woman's voice broke in on our conversation. 'That child looks so like one of mine it's amazing!' I turned. In the next bed, there was a woman of about forty. She looked half-Chinese, and appeared in good health despite her skinniness. 'Why bring your son here?' she went on accusingly.. 'He'll die, everybody does. You should keep him at home.'

'The chief said I should bring him,' I lied.

'It's a bad idea,' she repeated.

'Yes, I know,' I said unhappily. Then a thought came to me. 'But maybe he would be all right if you could take care of him a little, since he resembles your child.'

Then the woman told me her story. She had had six children, all dead now. Her husband too had died. Loneliness had brought her to the hospital. She was not ill, but in exchange for being looked after, she mended the clothes of the hospital attendants. Now she had seen someone she could look after in her turn.

'Yes,' she said, 'I'll take care of the little one.'

Suddenly, I saw there was a way forward after all. 'Please consider him as your son,' I said, trying to control the tremble in my voice. I hardly dared hope yet, but it seemed that here was a way for the intolerable burden we had chosen to bear to be lifted from us. 'As you see, I am sick. My wife is, too. It is possible that my wife and I will not see our son again. But I shall try. Look after him until then.'

That evening, I described to Any what had happened with a wild feeling of relief. 'You see, Any, my dear? We made the right choice. It's Nawath's fate to survive. He's going to be all right after all.'

The news, and my reaction, gave her new strength, not only to continue with our plan, but also not to give in to her own fierce desire to see Nawath again. She was afraid that if she saw him her resolve would crumble in the face of her own remorse, and that her feelings would undermine her will to go with me.

Still, for three more days, Any and I hesitated to commit ourselves to flight. Time was running out, yet we couldn't bring ourselves to abandon Nawath. I was torn between two evils: entrusting our son to the woman, or renouncing our decision. The situation was pure torture for Any. She said she would leave, but she wept continuously.

The third day, in an attempt to gain further reassurance, I visited Nawath again in the hospital. At the sight of him, my spirits lifted again. He looked much better. He was sitting on the side of his bed, swinging his legs. I hadn't seen him so lively in weeks. He was also rather dirty, I noticed, to my embarrassment. I hadn't washed him when we arrived, and no one had washed him since. The woman in the next-door bed looked up as I approached. 'Oh, you're back,' she said. 'He's all right with me. We like each other, don't we, Nawath?'

He nodded and smiled.

'Look,' she went on. 'He needs better clothes. I have a lot of clothes left over from my children. Why not take him for a bath in the river? Then I'll dress him properly.'

I took his hand, and we walked slowly to the river.

While I was undressing him, he asked, '*Pouk*, where's *Me*? How is she?'

Pouk and *Me* were peasant terms for Father and Mother, and therefore an approved part of the new vocabulary of the revolution. Daddy and Mummy – *Papa* and *Mak* – were no longer tolerated, prohibited as bourgeois, like many other words excised by the lightning strokes of ideology.

Had he guessed that he was not going to see her again? With great difficulty, fighting my tears, trying not to let him see my anguish, I struggled for words to reply to him. 'Your mother is not well. She's resting at home. She's too tired to come. If she wasn't ill, she would have come with me.'

I wanted somehow to prepare him for our departure, for solitude, for separation, for the distress that lay ahead. But I couldn't say anything directly. It was too dangerous for us all. The conflict was too agonizing to bear, and I found tears running down my face. I began to wash Nawath gently and carefully, trying to find the words I sought, speaking when I could trust myself to do so.

'My dear son, you know our troubles . . . a curse has come over us . . . we can do nothing but endure this period of misery . . . your grandparents, your uncles, your aunts, your cousins, your little brother Staud, your older brother Sudath, are all gone. They are in the other world. They have been rescued from this nightmare, from hunger, from hard labour. They are already in heaven. But you must get well, Nawath. You are in hospital to get well. You have a new auntie who loves you like her own child.'

'Yes, father. Yesterday she gave me palm-sugar. It was lovely.'

'You see? Be respectful and good to her. She has lost all her children. Perhaps . . . perhaps she could take the place of us. You see, your mother and I, we're very sick. Perhaps we will not live very much longer.'

'Are you very sick, father?'

'Yes, my darling. Perhaps the day when we must leave you is very near. But you, you're the strongest in our family. You are the last one left. You must survive to keep our blood alive. Your new auntie has clothing and perhaps even gold. She will certainly be able to find extra rice, fish and sugar. You have become her only child, so you must love her as you love us. If you don't see us again, it's because we can't come any more. Remember the name of your father – Yathay – and that of your mother – Any. Never forget these two names – Yathay and Any.'

Then I took off my wedding ring, a simple alloy one of no interest to the Khmer Rouge, and slipped it into the pocket of Nawath's trousers, which were lying on the bank beside me. 'Always keep this ring with you,' I said. 'Wear it when you are bigger.' He couldn't wear it yet. His fingers were too small. 'Don't lose it,' I went on. 'It's the only souvenir that you will have of your family. If you don't see us again, don't look for us. Follow the orders of Angkar. Do what they ask you to do, without grousing, without protesting.' It was my turn now to bestow on my son the advice that my father had given me. 'Above all, be careful about what you say and do. Don't voice opinions. Be suspicious. Pretend to be ignorant, deaf, mute. It's the only way of surviving.'

Nawath listened in silence, nodding, dry-eyed and serious – too serious for a boy of six – but I was proud of him and his courage, courage far in excess of mine.

'You must stay alive. May Buddha and all the good spirits watch over you. Remember: just stay alive, my son.'

Our path was set. Even though Any continually asked me questions – How did he look? Did he really seem better? What exactly did you tell him? What did he say? What was the woman like? Would she really make a good mother? – she was reassured. We decided to leave as soon as possible.

157

The pain of those days made it hard for us to think clearly. I thought briefly that we would have to delay to exchange all the things which we no longer needed to procure rice. I had already obtained some dried fish and two cans' worth of rice, but that wasn't enough. Anyway, for several more days, we hesitated, and consumed much of it, until it occurred to me that we could do without rations if we could be sure of finding food within a day or two of our departure. There was a way to do this, but it would need careful planning.

Any knew a young woman, Mom, a girl of about twenty who had worked on irrigation canals. During her work, Mom had made friends with people from Leach, and knew that there, indeed in all the villages of the Leach district, they ate better. She said that the average ration there was one can of rice to every three people per day.

Any had often told me about her talks with Mom, but I had not paid any attention until now. Suddenly, her knowledge was precious to us. I asked Any to see Mom to get information on the path we should take and the name of the worksite, so that I could forge papers for the trip.

At the canteen later that day, Any approached the girl and spoke to her about our scheme. Not only did she promise to help – she wanted to come with us to join her friends. I agreed at once. She was intelligent, in good health, committed to escape, and alone, for she had just lost her parents and her only brother had been assigned to a youth team elsewhere.

We needed a suitable way-station, not far from Don Ey, and Mom was able to suggest one at once – a quarry where people were often sent, in groups and individually, to break stones for the construction of roads and bridges. It would be our first destination.

To get us there, and beyond, I made out false passes by imitating the signature of the village chief. It was a risk, but not a large one. I had been given this kind of document several times to go fishing and ploughing. I knew the style. I still had some paper and my ballpoint pen. I had kept it carefully hidden, for the Khmer Rouge loved pens and used to clip them in their breast pockets, on the outside, to show off their status and intelligence. Amongst the New People, both paper and pen were rarities.

Nobody thought of writing any more, now that the postal service no longer existed.

I hadn't written anything for a year and a half, but since many of the Khmer Rouge were barely literate, I was not worried about the quality of my calligraphy. Actually, I made out two sets of passes. We needed separate passes because men and women were not supposed to travel together. The first set would get us, separately, to the quarry. We would then destroy these passes and there would then be nothing to link us with Don Ey. The second set would allow us to reach Leach. I authorized myself to go bamboo cutting in Veal Vong and the two women to visit the hospital in Leach, both perfectly acceptable destinations for anyone coming from the quarry.

On the day of our escape, we left the village at dawn. I was well in front of the two women. Dressed in a shirt dyed black, with a Chinese cap and Ho Chi Minh sandals, I could at a distance have been mistaken for one of the Ancients. Even so, I had no great confidence in our scheme. Nawath, constantly in our thoughts, seemed to have more chances than us. We might be followed; our false papers might be discovered; we had only a few provisions on us. And still I had no idea what we would do when we reached Leach. There was no thought yet of going beyond.

A heavy downpour the night before had soaked the ground. It was like walking through a shallow lake. We intended to cover the ten miles to the quarry in one day, but walking in that mud, through ankle deep puddles, was slow and tiring. Often we stopped to get our breath back and regain our strength. At each stop, to avoid any curious looks, I would sit off by myself in the forest so that if anyone surprised me I could say I was answering the call of nature. The two women sat beside the footpath. When they felt strong enough to continue, they gave me a wave and we set off again. By late afternoon, we were still a mile or two short of our goal, but there was a village near by. I waited for the women and we decided to risk trying to eat and sleep there.

Keeping a discreet distance between us, we presented ourselves to the Khmer Rouge in the communal canteen. Suspiciously, the chief looked me over. 'Where are you going, comrade?'

'I've been sent to the quarry,' I said, handing him the pass, and trying to control my nervousness. Just then, Any and Mom appeared behind me. 'Oh, here are two others who have been sent with me,' I said.

'Let's see your passes, then,' the chief said, and glanced from mine to theirs. Of course, they carried the same signature, and he was reassured.

'OK, you may rest here.'

The next morning, at dawn, we left before the village awoke. This time, the women walked ahead, past the quarry. After another mile or two, we destroyed the first passes and walked on.

As we walked, Any became so exhausted that I had to carry her bag as well my own, letting the women go on ahead again. As we approached Leach, it struck me that this arrangement would be an advantage for the women. The Khmer Rouge paid no attention to people moving about without baggage, since they would presumably have belonged to the village. But I would be suspicious – although I was dressed in black, my skin was not as dark as the Ancients and I was carrying two bags.

We had almost arrived at the village when a Khmer Rouge on a bicycle, with a rifle slung over his shoulder, accosted me. With a menacing look, he got off his bicycle, giving me a few seconds to think what I was going to do. 'Comrade,' he asked, rather rudely, 'Where are you going with those two bags?'

I hardly paused. 'Oh! That fellow's late again!' I said angrily. 'He's always late. He – '

'I said, where are you going, comrade?' he interrupted.

My mood changed, as if acknowledging his authority. 'I'm going to cut bamboo in Veal Vong. Do you know Veal Vong, comrade?' Then I hurried on, not allowing time for his suspicions to harden. 'We were in a group, but one of my comrades is slow. Now we've got separated. He's behind me somewhere and the others are all on ahead, I suppose. Did you see a group pass by yesterday evening or this morning?'

The Khmer Rouge seemed surprised by the question. He replied more politely now. 'There are so many. I don't know which ones were yours.'

I continued unconcerned, as if he were irrelevant to my real problems: 'You see what a mess I'm in now. Here I am with two bags, and I'm late. I know why he's hanging back. With this idiot carrying his bag, why should he ever catch me up? Anyway, if you – ' I broke off, noting that the Khmer Rouge was staring at my cap. He seemed more interested in my cap than in my story.

'Your cap is beautiful,' he said, dreamily.

What incredible luck. 'Oh yes!' I said. 'It's a beautiful cap, isn't it? Would you like to exchange it for yours?' He was a bit wary and didn't reply at once. I reassured him: 'It would be a pleasure to have your cap, as a souvenir,' I said, handing him mine.

It didn't fit. I could see the disappointment in his eyes. 'It doesn't matter,' he said sadly. 'Goodbye, and thank you, comrade.' And he cycled off.

I took a deep breath and walked on. Any and Mom were waiting for me. I told them briefly what had happened and we continued on our way to Leach.

While Mom went in search of the people she knew, Any and I waited outside the village, wondering what we should do to get ourselves accepted. Again, Any's mind reverted to Nawath. 'Did he ask about me?' she wanted to know, with tears in her eyes. 'Was he upset I did not come? Oh, Thay, will he really be all right?'

'Yes, Any, my dearest. It was right to leave him. He will be well looked after.' I had no doubts, no doubts at all, that he would live, even if we died.

After a while, Mom returned, and said she'd found her friends, who had invited us to join them. There I learned that we had no real problem after all – one of the officials, the chief of one of Leach's base camps, was open to bribery. All I had to do was offer one *tael* of gold per person, using Mom's friends as intermediaries, and we were in. We could stay in Leach's Camp No. 1 indefinitely.

9 FEEDING THE FIRE OF ENMITY

For the first couple of months in Leach – November and December 1976 – we survived as we had in Veal Vong, by supplementing our rations buying rice on the black market, with the occasional addition of sugar, fruit and fish. Though our hoard of spare clothing and jewellery inherited from my family was running low, I still had dollars, and these were valued in Leach. A hundred dollars bought fifteen cans of rice (a hundred-dollar bill being once again the basic unit of currency).

My job was clearing trees, along with a hundred other men. Our first assignment involved a scheme that was typical of the way the Khmer Rouge did things. We were marched off to a rice field in which grew a scattering of fruit trees and bushes. It looked like a perfectly serviceable rice field to me, perhaps better than most because it supported the fruit trees as well, mostly rather fine mangoes and tamarinds.

Our leader, Comrade Run, explained our task with obvious pride. Apparently, at harvest time the place was infested with sparrows that gorged themselves on the rice. The sparrows nested in the fruit trees. Eager to display true revolutionary initiative, to apply the sacred spirit of self-sufficiency that Angkar demanded, Comrade Run planned an assault on the sparrows. How? By destroying their nests. And how again? By cutting down the fruit trees. While people were dying of hunger a mile away, we were out chopping down fruit trees. The damage wrought by the sparrows was nothing compared to the damage we did to Leach's fruit harvest.

After that notable objective was achieved, we were turned loose on the forest to make new clearings. We were divided into ten groups. I belonged to a group of twelve who were considered the best workers and thus designated Group No. 1. In the morning, we walked in columns to the work site. At noon, there was an hour's break for lunch, then we returned to work until six p.m. At night, when the moon shone, we worked up until ten or eleven p.m. We would return to the village every tenth day to rest, but also to attend a political meeting.

There was, however, another unofficial side to our lives. Out in our forest camp, I and two others hung our hammocks a little apart from the rest, in the hope of having some peace, away from constant supervision. Sometimes, when our comrades and our group leader were fast asleep, we would sneak away two at a time to go back to the village. The third always stayed in his hammock to tell any snooping Khmer Rouge that the other two had gone into the forest to relieve themselves. On these trips, I would pass through a number of Leach's other subsidiary camps, each one a collection of eight foot by ten foot bamboo huts, thatched with palm leaves and raised on stilts. It was on these occasions I was able to continue making exchanges. I would make a deal on the way in with a broker – as in Veal Vong, the brokers were well-known to the New People – go home to see Any, collect clothing, jewellery, or dollars, and pick up the extra cans of rice on my way back. Any was the focus of this activity. Seeing her and talking with her was my only pleasure, my only strength. We were life itself to each other, each other's only hope.

We were forbidden to have extra food, but we managed. Though not allowed to cook rice, we could boil water, so when we saw our group leader, Run, coming, we would snatch up a water can, and put it on the fire, whipping away any rice that was cooking and hiding it in the bushes. Thus, whenever it was my turn to go back to the village, I could take cooked rice to Any, returning to the forest camp before dawn, so that on waking up no one noticed my absence.

One rest day, I decided to stay in my hut rather than go to the political meeting. It was foolhardy, but all I had to do was remain out of sight until I heard the gong, which rang to call the children to eat – an hour or so before the adults' meal – and also signified the end of the meeting. Then it would take the men about an hour to get back to camp. It would be easy for me to drift back in time for the communal meal.

When I left, I took with me in my scarf one can's worth of newly bought raw rice which I intended to cook that evening. At the campsite, however, I found to my surprise that everyone had eaten. Apparently, the meeting had been shorter than usual and my workmates had returned and eaten early. For a moment I was taken aback, thinking I was about to go hungry, until I saw that they had kept some rice aside for me. I was touched – in those harsh conditions, it was more than I would have expected. Eager for food, I unthinkingly put my scarf containing the rice into the nearest hammock and sat down to eat about twenty yards away.

Just then, the owner of the hammock, a friend of mine called Chorn, came back, went to lie down, and sat right on the bundle of rice. He jumped up in surprise, and prodded the scarf. His jaw dropped. 'Rice!' he said, in an appalled voice. Possessing extra rice was a major offence, and here was a whole bundle of it in his hammock. In panic, he held the scarf up and shouted, 'But it's not mine! This rice doesn't belong to me! Who left rice in my hammock?'

You would have thought he was holding a bomb. I flapped my hand and mouthed frantically at him to attract his attention. Too late – the camp chief, the boss of the whole operation, was already on his way across to us. Seeing him, Chorn protested even more loudly: 'It's not my rice! It's not my rice!' He kept repeating the words over and over, as if they were some sort of incantation.

'Whose is it then?' the chief asked. 'And whose scarf is it? You're sure they're not yours?'

'No! I found them under me when I lay in my hammock.'

The chief turned to the rest of us. 'Whose rice is this?' he asked, his gaze wandering from one to another.

Everyone knew the scarf was mine. Sooner or later the truth would come out.

I stood up. 'Comrade, the rice is mine.'

Then Run, my immediate supervisor, the group leader, whose responsibility it was to deal with the situation, stepped forward. It would, in normal circumstances, have been the prelude to my death. Fortunately, however, Run and I were not complete strangers.

Two weeks before I had seen Run sitting in front of his house, looking utterly crushed. When I asked him what the matter was, he said, 'It's my wife, Thay. She's very sick. She's in such pain she sometimes screams for relief.'

'Have you no medicine for her?' I asked.

'I've tried our medicines, but they're not effective,' he said. He was obviously a very worried man, for he had tried everything available to a Khmer Rouge. At once, I saw there was a chance here to get some more extra rations, for I knew someone who could obtain some tetracyclin, an antibiotic. There were doctors among the New People who still did what they could for us. They brought their medicines into the black market, as others provided food, clothing, jewellery, or watches. One tablet of tetracyclin was worth a can of rice. I would ask two cans – one for me, one for my supplier. But I had to proceed cautiously.

'Comrade, have you tried foreign medicine?' It was a harmless way to suggest the idea. If he disapproved of foreign medicine, I wouldn't be trapped. But he leaped at it.

'Comrade, do you happen to have any? Do you know where to get any?'

'Not me,' I said innocently, placing my hand on my heart. 'I don't want to be mixed up in anything illegal. I have never seen any foreign medicines, but I've heard about them in the camp.'

He couldn't care less about my guilt or innocence. He just wanted his wife to be free of the pain. 'Try to do something for me, Thay! My wife cries all the time. I don't know what to do. I'm desperate.'

I said I would do my best.

The next day, having done precisely nothing, I told him that, despite the risks involved, I had contacted a man who had two tablets of tetracyclin. Not, of course, that I could guarantee a complete cure. . .

'How can I get them?'

'The man wants two cans' worth of rice for one tablet. I can arrange that for you.'

'Come back tomorrow. I'll find the rice. Don't let me down.'

So we became accomplices. I found him the tablets, and he gave me the rice. The two of us shared a secret. If one of us betrayed his promise, in the eyes of the authorities we would both be guilty.

Now here was Run, bombarding me with questions as he had to in the presence of the camp leader and a whole crowd of others. 'The rice is yours? Where did it come from? Why did you leave the rice in your comrade's hammock? Do you want to eat more than others? You're a counter-revolutionary, is that it?'

I was on a knife-edge. Run had the power of life and death over me, and nobody would have reproached him for having me killed. He had reason enough – theft and black-marketeering were capital offences. Moreover, I knew he had another reason to show himself as an intransigent leader – by having me killed, he could get rid of a witness to his own crime. 'Who sold you the rice?' he shouted. 'You must denounce the person who sold it to you!'

I certainly didn't want to do that. The only thing I could do was make up something plausible and then somehow turn the conversation to my advantage. 'A soldier,' I said. 'I exchanged a pair of trousers for it with a soldier who was passing on his bicycle.' No, I had no idea of his name. I had never seen him before. 'Anyway, comrade, the rice was not for me.'

Run was taken aback. 'I don't understand. Why did you bring the rice here then?'

'I was going to trade it to find *medicine for my wife*,' I said, looking him in the eye.

There was the briefest of pauses.

'She's getting worse,' I went on. 'Angkar's medicines have not cured her. I have to find some tablets. You know how it is.'

I could see that he did.

'But why did you bring the rice to the worksite?'

'I told you: I thought perhaps one of us had medicine.'

'Who then?'

'Oh! I didn't have anybody special in mind, comrade. I – '

At this point, the camp leader interrupted. 'This is a serious crime, comrades! Comrade Run, it is up to you to decide how to punish Comrade Thay.'

Run tied my elbows behind my back, and led me away. From their terrified expressions, it was obvious my friends thought I was going to my death.

Run pushed me towards his hammock, away from the others, and told me to squat down in front of him. He sat back and began to lecture me. I would have expected nothing less, and lowered my head, playing my role as the ritual phrases of condemnation poured over me. 'Thay, you are a counter-revolutionary . . . you participated in exchanges . . . you don't know how to get rid of individualist leanings . . . you taint our group . . . you've been in re-education for more than a year and a half, yet you have remained a counter-revolutionary. . .' and on and on for an hour or more.

It occurred to me as he talked that he seemed to be so taken up with the need to show himself as strong that he was in danger of forgetting the favour I'd done him. If he went on like that, he would leave himself no other course but to have me cudgelled to death in the forest or sent off to a re-education camp. I thought I'd better take action.

As he drew breath, I said in a low voice, 'Comrade, remember your sick wife. Remember my efforts to help you. If you hurt me, I will denounce you.' I looked up at him, so there could be no doubt about my seriousness. 'If I die, you die.'

His eyes widened, and the colour drained from his face, and I knew I had a chance.

In a second or two, he resumed the look of an austere and inflexible leader, his face impassive. For another quarter of an hour, he continued his harangue, his voice growing louder and louder. It became clear to me that he was putting on a show for everyone to hear, especially the camp leader. I began to relax, wondering how he could retract his accusations without loss of face.

'Thay, you are a counter-revolutionary, but fortunately for you, you are a good worker.' Then he began to praise me, still talking in a loud voice – 'I have noticed you are the first to wake in the mornings and that you are the best worker,' and on and on he went about how I gave everything I had to my work. It was such an astonishing performance that I could hardly believe our undeclared conspiracy would not be discovered. Never had the most assiduous Khmer Rouge, the most perfect revolutionary, been garlanded with such praise. An hour before I was criminal scum; now Comrade Run found it hard to do justice to my merits. And he concluded: 'As a result, this time – and only this time – I will ask the chief to give you a warning so that you can cleanse yourself. It will be a serious warning, Thay. The next time, you will become fertilizer on our rice fields.'

After that, it only remained for the camp leader to give me a brief, formal warning – 'Don't do it again! Next time, you'll be fertilizer' – and I was saved.

* * *

It was at Leach, during the first three months of 1977, as life assumed a certain regularity, that I came to a better understanding of the Khmer Rouge system and ideology. I knew that the system varied with place and time, and that my information was limited, but it seemed to me that in Leach they had established a system that corresponded quite closely with their true intentions.

The basic unit of organization was the cooperative, of which the village of Leach had three. Depending on its size, a cooperative could typically comprise three or four camps, a gathering of fifty to a hundred houses with a communal kitchen. Mobile units formed camp sites in outlying areas. Above the villages were district and provincial administrations, but we were kept in the dark about these abstractions. We knew only three things: the camp, the cooperative, and the village.

The village also had several other organizations for collecting and distributing food – the central health organization, with two hospitals, and the military camp. In Leach we seldom saw military personnel. The soldiers stayed on the outskirts – we never knew where – so that they could monitor us discreetly without making contact with us.

Each unit had a tripartite administration – the chairman, vice-chairman and secretary. The village chairman controlled all the activities in his sector, assisted by the *chlops* – the security police. Angkar's orders were passed verbally down the chain of provincial leaders and district leaders, who would summon the village leaders. In general nothing was written down. The application of the orders, therefore, depended on the interpretation placed upon them by each leader, depending on his level of education and on his ability to remember the orders.

The central government published only a monthly journal, but it appeared irregularly, and did not get beyond the camp leader. Anyway, the majority of the Khmer Rouge were peasants with little interest in reading. Phnom Penh radio constituted the main source of information for the people, but radios were rare (though sometimes the camp leader had one, and sometimes he listened to it on the work site so that everybody could benefit).

There were however mysteries, shadowy zones about which I could obtain no information. Who supervised defence policy, railways, my own Public Works Department, transport, state security? Maybe there was nothing much left to supervise. So much was a blank. For certain, there were no schools, no money, no communications, no books, no courts.

And no prisons, at least not in that area. This was one of the Khmer Rouge's proudest boasts. How unlike capitalist society, where punishment wasted labour and resources! And how different from Buddhism! In Buddhism, punishment was meted out later in a supposed afterlife, an indefinite postponement of retribution that encouraged people to commit other sins. The Revolution had abolished all that. The man guilty of a serious offence was punished immediately. No delay – that was true justice. The Revolution purified the individual faster than religion did.

In the cooperatives, the management of the work and of the labourers had a single objective: the production of rice. By 1977, in Leach anyway, they had forgotten about the initial mass mobilizations to make embankments, dams and canals. Everything now was centred on the production of rice. Each phase of work had its own teams, specializing in irrigation, ploughing, fertilizing, planting and harvesting. Other teams took care of land clearance and hut construction.

People were classified by age as well as activity. The young men and girls formed the mobile teams. Those who were married and had children were called the 'old team'. The truly old people could not do hard manual labour. Instead, the old women took care of the children and the old men made mats or wove bamboo baskets.

Although according to Angkar the children had to go to school from five to nine years of age, in Leach there was no real school. The children were supposed to be taught reading and writing, but in fact they only learned revolutionary songs for an hour and then went to the fields to help adults clear wood.

Surveillance was constant and mutual. The need for this was one of the favourite themes of the speakers in political meetings. We were warned to be vigilant and invited to denounce friends. 'We all have individualist leanings. These may surface at any time. You must watch each other in order that you may detect them, to help us to purify you and to support the Revolution.' We, the adults, knew how to ignore such sentiments. The children, though, did not understand what was involved. Many denounced their parents, simply in order to 'purify' them, believing that they were acting for the good of their parents and for the good of Angkar. Adults became wary of talking freely in the presence of children.

Each sector of village activity was divided into teams. In the hospital, for instance, teams distributed medicine, gave injections, cooked, and fished. The duties, however, were interchangeable. Medics might find themselves giving injections one day and cultivating vegetables the next.

At all levels the Khmer Rouge insisted on self-sufficiency. Each camp was to provide its own rice, vegetables, water and housing. The aim to acquire 'self-sufficiency and universal competence' reflected national policy. The radio kept proclaiming that Kampuchea had no need of external aid. It therefore refused all contact with the outside world, even humanitarian aid. Any aid, or indeed trade, was theoretically considered a betrayal of the principle and as the beginning of counter-revolution.

And all this in the name of equality. Within a short while, Kampuchea was to become a perfect communist country, which, we were told in many political meetings, had never been realized yet anywhere in the world. Subjected to this Utopian idea, the individual was allowed life only as the perfect revolutionary.

The perfect revolutionary was submissive to Angkar, should not experience any feeling, was forbidden to think about spouse and children, could not love. In addition, he rejected all reactionary beliefs, i.e. religion. Under the constitution of January 1976, religion was banned. (Actually, their law stipulated that one could believe in any religion except reactionary religions. Except that all religions were considered reactionary.)

In an often-heard Khmer Rouge parable, the individual was compared to an ox: 'You see the ox, comrades. Admire him! He eats where we command him to eat. If we let him graze on this field, he eats. If we take him to another field where there is not enough grass, he grazes all the same. He cannot move about, he is supervised. When we tell him to pull the plough, he pulls it. He never thinks of his wife or his children.' Often during the meetings, the Khmer Rouge spoke about 'Comrade Ox' as the ideal revolutionary. This comparison should make us laugh if it did not make us cry. Comrade Ox never refused to work. Comrade Ox was obedient. Comrade Ox did not complain. Comrade Ox did not object when his family was killed.

Often we were told to show 'initiative'. But it had to be for the collective. True initiative was reprimanded as a manifestation of egotism. To take the initiative to cultivate vegetables for oneself was to court denunciation, unless of course you planted the vegetables for the community and never touched them yourself.

Money, too, was banned for the same reason. It would have financed inequality. Angkar could enforce equal wages, but how could Angkar enforce spending the money equitably? Some would save more than others. Inequalities would multiply.

All of this had to be drummed into us constantly at political meetings. The Khmer Rouge compared us to knives that had to be sharpened regularly. Our political consciences had to be honed repeatedly by the grindstone of political education. Political conscience and ideological determination, that was all we needed. Traditional education was at best useless, no more than a means to display superiority. The Khmer Rouge attitude to those with qualifications was uncompromising: 'To leave them alive contributes nothing. By exterminating them, nothing is lost to the Revolution.' Educated people were simply threats to be eliminated.

The system never worked. Rice produced locally was not necessarily destined for local consumption. Rice would vanish into the central warehouse, from where it would be transported to other regions. The people saw the meagre products of their labour vanish, felt cheated, and had no heart for their work. Naturally, yields suffered. As soon as our warders turned their backs, we tried to rest; and at harvest time, theft was a way of life. Thus self-sufficiency became its opposite: self-insufficiency.

In the end, all the New People (and many Ancients) who were subject to this system became enemies of it. How could it be otherwise, when so many of us had seen our families die? The Khmer Rouge knew it, knew that by 'purifying' us they were creating potential adversaries. Whatever the original purpose of the Revolution, therefore, New People could never be allowed the freedom to become Ancients. In the minds of the Khmer Rouge, we would always be a race of slaves.

As opposition grew, the Khmer Rouge had no other choice but to increase terror. They thus betrayed their own ideology. Aiming to enforce complete honesty, they themselves lived a lie. Official propaganda claimed Democratic Kampuchea to be a paradise. In fact it was a hell. Aiming to establish a classless society, they ensured the permanent existence of two classes, both oppressed by a third, the Khmer Rouge themselves.

There was no possibility of reconciliation. Instead of being 'purified' by the Revolution, the New People became progressively more impure. If the Khmer Rouge turned back, if they relaxed, they thought the population would revolt.

They were right. Numerous plots were nipped in the bud. The number of escapes increased month by month. Everything proved that people could no longer bear the regime. Instead of producing purity and subservience, they produced impurity and enmity.

The ideals were empty, the policies useless, re-education a myth. Why? Because the Khmer Rouge lacked intelligence and moral standing. Competent Khmer Rouge officials were rare. The Ancients who were promoted to the rank of official were often ignorant, applying and explaining revolutionary principles at random, without logic. They claimed to oppose the venality of Lon Nol's people, like those officers who did not update the list of dead and deserters in order to steal their wages. Yet, as I saw in Veal Vong, they did precisely the same. Instead of being repressed, corruption and individualistic leanings were encouraged. Each leader was his own God. The Revolution was a paradox – one mass of people exploited by another, for ever, both trapped by the system. Ends justified means. Ideals legitimized any crime. Absolute power had corrupted absolutely. Repression was the only possible policy, economic collapse the logical consequence, revolt the only answer.

Week by week, little dramas revealed the hatred and rebelliousness nursed by the system. I remember the case of a woman caught having intercourse with a Khmer Rouge. Some time before, her son had been deported, and she had been separated from her husband, a former Republican lieutenant. The Khmer Rouge she was caught with was not just anybody. He was the vice-chairman of Camp No. 2. During her interrogation, she denounced two other lovers: the *chlop* and the secretary of the camp. Together, the three were known as real brutes, torturers, perpetrators of numerous crimes. All four – the young woman and the three Khmer Rouge – were led into the forest and executed. We New People looked upon the woman as a true heroine of the passive resistance. She had had her revenge, and had struck back for all of us.

From mid-February 1977, I talked about guerrillas and uprisings more and more frequently, especially after I acquired an unexpected ally. While on my way to work one morning, I spotted a striking figure – a fresh-faced young man in his late twenties, very thin, standing under a sugar-palm looking up at a friend who was up in the tree collecting juice.

Then I recognized him. I had good reason to, for he was a distant cousin of mine and also an employee of the Public Works Department.

'Yann? Is that you?' I shouted. 'Yann!'

After a delightful reunion – doubly delightful, for I was given a whole cylinder of sugar-palm juice to drink then and there – he told me his story. He was living with his wife, three-year-old child and old mother-in-law in a nearby camp. I would have bumped into him sometime, and was surprised it had not been sooner.

After that we began to meet regularly, not only for the sake of the sugar-palm juice that I could share with Any. It was not long before we were discussing the possibility of initiating, or taking part in, uprisings.

Rumour was rife. A Khmer Rouge driver, who frequently took provisions from Leach to Pursat, told us there had been a raid on Pursat, and that five Khmer Rouge had been killed. Ten New People had followed the insurgents back into the forest.

Not long afterwards, I saw cyclostyled leaflets scattered along the road. The leaflets reproduced a handwritten text, urging deportees to revolt: 'April 17th will be the fatal day for the Khmer Rouge barbarians. On April 17th, 1975 we revolted against Lon Nol and his corrupt gang. April 17th, 1977 will be the last day for Pol Pot and his gang of *thmils*. Be ready.' That was all. According to my friends, the leaflets had been found on other roads as well. Suddenly, hope blossomed.

I knew Any and I would have to leave sometime. Eventually famine and hard labour would do for us both. But for all this time, I believed escape would lead only to death. All escape attempts ended in failure, or so the Khmer Rouge said. Later, perhaps, during the next dry season, I would try. Now the news of the coming uprising gave me a better reason for inaction. No need to plan escape – by staying, I could participate in insurrection. I couldn't doubt that it would happen. Everywhere people knew about it. It was imminent. It had to be – several signs confirmed it.

One of my friends, a New Person who was in my camp, had a visit from an Ancient who wanted to barter clothes. Ordinarily, it was the other way around, but this Ancient wanted clothes, coloured clothes, and he didn't care about the price. It was a strange proposal. The Khmer Rouge wore black, and coloured clothing had little value. Only dark trousers and shirts could be exchanged. Intrigued by the request, my friend came to me to see if I still had coloured trousers and shirts to spare. I was surprised. Why would an Ancient seek clothes forbidden by Angkar?

During subsequent meetings with the Ancient, my friend asked him that question. At first, the man dodged the issue, but eventually started to talk. He was a *chlop*, he said, but hurried on to say that he was sorry for everything that had happened.

'Not all Khmer Rouge are the same. Take me – I do not believe in this society of misery and hard labour. You should not condemn all the Khmer Rouge.' It was astonishing that he should say such things. 'You know the rumours,' he went on. 'The regime will not last much longer. What you read in the leaflets is true. We must be ready. You know why we want coloured clothes. When the time comes, those with coloured clothes will be on your side. They will be like the New People. We all need them.'

As it happened, we no longer had many coloured clothes. We had exchanged them, or dyed them, or deliberately damaged them to show how truly poor we were. But the *chlop* was not to be put off. He suggested that my friend join in a clandestine network. My friend was too wary to commit himself, but the man insisted he would pass on information anyway. 'If something happens,' he promised, 'I will contact you somehow or other.'

Then, in March, a reconnaissance plane flew over Leach. It was the first time since the fall of Phnom Penh that I'd seen a plane. Everyone stopped work and asked what it meant. Probably it had come to film us for Khmer Rouge propaganda, but it was possible that the plane was trying to spot guerrillas in the forest. That's what we wanted to believe. And we planned accordingly.

Convinced that an uprising was imminent, we – that is, the few in each camp who were set on doing what we could – plotted for all we were worth. In the end it came to nothing. We could not flee to the forest without food. The rice stocks were carefully guarded by the Khmer Rouge. If we killed the guard, we would surely draw in the rest of the garrison camped near the village. All we could hope to do was join the guerrillas during the attack. We sat and waited for information.

A week before the anniversary of the Revolution, about April 10th, our team leader announced a change of routine. There would be a curfew every evening – half an hour to wash and then sleep – added confirmation that the uprising would take place on schedule.

The day of the anniversary itself dawned. The year before, the victory of the Revolution had been celebrated for three days. Now the holiday was shortened to one day.

And a miserable affair it was. We were marched into a clearing where banners proclaimed the merits of the Khmer Rouge Communist Party (that in itself was a novelty – previously, Angkar had not called itself communist). Guarded by the military, we endured speeches by the chairman, the vice-chairman and the secretary, and watched dancers miming Revolutionary allegories inspired by Cambodian folklore, but with movements copied from Chinese ballet.

During the next two days – April 18th and 19th – we waited, tense with anxiety.

Nothing.

Then a new rumour circulated. Word had it that the guerrilla troops had withdrawn. We didn't know why. (Later, I learned that a general uprising throughout the country had indeed been planned, but the plot had been bloodily suppressed.) The harvest was just over, and the opportunity for action was slipping by. Soon no paddy would be left in the fields as possible supplies for guerrillas.

I wondered if Any and I truly had the strength to remain alive for another year. I had hardly anything left to barter. Every day I ran the risk of being discovered, as in Don Ey. I was still in relatively good health, but felt it was only a matter of time before I cracked up.

I decided to act.

10 INTO THE FOREST

From now on, I spent as much time as possible planning our escape. Lacking practically everything, we needed all the help we could get. An organization was already in existence – the men and women who we had contacted when preparing for a possible uprising. But there were too many of them. An escape was not the same thing as an armed revolt.

I talked over the problem with Yann. Although he was in another camp, since he was a relative there was nothing suspicious about my talking to him. Yann suggested that we include in our team a Captain Lang. He was a good choice – a tough and experienced officer of about forty, he had been wounded in the right leg in the civil war, and walked with a limp, but there was no doubt of either his courage or his endurance. Lang was in Yann's camp, working on hut construction. We met together briefly, just the once, for long enough to establish our cell. Thereafter, I hardly exchanged more than a few words at a time with him. It was Yann who acted as our liaison officer.

The first problem was to decide on a team. Eventually we settled on twelve possibles. All proved agreeable. There were six other men, and three women altogether – Any; Eng, a woman in Any's work-detail; and Eng's sister.

Then we allocated ourselves tasks. Between them, our six new members took care of gathering information about the number and position of military camps and the best routes to avoid both them and Khmer Rouge patrols. Beyond that, we needed as much information as possible about the mountains to our west, which covered most of the seventy miles to the Thai frontier. Lang was the co-ordinator.

My task was to gather food. For that purpose, the team passed on to me all the goods they wished to exchange. I began the careful business of making exchanges, gathering large supplies of rice without raising any suspicions.

Time was short. Our preparation started at the end of April, but we only had a month. In June the rains would forbid travel in the forested mountains. Even if we had food enough, the going

177

would become almost impossible, and with cloudy skies we would have no sun to give us a sense of direction.

Once, I got into conversation with an old man who knew the area. So experienced was he that I took him into my confidence. Wouldn't it be dangerous with all the Khmer Rouge patrols, I asked. 'Long ago,' he said, 'I was a tiger hunter there. There were hundreds of tigers in the forest and just as many tiger hunters. We rarely saw one. So there's really little chance of the Khmer Rouge finding you.' He said if he was my age he wouldn't hesitate: he'd go. The forest might be hostile, but it offered protection at the same time.

Certainly, it would be a protection in our case. The best way to Thailand for escapees lay through the heavily populated, flat north-east of the country, around Battambang and Sisophon. With any luck, the Khmer Rouge would concentrate their search in that area, not in the Cardamom mountain chain.

But the first main difficulty was to cross the space between the village and the mountains, which was riddled with Khmer Rouge. We were not armed, other than with knives. We would simply have to rely on our wits and nerves to avoid contact.

On the basis of the information we received, Lang asked one of the men to check out a possible route. The man belonged to a team of ploughmen. His oxen often passed the village boundary. Two weeks after having made the decision to escape – in the first week of May – our ploughman intentionally let his animals stray. Then he hid them and fastened them securely. On returning, he immediately pretended to panic and asked for authorization to seek the 'lost' oxen. After being showered with Revolutionary invective by his group chief, he was given a pass that allowed him to move away from the group and scout the surrounding area. He was thus able to identify the position of several military camps, two or three miles away. To the south, the way was clearer.

As for the date of our departure, we made no decision yet. For security reasons, all we decided was that we must leave by the end of May.

The decision gave me and Any new strength. It was the only course possible. We had to work towards survival, not only for our own sakes, but for Nawath's. Any mentioned him less now, but from her occasional questions, and the way she asked – the sudden silences, the anguished glances – I knew our decision preyed on her mind as much as it did on mine. 'Tell me how it really was, Thay, my dearest,' Any would beg, and I would describe to her some new detail of the way the beds were set, of the woman's affectionate glances, of Nawath's improved health and touching air of quiet acceptance, of how we had walked together down to the river, of what I told him while I was washing him. Every time I spoke about my parting from Nawath, and every time I thought about it, the tears would spring to my eyes. The words were seared into my memory. 'A curse has come over us . . . The rest of your family are all in the other world. They have been rescued . . . You are the last one . . . You must survive to keep our blood alive . . . You must get well . . . You have your new auntie . . . Be respectful and good to her . . . If you don't see us any more, remember the name of your father – Yathay – and that of your mother – Any.' And then giving him our wedding ring. And then those final words: 'Just stay alive, my son.'

'Is that all, Thay, my dearest?'

'Yes. There was nothing else.'

Every time we talked about our decision to leave him, we would tell each other yet again that we could not have acted differently, that this was the only way. Now it was up to us not to fail him. We had to escape, and live, to find him again, and show him that we had not abandoned him, that we did what we did because we loved him.

While I did clearing work, my wife transplanted rice. Later, she was mobilized to participate in the harvest work. She had belonged, among the different jobs in Camp No. 1, to a team of harvesters. She had to work near the village for two or three days then move somewhere further with the team. She was not absent from the village on a systematic basis. I, on the contrary, was often called up for external missions. While waiting, I had one major worry – that I would be sent away from the village on some other mission. I had to remain where I was to complete the exchanges, as well as be ready for our departure. But our clearing team was now about to move further afield. There was a good chance Angkar would assign a new work site to us far from Leach before we were ready to move.

I had to act quickly, but what could I do?

Once again, as at Don Ey, I decided to drop out of the system. Perhaps I could exploit the fact that my mobile team camp, my base camp at Leach, and the hospital were all separate entities. If each thought I was somewhere else, I could remain hidden and no one would ever know. The only problem then would be where to eat.

For a while, in order not to attract the attention of the Khmer Rouge, I worked hard, like a good ox. But not for long. I had no intention of exhausting myself before the date of our departure. I had to be as fit as possible for the long walks in the jungle. Now, the rule in my clearing team was that you could be ill for two days, but the third day you had to go to hospital and endure all the risks of reduced rations and contagion that that entailed. This rule I decided to turn to my own advantage.

One day, I said I had a pain that seemed to be tearing through my chest. It was a common enough complaint, for the impact of the axe on the tree trunks sometimes produced an agonizing feeling of being split apart. The group leader allowed me to rest.

Three days later, I complained of the same thing again. To avoid raising suspicion, I persevered with the deception for two days. On the third day, knowing what was involved, I went on moaning. 'It still hurts, comrade,' I said to the group leader. 'May I ask for another day off? I know that the regulations allow only two days of rest on the work site, but I'm really suffering. Tomorrow I'll be better.'

'No! Impossible! You must go to the hospital.'

'Chief, only one day – '

But rules were rules. I was given a pass to go to the hospital. That was what I needed – proof of genuine illness. Only someone who was really sick, who didn't think they would survive anyway, would risk going to the hospital.

Naturally, I had no intention of entrusting myself to the tender mercies of the medics. Instead I went to see the base camp leader, and told him I couldn't sleep in the open, and had been authorized to spend nights at home, being looked after by Any. That was all right by him, since I would not be around during the day. I just got up in the mornings and walked off, as if to work. In fact, I could move around the village pretty much as I liked, contacting others in the group and making exchanges. The mobile camp leader thought I was in the hospital, the base camp leader thought I spent my days in the forest. If I happened to meet a comrade from the clearing team, I could always say I had come out of hospital to visit my family. It was accepted that those who could still walk could do that. The only people I could not afford to meet were the mobile camp leaders. I just had to avoid their regular routes to and from the village.

The problem of food was easily solved. After making an exchange, I took the rice to one of my accomplices, gave him some extra rice to store, and remained there all day. While waiting there, out of sight, I ate some of the rice. At night, I returned home, and ate again with Any.

I ranged widely in my efforts to find rice. One of the best sources was an Ancient in the next-door village. It was something of a risk to go from one village to another, but once again I resorted to forgery – luckily my precious ballpoint was still working – giving myself permission from my base camp leader to move about. As soon as I arrived in the neighbouring village, about two-and-a-half miles from Leach, I contacted the Ancient who had rice for sale and then made a series of deals with him (and not only for rice – on one of these trips I acquired a fine, double-edged knife about a foot long, a vital addition for our trip).

I would return from these forays carrying whole sackfuls of rice – the equivalent of thirty cans – in my shoulder-bag. To mislead the Khmer Rouge patrols, I used to collect a bundle of wood. The Khmer Rouge mobilized a lot of people to cut wood in the forest. The wood served as my passport, and also served to disguise the weight of the rice. I abandoned it near the village, in case I was seen by anyone I knew. After all, I was supposed to be working in the clearing team. In this way, I was able to put aside not only the equivalent of 300 cans of rice – 165 pounds – but also some sugar and some dried fish, all concealed in caches in the homes of my accomplices.

With this wealth of food, Any and I recovered our strength, living this month as if it were our last. We had not eaten so well since Phnom Penh.

After three weeks, we had all the food we needed. But we were not completely ready to go. Lang told me he was still not yet certain of our exact route, so we could not yet set a date for departure. No need now for me to go on consuming our rations. Besides, I was nervous of being discovered. The longer I played this game, the greater the danger. I had to find a way to reintegrate myself into the system for a couple of days or so.

I forged myself a new note stating that I had been sent from the clearing team to the hospital, copying the original but changing the date. Armed with this document, I presented myself at the hospital, feigning illness. The medic read my faked order and agreed to hospitalize me.

There I had a stroke of good luck. By the toilet, in a pile of waste-paper – mainly bandages and old clothes taken from the dead – I happened to spot a few crumpled papers, among which I recognized some bank notes. I picked them up curiously, and was amazed to find myself holding two notes, one of five hundred French francs and another of twenty Thai *baht*. They had been thrown away by the Khmer Rouge, for in Cambodia they were useless. But where I was going, they might come in very useful indeed. I stuffed them into my trouser pocket and made my way back to my bed.

After two days of lying in my bamboo bed, addressing the occasional remark to my sick neighbours, forcing myself to be patient, I staged a miraculous recovery, and asked to leave. No problem there – I simply asked my nurse for a note allowing me to return, but adding that I would like to take a few days' rest at home before returning to my clearing team. A little additional holiday was neither here nor there to her. I returned home with the certificate of discharge.

In the meantime, my clearing team had changed work sites, moving further away from Leach. I didn't know exactly where it had gone, but wherever they were, I didn't wish to join them. That would ruin our escape plans. I had to make the best of my respite to find a working team near by.

I was playing a dangerous game, in preparation for a yet more dangerous one, and found myself constantly worried about how it would all work out. On arriving home that day, in an attempt to boost my confidence, I went to see an old woman who liked to read cards. She lived alone in a hut some sixty yards from us.

'*Yey* [Grandmother],' I said as she waved me to sit down on a mat, 'I want to know how you see my future in the coming months.'

She fetched her cards, made me cut the pack, then spread them out, and began to turn up this one and that one, muttering as she did so. Then: 'Thay, you will be travelling all the time from next month onwards.'

'But that's impossible! How can I travel?' I had not told anyone of my plans, so she could not have heard anything. 'We can't even go from one village to another.'

'Don't ask me. All I know is my cards tell me you will travel from next month onwards.'

'How will this travel end, supposing I do travel?'

She asked me to cut again, and again spread the cards out. 'I don't see anything else. The cards just say the same thing – you will travel all the time.'

All the time! That boosted my confidence.

First, though, I had to ensure that I was working near by when the time came. Asking around, I learned that the fertilizer group were short of workers. The fertilizer group gathered soil from termite nests, mixed the soil with cattle dung, then scattered this pungent mixture on the rice fields. I suggested to my base camp leader that he assign me to the fertilizer group.

'Comrade, you know I'm convalescing,' I begged. 'My illness was due to wood cutting and the clearing team is working far away in the forest. If I go back to that, I'll have a relapse. But if I'm with the fertilizer team, I won't be far from home, and I'll be able to sleep there.'

The man apparently remembered the three *taels* of gold I had handed over when we first arived in Leach five months before. He agreed. 'But,' he added, 'I can't guarantee you anything more. If the leader of your clearing team insists on you returning, there won't be anything I can do for you.'

So I joined the fertilizer group, working less than a mile away. There were twenty of us, in two teams of ten workers each. I helped dig up the termites' nests, while the others mixed and spread the fertilizer. I found it relatively easy work. I had enough to eat, the chief was not too strict, and the work schedule was flexible. We all got along well, and I slept at home at night.

This relative well-being, on top of weeks of regular eating, made me increasingly soft. Though I was not aware of it at the time, my commitment to escape was being eroded. I began to think that it might be possible to ensure survival right there, and then, when happier times came, find Nawath without facing the dangers of fleeing over the border.

One evening, Yann came to see me. Everything was ready, he said. The route was decided. It only remained for Lang and myself to agree a date.

'Wait, hold on,' I said. 'Don't let's be in a hurry. It's only mid-May. We have another two weeks. At the end of May, we can leave.' Secretly, I found myself wondering if it might not be possible to wait until the end of the year.

It was not to be.

I had worked for more than a week in the fertilizer group when, on the path leading to the village, I bumped into one of the three leaders – the secretary – of my clearing team. He was responsible for food, and came to Leach from time to time to get supplies.

'Where are you going, Comrade Thay?' he called out. 'You should be at the hospital, shouldn't you?'

I was shocked to see him. 'No, comrade, I left the hospital and I returned to the base camp. My camp leader has assigned me to the fertilizer group.'

The secretary appeared offended and I knew instantly what he was going to say. 'That's impossible! What do you mean? He can't do that! You belong to the clearing team. You should not avoid the task given you by Angkar unless the team disappears or you are no longer needed. You're a good worker. You have to return to help us.'

I did my best to wriggle out of it, talking about the pain in my chest, and being unable to sleep in the open, and being assigned to the fertilizer group, all to no avail.

Off we went together, first to the fertilizer group's work site, where the team chief denied any responsibility, saying it was the chief of Camp No. 1 who had sent me to him, then on to the base camp leader, who, as he had warned me, made no attempt to stand up for me.

'No more to be said then! I'll take him back with me.'

Now I became frightened. The work site was eight miles from

the village, too far away to allow me to fetch supplementary food. Trips between the base camp and the work site would be unthinkable. Everything would be lost if I went there. I would lose my strength again, and that would be that.

'We leave tomorrow morning, Comrade Thay. Be prepared. You'll carry your shoulder-bag and blankets. Don't forget anything. Eight miles is a long way. You won't have time to come back.'

Back home, I tried to think more calmly. No question that we had to escape the very next day. Exactly how, I had no idea.

As soon as the communal meal was over, at dusk, I went out to warn Yann and a couple of others that escape was imminent.

He couldn't believe it. 'Why so soon? I'll hardly have time to warn the others.'

I explained, conjuring reasons out of the air. The rainy season was almost upon us. Informers could not have time to discover our project. And cowards would stay behind. After all, the cowardice of only one man had upset my first escape attempt in Veal Vong.

In my desperation, I tolerated no opposition. When one of the men prevaricated, saying he was frightened, claiming he had heard that three days before a family was shot escaping, I refused to accept what he was saying.

'Oh, that's the sort of rumour that the Khmer Rouge always spread!' I said, and then began to improvise wildly, determined to match any claim made by the Khmer Rouge. 'Do you know why I want to leave now? Somebody told me they had heard on the Voice of America last night that three families had succeeded in reaching Thailand' – a complete lie; I just made it all up on the spur of the moment – 'If they can do it, why can't we? We're well prepared, we've thought of everything. Come on! Three families! And one of the families was from our region. Why should we fail? We have no children. The three women are healthy – '

'All right! All right! I'll leave too!'

So word was passed down the line. We would meet after the meal the following evening.

Now I had to get rid of the troublesome secretary. He'd told me to meet him at six a.m. in front of his house, saying he wanted me to carry rice to the camp site. Instead of going there at the appointed hour, I waited at home, knowing that he would come to get me. I told Any, 'When you see him coming, start screaming and twisting as if you're in pain. Pretend you have a terrible stomach ache. Do anything to show how much you're suffering.' Then, glimpsing the secretary approaching, I went out from the other side of the house, skirting the camp and making my way to his place.

Any put on a good act. When the secretary appeared she was screaming in apparent pain. 'Oh, comrade, my stomach!' she moaned. 'Thay went to your place to ask your permission to stay for another day to get medicine for me. Ah, my stomach!'

'Impossible! He can't stay in the village! He must leave today with me! I must go and find him.'

'Well, he went to your place. You should have passed each other.'

'All right,' he said in exasperation, 'I'll find him there.'

I met him on the footpath, as I had planned. Before he had time to open his mouth, I launched into my story, about Any's pain, and getting his permission, and the need for medicine, and her helplessness. 'She can't even collect firewood to heat water, comrade. She only has me. Just one day, comrade! Tomorrow I'll go to the camp! It's a promise!' I was so convincing I almost convinced myself. There were tears in my eyes. Even if my emotions did not exactly match my words, they were real enough. I couldn't believe he would refuse. 'If my wife isn't better tomorrow, I'll entrust her to Angkar and leave her at the hospital. Only one day!'

To my horror, he shook his head. 'No, no, it's impossible. You can explain your situation to our chairman out at the camp. Your wife is your wife, but you have to have the permission of the chairman. Now, come on and help me carry the rice.'

Unhappily, I agreed to follow him. I could hardly do otherwise.

At that point, he noticed I had nothing with me – no change of clothing, no hammock, no blanket. 'You're not bringing your shoulder-bag?' he asked in surprise.

'No, since I'm going to ask the chairman for a pass.'

'What if he refuses? Too bad for you if you have nothing to sleep with.'

At his place, we loaded the bag of rice on his bicycle rack. I wheeled the bicycle while he walked behind me, and we headed for the camp site, with me racking my brains to find a solution. What if the chairman refused? We were to meet, all twelve of us, that night. If I got permission, we could get a night's march ahead of our pursuers before the alarm was given. Otherwise all was lost.

While we were walking, I noticed he was wearing a wrist-watch, a Citizen, one of several popular Japanese makes. On the black market there were two categories of watch, automatic and non-automatic, with several different grades of automatic, headed by Omegas. Every Khmer Rouge loved the idea of owning an automatic Omega. They were, of course, very scarce. We had gone three or four miles – about halfway – when an idea struck me.

'Comrade, excuse me, what time is it?'

'Ten o'clock.' He was still angry with me for changing his plans and didn't want to talk. 'Ten o'clock! You made us lose a lot of time! We have to hurry. I have to cook the rice before the others can eat.'

'Yes, comrade. Oh, your watch – it's Japanese, isn't it? – a Citizen?'

'Is that what it's called?' he replied.

'Yes, a Citizen.'

'Ah. A Citizen. A Citizen.'

'Right. It's not bad as watches go, but why didn't you get an Omega?'

The word Omega caught his attention. 'I tried,' he said, 'But they're difficult to find.'

'Yes, comrade, I know. A friend of mine has one. He told me it was very expensive. He said you need a lot of rice to get one.'

'Well, perhaps I have some rice.'

Progress, I thought. Of course, a Khmer Rouge could not obtain rice legally, but almost certainly he had bought his Citizen with rice in the first place.

'As it happens,' I said nonchalantly, 'He wants to exchange the watch. Only because his son is sick, you understand. He's very discreet. If you had rice, I'm sure he would agree to part with it. With the rice, he could find medicine.'

'So – how much would he want?'

I had him.

'I suppose, oh, sixty cans' worth.'

'Sixty cans! That's expensive.'

'You're the cook, and he's a reasonable man. You could give him twenty cans first and then the rest in instalments, ten cans at a time. Perhaps you'd like me to speak to him about it, because it must be done quickly or someone else will beat you to it.'

After a pause, he said, 'But I don't have enough rice.'

'Oh.'

We fell silent again. Then I said, as if a new idea had struck me, 'Do you have dried fish?'

He said he did. And I remembered seeing some coconut palms near his hut. 'Very well, comrade, how about thirty cans' worth of rice, two coconuts, and some dried fish?'

'Thirty cans and one coconut. That's it.'

'I'll put it to him. If only I could be certain of getting permission from the chief.'

Accomplices now, we stopped for a few moments to rest, and spoke of other things.

As soon as we arrived in the camp site, the secretary led me to the chairman, and explained how he had found me. The chairman knew I was a good worker, and was happy to see me again. 'Well, Thay, what do you mean by abandoning us like that?' he asked lightly.

'Comrade, it was the will of Angkar. They just assigned me to the fertilizer group. I don't know why.'

'Well, you're back, that's the main thing. We won't let you go again.'

'Pardon me, comrade, I didn't bring anything to sleep on. May I return home this evening?'

'Oh, you! Always wanting to dodge work!'

'No, it's not just for my sake. My wife is sick. I must try to get her some medicine. If she doesn't recover, I'll take her to the hospital. I promise you I'll come back early tomorrow morning.'

'Always a good story! Do some work first, then we'll see.'

'But, comrade, it's not a story. Ask the secretary. He'll tell you the condition she's in.'

'Come on, Thay, your wife's not really sick, is she?'

'Ask the secretary!'

The chairman turned to the secretary, who nodded. He had seen her. Besides, he wasn't about to risk losing his Omega.

'So, can I go?' I asked eagerly.

'Have your lunch first and we'll talk about it then.'

'So, I *can* go?'

'All right, go!' the chairman said, grumpily. 'Leave after lunch. But tomorrow be here very early. It's the last time you can do such a thing.'

'I'll wake up early. I'll be here by six a.m., I promise!'

I swallowed my meal and fled.

The few minutes to twilight which followed the communal evening meal was an ideal time to move about without arousing suspicion, because then night workers began to appear, mixing in with the day shifts. When Any returned from work, we quickly got ready. In my shoulder-bag – made, as bags usually were, from a single trouser-leg tied at each end – I had my provisions: cooked and raw rice, two lighters, cooking utensils, a condensed-milk can for cooking in, a plastic box for salt and sugar, a small metal box for pieces of dried fish, a water bottle and my knife. In my pockets, I had a piece of map, my ballpoint pen and my bundle of foreign money. In case of rain, Any and I also had a change of clothing each.

Slowly, surreptitiously, we gathered in three separate groups of four at the edge of the village. Darkness fell, revealing a clear, starlit night. Two other conspirators had joined Any and me, and we walked on slowly into the forest, to the next meeting point, a huge tree we all knew. Then, when Yann, Lang, Eng and the others had joined us, we set off along a trail southwards, in single file, each person following the shadowy figure in front, keeping in touch with each other by whistling, imitating the sound of birds.

Half a mile from Leach, deep in the forest, the trail gave out. On, then, away from Leach, through the virgin jungle. Two of our companions, a former adjutant and a former staff sergeant, knew the area, and led us on southwards. I felt exhilarated, keyed up. Liberty or death! My head was clear and I was confident in my companions.

We walked on right through the night, always heading south, stepping with infinite care, feeling our way through the darkness, guided by the rustles and whispers of the person in front. Everybody had to stay as silent as possible, for there was always a possibility of being surprised. It occurred to me that we were not many miles from Veal Vong now, and there could well be patrols out. Khmer Rouge soldiers didn't always stick to the road, making their way through the jungle on foot, and occasionally on elephant. They knew the region well, and were much more mobile than we were. Once, we came to a river, almost dry now. Out in the open, we picked our way carefully across the hard-packed river-bed, with the starlight showing us the meandering remnants of the water.

Ignoring our growing exhaustion, we continued on through the whole of the next day with only brief stops to regroup and regain our breath. Any in particular had difficulty keeping up. But Eng was with her, and occasionally I would drop back to hold her hand. She never complained, and always gave me a little smile of thanks when I muttered some encouragement to her.

At the end of that day, we guessed we had covered some fifteen miles. It was time to head westwards. There was still one serious obstacle to cross before we were completely free from the threat of patrols – a strategic road. We reached it towards the end of the afternoon, and decided to sleep there before pressing on. Finding a spot that was well camouflaged by high grass and foliage, we rolled up in our blankets, or hung hammocks on the low branches of trees. Any and I put our hammocks on the ground, lay down, and prepared for sleep, hugging each other tightly, on this our first night of freedom since leaving Phnom Penh.

'Nawath's all right, isn't he, Thay?' Any whispered in my ear.

'Of course. You'll see.' I felt elated by the way things had gone so far.

'And the others? What about the others? My parents? And Anyung?' Her words, uttered with such longing, opened up a flood of memories. Once, the only response would have been to weep. But now, for the first time in years, I felt optimistic. 'I'm sure they're fine,' I said. 'After it's all over, after we get out, we'll find out.'

Then, almost instantly, we collapsed into exhausted sleep. The place was mercifully free of insects – as was the whole forest at this time – except that in the morning we found the corner of Any's hammock, where the string attached, had been eaten away by leaf-cutter ants. Now we could use it only as a blanket.

When day broke, our scout went up on a little hill from where he could see the road and waved the all-clear. Agreeing to stop for a break a mile or so beyond the road, we dashed across one after another. I found myself lying last, with Any and her friend, Eng. I could see a few of the others flitting along just in sight two hundred or three hundred yards ahead.

As we were approaching a small clearing, one or two of those in front stopped. Apparently they were waiting for us.

But suddenly, the last one in the line turned and started making signs I could not decipher. Then I heard his voice, a forced whisper of alarm. He was too far away from us to understand what he was saying, but from his urgent signs it was clear there was something wrong. We froze.

Then, from ahead, came a sudden panic-stricken shout, repeated several times: 'Split up! Split up! Split up!' And I saw those in front scatter into the forest, away to the left. I assumed they were going to hide.

They vanished. All was silent.

We held back, watching, hardly daring to breathe. There was only one explanation – there had to be a Khmer Rouge patrol ahead.

I waved Any and Eng back and to one side, where we hid in the bushes, silent and frightened, behind a large rock, imagining the Khmer Rouge pacing towards us, hoping they'd gone, waiting for our friends to call out the all-clear.

As time passed, I found myself thinking of my father and his prayer. If there was a time I needed help, it was now. *Neak mo puthir yak. Meak a-uk, meak a-uk, meak a-uk.* I began to recite to myself, not even moving my lips, remembering his advice, 'It will help you' – *Neak mo puthir yak* – 'but don't be audacious!' – *Meak a-uk, meak a-uk, meak a-uk* – 'It will help you to stay alive if you help yourself.'

Neak mo puthir yak . . . neak mo puthir yak. . .

We waited in that humid spot for more than two hours, until the sun was right overhead. Every now and then, I peered round our rock, staring through the surrounding undergrowth. Nobody. Nothing. Not a sound except the buzz of an insect, the squawk of a bird, the wind in the canopy above. What had happened to everyone? It was a mystery.

Eventually, I told the two women to stay where they were while I tried to find out what had happened. Carefully, I began to prowl through the jungle, taking care not to make a sound, easing forward from tree to tree until I was where I had last seen our companions. There was no trace of them, not even a footprint. Where had they gone? Impossible to know. If there had been Khmer Rouge, there was no trace of them. I wandered this way and that for twenty minutes. In the end, I began to call, then yell.

Nobody answered. The jungle was deserted. We were alone.

I tried to reason out what might have happened. Obviously, having seen a patrol, our friends had abandoned the planned itinerary. They'd probably given up marching westwards altogether. Or perhaps they had tried to outstrip their pursuers, or go around them. In that case, they would be two hours ahead of us by now. Or perhaps the Khmer Rouge had arrested them. But without a shot? It seemed unlikely. There was just no way of knowing.

Wearily, I took out a lighter, and made a fire. We cooked some rice and ate, then continued our search, with no luck. There was nothing left for it but to continue westwards, towards the setting sun.

After a night spent sleeping on our blankets, we set off again. Not long afterwards, from far away, came the sound of gunshots. Instantly, I waved us under cover. So there were patrols in the area. Now I was convinced: Yann, Lang and the rest had been caught, or killed, and we were alone.

The forest became thicker, and the hills steeper. We walked on westwards, always westwards, guided by the sun.

For three days we walked, moving silently, in constant anxiety. If we heard an animal – probably nothing more than a squirrel or a deer – we flattened ourselves into bushes. At dusk, when it became impossible to make any further progress beneath the forest canopy, we stopped for the night, made a small fire, and cooked rice. Fortunately, there were few showers, and they were light.

Eng, a few years older than Any, only mentioned the disappearance of her sister once. 'Do you think she's lost?' she asked timidly. Her sister had been the only member of her family left alive.

'Well, when they ran, I think she was with Lang. She should be all right. Lang is very experienced.'

There was no further discussion.

Day after day, we walked on, less cautious now, up and down hills, always higher. Occasionally we crossed rivers, all shallow, for the rainy season had not yet started. Sometimes it was not easy to find fresh water, and on several occasions we drank from stagnant ponds. In the morning, our shadows showed us the route to be followed. At noon, we stopped and ate. I stuck my knife into the ground vertically, watching for the shadow to begin to lengthen. Then we headed westwards again.

Though the mornings were almost always clear, clouds sometimes built up in the afternoons, hiding the sun. If they did, I would find an isolated tree, feel which side of the trunk was warmer, and thus get a rough idea of where the west lay. Then I would look for reference points – hills, tall trees, or even clouds – and on we would go, using these as markers. It was not reliable, but it was better than nothing.

And so, for a week, we walked, without seeing a trace of human life.

Meanwhile, our stock of rice declined. We only had the equivalent of twelve cans – less than seven pounds – to last us until Thailand. That, plus some salt, and a bit of sugar. I calculated we could last two or three weeks, no more. But I had no idea how long the trip might take. I had the impression, during the first week, that we were walking quite quickly, and guessed that at that pace we could cover the seventy miles to Thailand in less than three weeks.

That soon proved over-optimistic. The terrain and the jungle became ever more difficult. Certain parts of the forest were impenetrable tangles of vines and brambles. We sometimes had to make long detours that wasted time and energy. Sometimes, when a mountain slope was too steep, we had to turn back. At best, we made six miles a day, and not always in the right direction.

And we consumed rice faster than I'd expected, about half a can a day. I became worried. What if we were separated suddenly by a patrol, or for some other reason? It seemed to me important that we each had the means of surviving alone. We shared the remaining rice between us.

There was no conversation, for we were afraid of making any unnecessary noise and struggled on wrapped in our own thoughts. Only when we were resting at noon and in the evening would we talk, our heads close together. As the one who was supposed to be in control, I found myself a little isolated. The two women, however, were good company for each other. In that first week, their spirits remained high. They liked to talk about what they would do after we crossed the frontier. Eng said she and her sister would probably join relatives in Paris. What about us?

'Oh, we're not sure, yet, are we, Thay? We could go to France as well. But Thay still has friends in Canada. Perhaps we'll go there.'

Their confidence astonished me. It may have derived from me, for I was careful to hide my fears.

'Thay,' Any asked one night, as we were on the point of sleep, 'Do you really think we'll make it?'

'I'm sure we will. Otherwise we would not be here.'

'Thay,' she said after a pause. 'We will see Nawath again, won't we?'

It was the closest she ever came to expressing doubt. Since the first camp, the night after we left, she had stopped mentioning the past – no comments about the horror of the last three years, no more questions about Nawath. I believed her confidence to be complete. Certainly she never expressed fear at our present situation. Now I saw that she had her doubts. It was just that, like me, she was determined not to show them. It was as if we had an unspoken understanding that our optimism should not be set at risk by discussion.

'Of course we will,' I said. 'I promise you with all my soul.'

* * *

Day ran into day. Life became a universe of greenery, leaves brushing us, our slacks and shirts torn, legs and arms scarred by thorns, ascent after ascent, the same snares, the same high grass and dense vegetation, always a problem of finding our bearings, always the risk of going round in circles, streams up to our waists, rocky hills which tore our palms. We had only one thing to be grateful for – the forest was clear of insects. We hardly ever saw an animal, let alone a dangerous animal, on the floor of the jungle. Sometimes we came up against thickets of bamboo, tangles of branches that we had to crawl through if we were to continue our course. Time was running out, and the rains were almost upon us.

After a few days, the only person to break the silence was me. It was obvious that the two women no longer had the strength to keep up a show of optimism, and I took it upon myself to keep their morale up.

One morning, when depression seemed about to overtake them, I found myself making a speech, haranguing them in revolutionary spirit, but driving us all on towards freedom and life rather than captivity and death. It seemed to work, and it became a habit, a ritual with which we began the days. 'Like the Khmer Rouge,' I told them, 'We are on the lookout, on a war footing. We walk for twelve hours, and when night falls, we eat our rice. We're no worse off than we were in Leach and we have the advantage of walking at liberty, of getting closer day by day to real liberty.' As we walked, if I discerned a sign of tiredness in either of the women, I drove them on, encouraging them, persuading them, cajoling them, ordering them to continue.

It was a relentless struggle against the clock. If we made progress, fine. If we did not, it was that much rice lost. The sands of time were slipping away, measured in grains of rice. Our success depended on our food, and our lives too. Consuming energy the way we did, there was no way to cut down. All we could do was bulk out our rice-and-water soup with the occasional mushroom. There was very little fruit, and we had no time to stray from our path to search for it.

There seemed to be scarcely anything alive in the jungle, certainly nothing we could catch. We heard almost nothing, except birds. Once or twice, there were crashing sounds, perhaps of wild pigs, and sometimes monkeys leaped and screamed overhead. Once, we saw the footprints of a tiger by a stream. But otherwise nothing.

We became like game ourselves, suspicious of being seen if we thought ourselves exposed. In the hollows of valleys, we were afraid of being spotted from above. On the sides of mountains, we made as little noise as possible so as not to be heard. At any unusual noise, we would exchange signs and stop stock-still, silent, wondering if it was our passage that had startled some small creature, or if it had fled from a nearby patrol. If the noise repeated itself, I would creep through the undergrowth to check it out. I seldom saw anything.

If the women fell behind, I sat down and waited. I never wandered away from them, always staying within eyesight so that they wouldn't panic. We took our long rest at noon, and in the evening stopped for the night, looking for a dry, smooth spot where we could stretch out in shelter.

One day, perhaps the ninth day of our trip, we reached the crest of a mountain. From the duration and difficulty of our ascent, we were probably above the 3,000-foot mark. We stopped on the edge of a sort of a dome, clear of trees in front, from where we could see all around. Beneath us lay a valley, swooping up beyond into another range of forested mountains. We knew how far we had come, and over what sort of terrain; now, horrifyingly, we could see the difficulties ahead. The mountain crests seemed to march on endlessly to the horizon. And how far beyond?

But on the other side of the valley, in front of us, I could distinguish some huts, almost at the bottom of a slope, on a natural terrace. They were so far away I could hardly make them out, but I could see smoke rising from them. There were modest rice fields to one side of them. Perhaps there were soldiers down there. There was no way of knowing. Even if they came out of the houses, we would not be able to identify them. We would just have to keep on guard, paying extra attention to the movements of wild animals disturbed by a Khmer Rouge patrol.

Night began to fall. We decided to sleep right there, regaining strength for the climb down the next day. It was a good camp site – a grassy plateau, backed by trees, with a large boulder that offered protection. We began to prepare our meagre dinner in the glow of the setting sun. I lit a small fire with some twigs and dry wood, near the boulder, leaving Eng to take care of the cooking. There was little danger – the smoke disappeared into the tall trees above us. Any and I prepared our beds.

Even as we worked, a stiff wind sprang up, scattering a few sparks from the fire. I told Eng to be careful, to cover it with damp leaves so that the villagers didn't notice any sudden blaze. After Eng had finished cooking, she broke the fire apart with a branch and we gulped down our rice soup.

We were about to lie down, when I suddenly saw flames licking at the dry grass around the fire.

'Ai! Fire!' I shouted, leaping up. I broke a branch from a nearby bush and began to beat the flames, but the wind fanned the blaze and within seconds it had spread across the grass, to the base of the nearest trees. It was already beyond control. I threw the branch away, and turned to the women, who had been watching in growing horror.

'Quick!' I shouted. 'Grab the things! Get away!' I wasn't actually afraid of being overwhelmed by the fire, for the wind was taking the flames away from us. But now that it was dark, the villagers would surely see. 'We must get away from here before the Khmer Rouge arrive! Hurry up!'

In panic, with smoke billowing around us, we gathered all our things into the bags, and rolled up our blankets. Then we ran, with me leading the way, across the slope and down a little into the almost benighted forest, away from the fire. Groping my way in the gloom, leaving the flickering flames behind, I heard Eng behind me and glanced round to see that Any was with us. Yes, she was there, a shadow twenty or thirty yards back. 'Hurry up!' I shouted, and blundered on.

We had gone some two hundred yards when Any cried out: 'The can! We forgot the can!'

She was referring to the condensed-milk can in which we cooked our rice. It was vital, not simply as a cooking utensil, for there was still some rice in the bottom of it. I turned, and thought I saw Any hurrying back towards the fire, a dim movement of shadow against the distant glow. I screamed at her: 'Don't go! Any! We can't stop! Come back! We don't have time to go back!'

If she heard me, she didn't reply. She was gone, swallowed by the gathering darkness.

Eng joined me. 'Best sit down here and wait,' I said. Perhaps it wasn't so bad. The fire was running away from us. Any would find the can, and be back with us in a few minutes.

We waited.

As time passed, I became more and more anxious. What had happened to her? I remembered I'd heard a small stifled cry as she turned back. She must have tripped on a stump, I thought. Maybe she was hurt.

We went on waiting. Nothing, still nothing. More minutes passed. I became increasingly worried.

Eventually I realized I would have to look for her. Telling Eng to wait for me, I moved off, guided by the occasional distant glow of the fire. Close to, and all around, it was pitch-dark. Slowly, feeling my way, pushing through bushes, shouldering past saplings, zig-zagging round trees, I reached the spot from where we had come and stared around in the darkness. The grass was burned out, and as black as the forest shadows. Beyond, the fire had not caught any of the trees, only the underbrush, and was already burning low.

Any was nowhere around.

'Any!' I called, wondering if the villagers could hear, then louder: 'Any! Any!'

No reply.

I wanted to call on the whole world to help find her. I shouted out as loudly as I could. The space around me was empty. I was in a womb of darkness. No reply, not even an echo. I could see nothing.

At once, in rising panic, I retraced my steps, trying to pace out Any's itinerary and to re-enact her movements to understand what had happened to her. I called again, and again. Nothing. As I forced my way through the undergrowth, with bushes tearing at my clothes, I found roots and brambles catching in my sandals. I kept tripping and stumbling. In a fury, I tore my sandals off and threw them away. Then, desperate, I began to go around in circles, searching right around our camp.

Or at least I thought I was going around the camp. Time passed, I shouted, I barged through leaves and branches, floundering in a nightmarish web of twigs and slapping leaves, with roots banging against my toes, and trees rising up to bruise my shoulders, arms and head. Still no sign of Any. I began to imagine the worst. Had she been caught by the Khmer Rouge? I didn't think so. They would have heard me, and found me immediately. No, I had to accept it: Any was lost in the darkness and the labyrinthine forest.

Perhaps she had believed she was coming towards me, when all the time she had no hope of finding me. By the time she realized she was lost, the fire would have been dying invisibly somewhere behind her and she would have gone farther away in another direction.

There was nothing more to be done, except wait until morning. I decided to return to Eng. She was – she must have been – less than two hundred yards away.

But in which direction?

I stopped, appalled. Now I realized by myself how the jungle could be deceiving.

I moved again in the direction I thought I'd come from, bumping into trees, knocking into low branches. I called out to Any and Eng. No one answered. I listened, holding my breath, willing my heart to cease its racket, and heard nothing, not even an animal.

I was lost.

At a stroke, in a few minutes, my world had vanished. I had never been so alone.

I must have walked for three hours, bawling out for Any and Eng, before I decided to sleep on the spot, in the jungle, and to wait for dawn before resuming my search. I had no fear of anything – of darkness, of the Khmer Rouge, of animals. My only concern was Any, my darling Any, with whom I'd survived so much, with whom I had prepared this escape.

I slept deeply, escaping from sorrow and exhaustion.

The next day, I was awake even before daybreak. Then, at first light, I set off, searching for Any and Eng, calling as I went, hearing nothing. I screamed like the devil himself. I shouted myself hoarse. Still no reply. On I went, my legs heavy, kept alert only by pain and distress. I don't know how many miles I covered in this way between dawn and noon, unable to resign myself to

Any's loss in such absurd circumstances. Round and round I wandered, back and forth, criss-crossing the whole area, shouting until I could shout no more.

Eventually, desperate with sorrow, deprived of reason, I sat down in a clearing and decided to end it there, in that forest, which had taken Any and Eng. I felt hopeless, ready to founder on despair.

After a while, I realized I was hungry. I still had two weeks' supply of rice, but I no longer had anything to cook with, except a tiny can, in which I'd kept pieces of dried fish. I emptied the can and its contents and filled it with rice. It contained hardly more than a mouthful or two. It wouldn't be easy, but I had to eat, to console myself, to think more clearly. I had two lighters with me, the two lighters for our small group. Pulling one of them out, I thought of the two lost women. They had no lighter, no matches, nothing to make fire with, to warm themselves, to cook food. I set fire to a few branches to cook my rice, and ate.

As I did so, an idea struck me. What if I made a bigger fire? Seeing the smoke they could, perhaps, orientate themselves and find me. I no longer feared alerting the village nearby. I no longer cared about danger.

I fed the fire and let it spread. The surrounding grass caught, sending the underbrush nearby up in flames, and then the trees. I stood there watching them, backing off as the fire grew. A voice inside me kept saying: 'Hide! If Any comes, you'll see her. Don't stay in the middle of the clearing. What if the Khmer Rouge find you? You'll be no use to anyone then.'

So I hid myself at the edge of the clearing. The forest went on burning.

Nobody came.

One hour, two hours passed until a good part of the forest was ravaged. I watched whole trees burning like matches. An immense cloud of smoke rose above me, visible for miles around, if anybody happened to be looking.

Any did not reappear.

I no longer felt like moving or walking. I didn't know what to do. At that moment, life no longer meant anything to me. It was as if I had become a blank, all memory erased by this last terrible blow.

All afternoon, I stayed in the clearing, waiting, watching the blaze.

When the sun began to sink, my voice called me back to reality. 'Why stay here?' I told myself. 'You will die. Time is short. Hours lost can never be regained. Nobody's coming. You can't do anything more. Leave now.'

The voice tormented me. Still I hesitated. I couldn't go – I couldn't abandon Any. Yet my voice told me I could not stay. Here, eventually, death was certain. However slight my chances, they would be better if I moved. Movement – that was all I thought of. Better to meet death moving than sitting. I no longer thought in terms of survival, let alone of finding Nawath. Those possibilities were too remote for consideration.

Anyway, what did I have to survive with? One pair of trousers and a shirt; a spare shirt, three cans' worth of rice, and a minute tin can in which I could cook a derisory mouthful of rice, all in my shoulder-bag; in my pockets my ballpoint, two lighters, my piece of map, and my bundle of foreign money; and at my waist my water-bottle and my knife, the fine double-edged dagger. Not enough to make thoughts of survival worthwhile.

After another hour, with the fire still crackling, burning its way slowly through the jungle two hundred yards away, I made the decision to leave.

I was empty. My body no longer existed. Submerged in sorrow, I felt stripped of the cares of the world, of all fatigue and illness, even of sensation itself. Barefoot, scratched and bruised, I no longer felt any pain.

Challenging death to take me, eager to welcome him if he came, eager to be free of all earthly ties, eager to rejoin my family, I turned towards the setting sun.

11 ALONE

I headed west, a dead soul, pushed on by my voice. I felt strangely light, freed of hope, freed of fear. I, who had once been so ambitious and so confident, had lost everything. I had been unable to save two of my children, I had abandoned a third, and now I had lost my wife. I had nothing left to lose. What was there to fear? No longer fearing destruction, I was indestructible.

I walked mechanically for three days, sleeping at night, but not eating. The thorn-bushes, the sharp-edged grass, and the stones on my bare feet did not touch me. I felt no pain. I was a sleep-walker.

On the afternoon of the third day, I came across a large mountain tortoise, about a foot long. I realized I was very hungry. Hunger spurred me back to reality. Death might still be waiting, but I would at least die fighting to reach my goal. I grabbed the tortoise and gripped it under my arm. It would be my supper.

To cook it, I lit a fire, no longer taking care to keep the blaze small, reversed the tortoise and placed it on the flames so it became its own pot. After a while, I smashed its shell with a stone, and dug out its flesh with my knife. Its meat was fine and delicate. I ate well, and still kept half the tortoise for the following days, cutting the remaining flesh into three large pieces, which I stored in my bag and a trouser pocket.

The next day I left at dawn, intending to stop at noon in order not to lose my sense of direction. But the smell of the grilled meat so whetted my appetite that I stopped early, near a stream, to refresh myself and to eat a little. I stretched out beside the stream, took my bag from my shoulder and pulled out a piece of tortoise to chew. After a brief rest, I drank some water and continued on my way.

All at once I felt better than usual. I seemed to be walking faster. I was surprised, and pleased that I was moving on towards Thailand so quickly. I had covered several hundred yards at this brisk pace when I had a strange feeling, a sort of inexplicable uneasiness. The ease with which I was walking was not normal. I thought for a few moments the tortoise meat must have given me exceptional strength. I climbed quite a steep slope, at a good pace, without even panting.

Then came a sudden appalled realization: I had left my bag beside the stream. I was not in the habit of taking it off for a short rest, and simply hadn't thought of it.

Well, it wasn't a catastrophe. I turned back to retrieve it. The stream was only about three hundred yards away. I retraced my steps.

At least, I thought I did. I thought I recognized the way. I even found a stream and walked along it. But it was the wrong stream. I couldn't find the place where I had stopped. At countless turns, at countless large trees, at endless little ups and downs, I thought I knew where I was. Time and again, my intuition proved itself wrong. It seemed nightmarish, incredible, that I was incapable of retracing a path of three hundred yards. But after three hours, I had to admit the bag was lost.

With it, I had lost my rice, my spare clothing, my can, and the bag itself which was useful as a pillow. Now I was stripped of almost everything. All I had in the world was a water-bottle, two lighters, the knife, my shirt, trousers and underpants, and in my pockets my ballpoint, the last of my money – three 100-dollar bills, a 500-franc note, and 20 Thai *baht* – the piece of the map left over from Sramar Leav, and a final piece of tortoise flesh.

My voice spoke to me: 'You must go on without your bag, or you're done for! You will move faster without your bag.'

So I set off once more, walking without thinking of anything, following the afternoon sun.

In the evening, I ate the final piece of tortoise meat. Then I slept, deeply.

Next morning, I resigned myself to living off the jungle. As I walked, I came across some mushrooms. Warily, I picked one. I remembered how people had died from eating mushrooms in Veal Vong. But I had no choice. Besides, there were lots of mushrooms. If I could eat them, I would have enough for a whole day. The one I held in my hand looked and smelled like an ordinary edible mushroom. I tasted it – foolhardy, perhaps, but I had no other way of ensuring that it was not poisonous. It seemed all right. I ate the whole mushroom, and put the others in my pockets.

That experience gave me my ground rules. Thereafter, I would always take a small bite of any wild fruits or vegetables I found, and I would only try those that were present in appreciable quantities, to make the risk worthwhile. I reckoned that if I felt no reaction within the first few minutes, they were not going to harm me in the short term. Whether anything I ate would have any long-term effects didn't bother me. I didn't care about the distant future.

The next day, I came across some repugnant-looking plants with huge leaves and soft spongy stems. I remembered seeing them several times in the forest. I tried one of the stems, raw. It tasted all right to me. I gathered a bundle of the stems, and in the evening, I grilled them on my fire, putting some of the stems into my pocket for the next day. As I was doing so, the lighter I was using ran out of fuel. I threw it away and pulled the second one from my trouser pocket.

I suppose I was lucky. Only once – a couple of days later – did I have a nasty experience. I bit into a harmless-looking green fruit – something like a pear – and instantly it was as if someone had set fire to my mouth. I spat, and scrabbled at my mouth, but the pain remained. I had never tasted anything like it – not the same sort of burning as pepper or chilli, but much worse, like acid. All that day, I walked with my mouth open, panting, trying to ease the pain.

By now, I was pathetically emaciated. My will alone kept me going. My thoughts were a blank, deliberately, so as to avoid all dark thoughts, anything which could have slowed my progress. I thought only of one thing – keep going, walk westwards. Nothing else mattered. I was a robot.

When I gathered fruit, I stopped for no more than a few seconds. I ate while walking. I never wanted to take the time to go hunting for food. The loss of time would wear me down, would threaten me more surely than the Khmer Rouge. Time gained was life snatched from death.

To encourage myself, I compared myself to the animals. If the animals could live in the jungle happily all their lives, why could not I, with my intelligence, survive one month? This notion made me even more determined not to give in. Like an animal, my life was governed by sunrise and sunset. But I was growing weaker.

ALONE

I began to wonder if I would make it. Every evening, I made a note of the distance I thought I had covered. One day, I wrote three miles, the next six, the next perhaps four. Each evening I added up the total distance travelled. Eighteen days after leaving Leach, nine after Any's disappearance, I guessed I had gone almost a hundred miles – more than the total distance from Leach to the border. And yet I was certain that I had not reached Thailand. The way I zig-zagged along, the way the ground rose and fell, I might have to walk double or triple the distance. I might not even be near the border. There was no way of knowing.

That afternoon the ninth after I lost my Any – descending the side of a hill, concentrating on weaving through undergrowth and round trees, I burst out into sunlight. I was on a track, a hard-packed earth road, marked by motor vehicles. I was amazed to find it in the heart of a jungle, for it was the first sign of human presence I had seen in almost three weeks. It headed south-west. To go south-west would greatly lengthen my journey. Too bad, I thought. I followed the road to see where it was heading, glorying in the luxury of walking in a straight line, on a hard surface, unencumbered by leaves and branches.

Further on, I gathered half-a-dozen jack-fruit seeds. The jack-fruit is a large yellow fruit, fibrous and sweet, with seeds that contain a sort of flour which is edible when cooked. It was a real windfall. The thought of finding more seemed an added reason for staying on the road.

Striding along that path, I realized I had emerged from my dark despair. Despite the physical exhaustion, despite my weakness, despite the loss of Any, I found that my morale was inexplicably high. I supposed it was because I had nothing more to lose. If I survived, I gained my life; if I died, I regained my family; either way, I won. I had passed the stage of physical fear. That was what kept me alive – the feeling of having overcome fear. I could give myself utterly to my battle against time. A new, unknown force, undreamed of a few weeks earlier, drove me on, putting life into me. Physically, I was a wreck, a scarecrow, barefoot, in tattered trousers and a torn shirt, but my condition did not affect me. In the evening, I stopped for the night some way off the track, and

205

grilled my jack-fruit seeds. As usual, I lit a fire to keep me warm
and dry in the dampness of the mountain air.

The next morning, I prepared to set off very early, aiming back
towards the road, without even considering that walking along it
might endanger me. About a hundred yards from my resting
place, as I neared the road, I heard noises.

Footsteps.

Someone was near, on the road. I knelt, peering through the
leaves, and saw a Khmer Rouge patrol advancing up the road.

There were six soldiers, some fifty yards away. The leader was
lighting a cigarette, head down. Calmly, carefully, silently, I
eased back into the forest, waiting in the grass and bushes. They
were so close I could hear them breathing as they went past.

I let a few minutes go by, thankful for my luck. If I had reached
the road a few seconds earlier, I would have stepped out right in
front of them. Clearly, I could no longer follow the track. It was
too risky. I would have to continue through the forest.

I looked for the morning sun, and headed away from it. The
jungle here was thick and varied, with frequent barriers of
bramble bush or bamboo, but at least it was flat, for I seemed to
be walking on a plain or broad valley between two mountain
ranges. Sometimes I had to crawl beneath the barriers, unwilling
to waste time by walking around. I didn't mind that, but climbing
became more and more difficult. On slopes, I began to stumble
more frequently, cutting my knees on stones.

As before, I ate wild plants. My pockets were soon stuffed with
mushrooms and leaves. And over the next few days – I am not
sure how many, for the days are undifferentiated in memory, a
scattering of incidents against a background of endless walking – I
found three more tortoises, which in all probability saved my life,
for each time I found one, I was on the brink of collapse. Once, I
stumbled on a pheasant. It flew right up at me. Glancing down, I
saw I had surprised it in the act of laying an egg, which I cracked
and gulped down. It was delicious.

On another occasion, I heard a buzzing, and found a swarm of
wasps in the hollow trunk of a dead tree. I couldn't eat the wasps
or their nests, but there might be larvae in there. I built a fire of
leaves in the tree trunk. As it caught, the wasps were driven out
by the smoke and the heat. The fire burned for about an hour or

so before it died down. As it died, I cut away the charred wood, scooped out the ashes, and there were the larvae. The top ones were burned to a crisp, but underneath were dozens of little curved larvae looking like cashew nuts, each in their compartments, perfectly roasted. I ate well, filling my pockets with the rest to eat later on.

After another few days, rain became increasingly frequent, and I found it more and more difficult to start a fire. At first, I could scratch away the damp wood from the surface of the twigs and branches to light the dry parts of the wood underneath, or roll up bamboo leaves to act as firelighters. But eventually, as the rainy season got under way in earnest, everything became too saturated to light. One evening, I even burnt half the remaining section of my map to start a fire, keeping the other half for recording my progress. Anyway, that was the end of my fuel. I threw the lighter away, and settled down to warm myself as best I could at this, my last fire.

Next day, as I started off, I looked up and saw what I thought were griffin-vultures wheeling in the sky above me. There were three of them, great dark brown things. When I rested at noon, they landed near by and looked at me, as if awaiting my death, staring with indifferent, lacklustre eyes. I couldn't ignore them because they had a strange disconcerting cry, like the bark of a dog. They yelped at me, as if baying me to my death, and that night, they watched over me. At the break of day, when I opened my eyes beneath my covering of damp leaves, there they were, on a branch nearby. Actually by then they didn't bother me. I was glad of their company.

The griffin-vultures were not my only companions. The forest here seemed to be richer in animal life, perhaps because we were in a valley, perhaps merely because we were further from inhabited areas. I began to see more monkeys, little beige things with white chests. My stumbling presence threw their noisy colonies into disorder, setting them leaping from tree to tree, throwing dead branches at me, as if to frighten me. I stared up, seeing mothers and babies, envying the happiness of their family life. But at the same time, I couldn't help thinking that if one of the little ones had tumbled from its mother's grasp, I would happily have eaten it raw.

Once I found myself practically face to face with a wild boar. I came through some bushes, and there he was, scratching at the earth, an old male, solitary, heavily built, with a nasty set of tusks. We were both equally shocked, and stared at each other. I saw him settle himself, as if he was about to charge. I didn't move an inch, not showing the fear I felt. After a few long seconds, he turned and fled. A patter of leaves, and he was gone. My unintentional piece of bluff taught me a lesson. When face-to-face with large animals, I knew how to act.

Then, as flat forest began to give way to foothills again, I saw a couple of wild dogs which scampered away in terror. Clearly, there was no chance of catching them.

As the foothills became higher, my luck turned a little. In a rockpool, I found some freshwater crabs and a small fish, which I scooped out with my cupped hands.

Then, just as I was pulling some small fishbones from between my teeth, I spotted another tortoise. I wanted to kill it quickly with my knife, and tried to cut through its shell. That was just a waste of effort. Then I thought of cutting its head off or slicing its throat, but the blade wouldn't reach far enough into the shell. Finally, I smashed it against a rock. After five or six tries, the shell cracked like a nut. Then I killed it, and cut the tortoise out. I ate its flesh raw, and kept the four feet for the following day. Looking back, it was a terrible thing to do to any living thing, but at the time, I didn't give it a second thought.

That same afternoon, or perhaps the next, I succeeded in killing a snake, a small green one no longer than my forearm. Although there must have been plenty of snakes in the jungle, this was the first one I had seen. I spotted it weaving through the low branches of a tree, looked around for a dead branch, and smacked the snake behind the head. Then I skinned it, and ate the flesh. In Cambodia, there are some snakes that are considered a delicacy when cooked, and I had myself eaten grilled snake back in Don Ey. But there was nothing delicate about this. If raw snake is an acquired taste, it is not one I would ever care to acquire.

The vultures, with their raucous voices, accompanied me for a week before they decided that I wasn't such easy prey after all. The monkeys, however, reigned all over this part of the jungle, up into the mountains. They made a terrific din when frightened, barking and leaping about, fighting and playing among themselves. Their carefree ways astonished me. While I'd been living in hell, the animals of the forest had all the while been in their own familiar and secure world. The thought reassured me, reminding me that I was safer here in the wild than in Democratic Kampuchea.

It must have been about this time that I started to feel I was very near Thailand. The frontier, as marked on my map, was not far from a river called Me Tuk, meaning 'Mother Water'. I had crossed several little rivers, thrusting my map and my money into my water-bottle to keep them dry. Since I was nearing the sea, each one I crossed was larger, more swollen by rain. Each time, I thought it must be the Me Tuk, only to be equally convinced by the next one.

Three or four days after re-entering the mountains – it's impossible to remember an exact sequence of events – I saw traces of a camp site near a river: ashes, unburned wood. I assumed at first it was a Khmer Rouge base for I could not think who else could have camped in this frontier region. Then I wondered if I had arrived in Thailand. Why not? Perhaps I had crossed the frontier without knowing it. I looked around to check, and saw soft drink bottles – Green Spot orangeade and Coca-Cola – scattered around. But the stickers on the bottles were in Cambodian. They must have been pre-revolutionary stock. I picked one up and tipped it to see if there were any drops left. I put it to my lips, and tipped back my head, anticipating the taste of a vanished age – ice-cool liquid fizzing down my eager throat. I must have stood there for several seconds, riveted by imagination and memory, before I felt a single, tasteless drop of condensation on my tongue. I dropped the bottle back among the others, and stared again into the surrounding jungle.

How much further was there to go? I had no idea. All I knew was that I would have to be on my guard. I didn't want to bump into a patrol, now that I was so close to the border.

That afternoon, it rained, as it did every afternoon, a violent downpour that set me shivering. Beneath the dripping canopy, there was no shelter. I walked on, trying to keep warm. The skies cleared again.

As dusk fell, I found myself climbing. Maybe if I got to the top of this hill, I thought, I could see where I was. The sky was clear now, and with the coming of night the moon shone brightly, giving me enough light to pick my way between the looming tree trunks.

I had almost reached the summit when I was assaulted by a weird series of noises – like laughter, weak and far away, but so astonishing, so diabolical, that the hair stood up on the back of my neck. The sound was like distorted human voices, coming from one side, up in the trees. As I stood and listened, I found myself less frightened than intrigued. I was used to bizarre, inexplicable noises, but I'd never heard anything like this. I turned towards the noises. There were more screams, more of this berserk laughter, as if I was being welcomed into some devilish rite. Then above me, the outlines of misshapen shadows leaped about, silhouetted against the moon-lit sky. I could see they were not monkeys, at least not monkeys that I had ever seen before.

I stopped. The screams ceased. I took another pace. More diabolical laughter. There was nothing coincidental about it – the noises were in response to my movements. They reminded me of the weird caterwaulings I had read about in ghost stories and legends. In normal circumstances, I would have been paralysed by fear. But I realized almost at once that I was not being directly threatened.

I decided to change direction, and walked away to the left. No cries pursued me. Suddenly, everything returned to normal. The moonlit forest was silent again.

Thirty or forty yards on, I found a good spot for sleeping, a well protected and sheltered place beneath a fallen tree. I fell asleep, puzzled by my experience. It was exactly as if the voices had warned me away from one direction and guided me towards another.

Up at dawn the next day, I continued on uphill and down, coming to another two abandoned military camp sites, clear indications, I thought, that I was at last approaching the border. The first, forsaken for a long time, had some maize plants growing to one side. I harvested five thin ears of corn.

Then on again, through the jungle, until I emerged at the bank

1 Phnom Penh in 1970, a lively and prosperous city. (*Associated Press*)

2 The city in 1979, still devastated by the savagery of the Khmer Rouge.
(*Syndication International*)

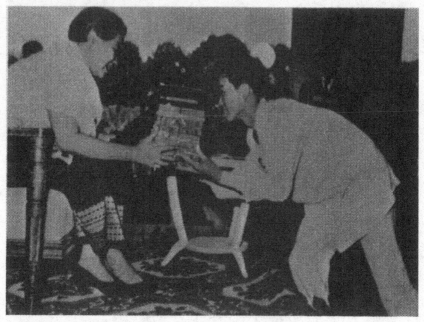

3 Pin Yathay, aged 17, receiving the national prize for mathematics in 1960 from Prince Sihanouk's mother, Queen Kossamak.

4 Huot Tat, the Buddhist Patriarch and Pin Yathay's great-uncle, during a pre-1975 book fair.

5   In a picture taken in 1973, from left to right: Pin Yathay's mother-in-law, his wife Any, his brother-in-law and his father-in-law. In the foreground are Sudath and Nawath, two of Pin Yathay's sons.

6   Nawath in 1973. Today his whereabouts are still unknown.

7 Women and children huddle together as the Khmer Rouge increase their bombardment of the capital, ten days before its surrender. (*Associated Press*)

8 April 1., 1975. Children run from buildings set alight by rocket fire near Phnom Penh airport on the day the city fell to the Khmer Rouge. (*Associated Press*)

9 A family leaves Phnom Penh during the mass evacuation ordered by the Khmer Rouge. (*Associated Press*)

10 As their fuel tanks emptied, cars had to be abandoned as the people were driven further and further on. (*Syndication International*)

11 A Khmer Rouge soldier orders shop-keepers out of their shops at gun-point during the evacuation of Phnom Penh. (*Associated Press*)

12 Khmer Rouge soldiers guard the border with Thailand three days after the take-over. (*Associated Press*)

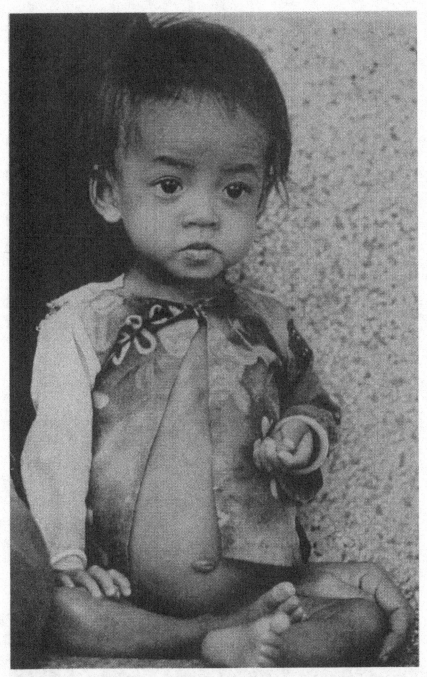

13 Thousands of Cambodian children suffered from severe malnutrition with often fatal consequences under Pol Pot's regime. (*Syndication International*)

14 Pin Yathay with Mr. and Mrs. Robert Stearns. On the day Thay arrived in Thailand, it was Robert Stearns who questioned him in English and established that he was not a member of the Khmer Rouge. They are seen here in Mai Rut, a refugee camp.

15 Evidence of the massacres carried out by the Khmer Rouge in the name of 're-education'. (*Syndication International*)

of another river, larger and deeper than any I had crossed before. The current was strong, and there seemed to be a real risk, if I ventured into it, of being caught by the eddies and being crushed against rocks. I was weak, but I had always been a strong swimmer, so I went upstream along the bank to find a clear space without rocks and without swirling water. I waded in, struck out, and found myself carried across to the other bank.

Clambering out on the rocky bank, I found the second camp site, recently deserted. The remains of food were scattered among the debris of ashes and unburned wood. I found some fishbones on which there were still some pieces of flesh, and some grains of fermented rice. I carefully washed the rice in the stream between my cupped hands, and sucked at the fishbones, before passing on.

With my eyes riveted on my morning shadow whenever the sun broke through the canopy, I cut through the bushes, heading up again. At the crest of the next rise, I came across a trail. At first, I didn't see any need to take precautions. I seemed to be in my own castaway's universe, impelled by one overriding ambition – to cross the border as soon as possible. Then I saw traces of footprints and dead leaves freshly turned. Now I became wary. I imagined I was looking at evidence of the passage of people fleeing towards Thailand, and their pursuers the Khmer Rouge. If the trail led to Thailand, then that was the way I should go as well. I turned along it, and began to follow it, ready to leap aside at the first sound.

As I walked, I felt something irritating my groin. I scratched myself through my trousers, felt a lump and pulled at whatever it was through the cloth, felt something fall down the inside of my trousers, and there at my feet lay a small black squishy tube. A leech. I looked at it in surprise. I had seen leeches before, but only in water. As a city person, I had no idea there were terrestrial leeches. Then I saw on my left foot another of them, already bloated with my blood. Revolted, I cut it away with my knife, and walked on.

I hadn't gone far when I discovered, to my disgust, that the forest was alive with leeches, perhaps because of the area, because of the rainy season, or because of their breeding cycle. In any event, they conspired to assault me at every opportunity. If I was not careful, I would be sucked dry by them. They climbed on to my feet, up under my trousers, inside my underwear, into my groin. After an hour or so, I realized I had to stop every few minutes to cut them away from my legs and between my toes, if I didn't want them to lodge any higher. It was impossible to avoid them. They were everywhere, in the grass, under leaves, on the bushes. And they became large very quickly, within a few minutes, as fat as a little finger, half a dozen at once, attaching themselves to feet and legs. All I could do was pull them off, cut them off and crush them regularly. By the end of that day, my disgust had gone, and the task had become mere routine.

The path led to a plateau of jungle which, as dusk was falling, opened out into a grassy clearing where there was a pond.

Suddenly, while I was moving from the grass into bush, I heard a cough. I looked up. A Khmer Rouge soldier was about twenty yards away from me, beyond a tree.

Instinctively, I crouched down, trying to huddle up, to make myself as small as possible in the bushes. The soldier, wearing a chequered scarf, a black shirt and shorts, had a Chinese machine-gun slung across his shoulders. He was coming towards me. I heard my heart beating, and willed it to be silent.

The guard passed about a yard away from me, just the other side of my bush. I could see him through the leaves. He was not young – about forty or forty-five – but he appeared strong, a dark-skinned peasant, in good health. He was so close I could have touched him if I had reached out. My heart was beating so loudly I was afraid he could hear it. But he went right on past, going towards the west, the same direction as I was headed.

I waited for him to disappear, then crawled away, back the way I'd come, without making any noise, and then cut away south-west in the deepening gloom.

Coming to a large tree trunk covered with thick leaves, I decided to sleep there. I was awoken in the night by two shots not far from me. The Khmer Rouge hunting, I thought, for the moon was shining brightly. Perhaps there was a patrol or a camp a few hundred yards from my refuge. Could be dangerous to stay there. At dawn, if a patrol came by, I could be picked up. I left my refuge right then and there in the middle of the night, moving infinitely slowly, stepping over branches and moving round saplings by the light of the moon.

I walked for the rest of the night, and the whole of the next day. I heard and saw no one. I knew now that I had not crossed the frontier, but it seemed that I had successfully crossed, more by luck than judgment, a zone swarming with Khmer Rouge.

Determined not to prejudice my chances, I immersed myself in the forest, reverting to my now well-established routine, removing leeches, constantly on the alert for strange noises, and looking around me all the time for anything edible. Even if leaves and mushrooms were not rich in nutrients, I could at least use them to stay on my feet. It seemed I was hardened by my two years under the Khmer Rouge, that my body had learned to tolerate the intolerable – hunger, diarrhoea, dysentery, fever, parasites. At least that was what I believed. Why else would my stomach have accepted such an assault?

That afternoon, I saw two black bears. One was sliding down the trunk of a tree, at the foot of which the other waited. They were thirty yards away from me when I saw them. We were about the same size and height, the bears and I. I must have surprised them while they were looking for bees' nests.

Honey.

The thought inspired me. Without a second thought, I walked towards the two animals. Instantly, they fled into the forest. I then wandered round, hoping to collect some honey. No luck. If there was a nest, the bears hadn't found it.

That night, I tried to find a suitable shelter to sleep. Clouds were moving in, and rain threatened. There seemed to be nowhere. Finally, in desperation, I lay down under a sagging tree.

It was not a good spot. When the rain came, an hour or so after dark, the ground flooded. I sat for a minute or two in soaked misery, in a regular stream of water, with rain trickling on to me from the tree above. There was no point staying there. I groped my way out in the darkness, not knowing where I was going or what I was looking for. Arms waving in front of me, I felt my way from tree to tree.

Then, astonishingly, I felt a tree trunk that had a crack in it, as if the trunk had been split by lightning. I felt all around. The trunk was still upright, and seemed firm, and the hole was almost large enough for me to step into. I pulled out my knife and began to work on the soft rotten wood. Within a few minutes, I had enlarged the cavity enough for me to slip inside. The split was almost exactly the same size as I was, just over five foot high, and a foot across. Inside, protected from the rain, I felt better. The narrow sides held me upright, and I slept. It didn't bother me to sleep standing. By now I could sleep in any position.

Suddenly, an indeterminate time later, I was awoken by a noise above me, inside the tree. It was an animal of some kind, trying to get out. I reached up. Little claws scratched my fingers. I grabbed, and seized something floppy and leathery. A bat. I held it tight in my hand, ripped it from its perch, wrung its neck, and slipped it into my pocket.

The bat was a good catch. Perhaps there were more. I was wide awake now, and waited for another opportunity. Then, through the pattering rain, I heard the whirr of wings, and waved my arm around, hoping to catch the bat in flight. I felt nothing. A foolish idea. Immediately, I went back to sleep, as if I'd been switched off.

When I awoke again, it was dawn. I climbed out of my hole, pulled out my bat, cut its wings off, skinned it, and ate it raw for my breakfast. It tasted good, as good as tortoise meat. I think that just then any meat would have tasted good to me, even snake. The bat would enable me to last for another day, maybe two.

The next day, I remember, was a good day. First, I found a crab, then a tortoise. Having eaten the crab, I could afford to save my tortoise, carrying it with me until nightfall, when I sheltered under a rock. There, prevented from sleeping by a violent rainstorm and a fit of shivering, I decided I needed more food. Feeling for a rock, I smashed the tortoise, cut it up – still working by feel – and ate some of it. Fortified, I put the four feet into my pockets to take me through the next day and then slept until morning.

At dawn, free from worry about food, I walked quickly. It seemed the only thing that drove me was grim and dogged determination. Existence was reduced to fundamentals – food, time, energy, escape. I knew I couldn't go on much longer like this, knew that any moment my body would cease to obey me. My body was reduced to nothing more than skin and bones.

Already, I could no longer climb a steep slope. I kept telling myself that the countdown had begun. That diabolical laughter in the moonlight – had that been in my mind, the result of fatigue? I remembered I had walked a great deal that day. Then, instead of stopping as usual at nightfall, I had gone on. Was that what happened when you died of exhaustion? Perhaps, as the end neared, other hallucinations were in store.

Armed with my four tortoise feet, I decided I had to reach Thailand that very day. I clung to that hope, the hope of survival and freedom, to drive me on. At each ridge, at each valley, I thought: this is it, the last one. I crossed a river, then climbed a high hill, hoping I would see the sea from the top.

There, before me, were still more summits, other mountains to climb, and behind me I could see the country I had travelled through, a succession of jungle-covered ridges. I couldn't believe I had overcome all that, could not accept I could accomplish more.

Not far from the peak, I staggered into another abandoned Khmer Rouge camp. There was still a bottle of fish sauce, half-full. I drank a little straight from the bottle. It tasted wonderful, a real tonic, an instant strengthener. I looked around, hoping to gather some indications as to where I really was. There were food cans scattered on the ground. I looked at the labels.

The labels were written in Thai characters.

Thai writing! I could hardly believe it. The last river I had crossed must have been the Me Tuk. I stood there, trying to take in the implications of my find.

Thailand! Freedom! A smile spread across my face as I realized I had made it.

I threw the can into the air with a shriek of delight, and as it crashed down through the foliage above, I pressed on, still smiling, knowing that any moment now I would find an inhabited village or come across a Thai soldier.

It began to rain again. I was freezing, dripping wet and chilled by a cold wind. I trembled like a leaf, wracked by cold. But elation carried me on. How could I explain myself to the Thais? It was most unlikely that any of the border guards would speak Cambodian, but there might perhaps be an officer who spoke English or French.

Cowering under a tree, I tried again to add up, on my damp piece of map, the distance which I had covered. I made it a hundred and forty-four miles – over twice the distance from Leach to the border.

That settled it. I was in Thailand.

I gathered myself for a final effort. 'Get on with it! Move!' I told myself. I was not afraid of dying, but I didn't want to collapse when I was already technically free. I was so close to my goal I could smell it. I began to anticipate the wonder of it. It is only in times of famine that you realize the joy of being fed; it is the pain of the disappearance of a loved one that reveals the true nature of love; it is only in captivity that you can gauge the bliss of liberty. There was only one thing to do – to walk, to keep on walking and to think of nothing else.

But still my mind turned. So: I was free. I would soon eat my fill. But why, after all, did I want liberty and food? What could it mean to me, what had driven me on, what was the purpose of life itself, now that my family, my children, my wife, were all torn from me? It came to me then that there were reasons, reasons beyond my own small concerns. I had to survive not only for Nawath, but also for those who had died – for my parents, for Any, for the other children. Only through my survival would their lives have continued meaning. Stay alive, my son, my father had said. Now I knew why. In me, he lived on. Through me, even the dead would live.

And there was another reason to survive. Now that freedom was within my grasp, I wanted to tell the world what had happened, to testify to the Cambodian holocaust, to describe what we had suffered, to tell how the Khmer Rouge had programmed the death of several million men, women and children, how a beautiful, rich country had been demolished, plunged into poverty and torture. I wanted to live to appeal to the world to help the survivors escape total extermination.

I felt increasingly confident that I would succeed, for a strange reason. I had that morning developed a tic, a twitch, in my left eyelid. Some superstitious Cambodians used to say that a tic in the eye meant good luck. For me, it had always worked, foreshadowing some professional success, or a chance meeting, and worked with an interesting variation – if a tic in the left eye was good luck, one in the right eye meant even better luck. My right eye was still its normal self, but a left-eye tic was good enough for me. 'And here I am in Thailand,' I thought. 'I'll be eating rice today. My eye never lies.'

I was still thinking along these lines when a new obstacle presented itself – a rather large, fast-flowing river. I went upstream along the bank to find a spot which was not too rocky. Rather than swim across fully clothed, I took off my clothes, pushing the map and the money into my water-bottle as usual, and jumped into the water wearing only my underpants, holding my clothes above my head.

On the further river bank, I headed west again. I would soon be arriving at the first Thai village. I found a path that led up to a large plateau. It was almost smooth from frequent use, probably by Thai wood cutters and foresters. I had nothing more to worry about.

I was wringing out my clothes, when suddenly there came a shout.

I glanced round.

Three young soldiers, aged no more than fifteen or sixteen, were aiming their guns at me from twenty yards away. They wore black.

Khmer Rouge.

12   FREEDOM

Strangely, I felt no fear. Instead, I smiled. I don't know why. I couldn't help it.

Apparently, the soldiers thought my reaction indicated I was being used as a bait for an ambush, for the three of them abruptly backed into the undergrowth, squatting into combat position, pointing their guns at me.

I reassured them, telling them that I was alone.

'Don't move! Stand still!' the oldest of the three kids ordered. He approached me warily, seized my clothes, and searched them, taking my knife and water-bottle. He noticed that the water-bottle made a noise, and asked me what was in it.

'American money.'

My reply intrigued him. He withdrew the rolled notes from the water-bottle – the three 100-dollar bills, the 500-franc note, and the 20 Thai *baht*, all wrapped in the piece of map. He threw away the incriminating map without a glance. That suited me fine. Now I was free to improvise my tale.

I was led off through the jungle for some three hundred yards, and emerged on the banks of an even larger river. There, down a slope, in an open area, separated from the river by a line of trees, was another camp. It had clearly been there for some time. Hammocks were set up, shielded by plastic sheets. Other plastic sheets had been made into half a dozen improvised tents, shelter for twenty-five to thirty men.

I walked into the camp, with one Khmer Rouge on either side of me and one behind. I stood there for a minute, feeling surprisingly calm, waiting for what might happen. A man of about thirty came out of a tent and signalled me to be taken to a tent with several beds in it. I was sat down on one bed, which was nothing more than a bench of bamboo poles. The officer, for that is what I took him to be, sat down on another bed opposite me. 'Well, did you come from Thailand?' he asked.

He probably thought I was a Cambodian resistance fighter based across the border.

'No, comrade, I want to go *to* Thailand. I'm from Cambodia.' I spoke simply, without displaying any emotion. I was a blank, with no sense of how to respond. It was as if I was waiting for some sign, some indication of how I should act.

'Not from Thailand?' he persisted.

'Comrade, look at me. Would I be this skinny if I came from Thailand? I'm only skin and bones. I want to go to Thailand because I was told that it's like our country was before. They have freedom and happiness there. It's not like our country now.'

Such words might well have been suicidal. I didn't care. I was going to be shot anyway. Strangely, though, he seemed more impressed by my honesty than by my hostile attitude. He was polite, but I recognized that sort of politeness, the politeness that creates a sense of false security and lowers vigilance.

'Where do you come from in Cambodia, comrade?'

'There were twelve of us when we started, three women and nine men,' I said evasively. Without knowing why, I didn't want to mention Leach. 'I come from Krakor, a village near the great lake of Tonle Sap.'

'Weren't you comfortable there? Didn't you have enough to eat? Aren't there a lot of fish in that area?'

'Yes, comrade, I ate well. But my family died, and so I decided to leave.' I told him briefly about losing the rest of the group in the jungle. 'So I was left alone to roam the forest. I was completely lost. I didn't know that area, nor the direction of Thailand.' Automatically, I found myself adopting the role of an idiot. You always had to pretend ignorance with the Khmer Rouge. They didn't like arrogant types. 'I continued to walk alone in the jungle,' I went on, in a tired and resigned tone. 'I walked for more than three weeks without rice. You can search me. All you'll find is a bit of tortoise in my trouser pocket. I ate raw tortoise.'

So, with my tortoise meat as evidence, I began to tell him of my trip. 'You see, comrade,' I finished, 'I really want to go to Thailand. But I don't know where it is. Is it anywhere near here? Where are we?'

While speaking, I thought of the river, next to the camp. It was larger than anything I'd seen so far, around two hundred yards across. This, surely, was the Me Tuk. But I wanted to check without arousing suspicion. 'Where are we now?' I repeated.

'What is this region?'

The leader avoided the question. 'We're nowhere. We were just told to take this position, and here we are.'

'But which river is that? The Pursat River?'

'No, no! The Pursat can't be as wide as that. Didn't you see how wide that river is? That's Me Tuk, the "Mother Water",' he said, patiently, as if explaining to a child, automatically using the local phrase for the river, unaware (I supposed) that the phrase had also been adopted by the map-makers.

So: across the river, and not far beyond it, was Thailand.

'Anyway,' I continued, 'I found this path, and met your comrades. Now I'm happy. Now I can eat. After that, you do whatever you wish. If you want to shoot me, shoot me! But give me some food first, I'm hungry and I'm frozen.'

I must have struck him as mentally retarded. They could never have seen a fugitive who was as candid as I was. I knew nothing of Khmer Rouge ways, nothing of any frontier. I was delighted to have come across the Khmer Rouge patrol. I would willingly accept anything as long as they gave me food. I happily showed my injuries – the leech bites, the scratches, the cuts. They were surprised at seeing me alive, and I seemed to respond to their attention, disarming them, concealing from them that I was not as weak as I looked, and certainly stronger than my complaints and lamentations made me seem.

After the interrogation, I was given some bananas. I began to gobble them up like a greedy child. They advised me to eat slowly, looking at me with wide eyes, as if they expected me to fall down dead. As I was eating, other soldiers came up. One of them asked who I was and where I was from. My story was repeated. 'Three weeks!' said one of the crowd in admiration.

When I had swallowed the third banana, I asked for some rice. On tasting food, I began to crave it obsessively. But I was out of luck. 'No, no! There's no more rice. We have eaten, it's three o'clock in the afternoon. Wait for the evening meal, and eat bananas until then.' I stuffed in the rest of the bananas, but still said I was hungry. They could hardly believe it, but volunteered to boil up some green bananas for me.

They lit a fire. A fire! The first I had seen in two weeks. Shivering, I stared at it, longing to stand by it, while the Khmer

Rouge who was in charge of me boiled up the bananas. 'Who told you we would shoot you?' he asked suddenly.

Apparently, my act had not been foolproof. If I knew the Khmer Rouge shot people, I knew more of their methods than I pretended.

'I know that I am a fugitive, a . . . a . . . counter-revolutionary,' I said, deadpan, as if parroting some word I had heard others say. 'I tried to escape, so your comrades will shoot me.'

I knew without thinking how to act and what to say to cover my tracks. It was as if I had summoned up the skills of my father, those that owed less to rationality, and more to instinctive wisdom. Perhaps it was because I actually believed that they were going to shoot me, and that I didn't give a damn. That way, I would join my family. I had only one desire at that moment: to eat my fill before dying.

'But, comrade, we don't shoot people in Democratic Kampuchea. We're short of labourers, short of people to help rebuild our country. So you had bad thoughts, so you wanted to leave Cambodia. But you don't even know where the frontier is! Why, it's still two or three hundred kilometres away. But I've no idea which direction. Shoot you? No, no. Whatever gave you that idea?'

I showed no surprise, staring at him with my mouth open, pretending to believe him.

'Yes, you're lucky you met us. We'll give you food and Angkar will not harm you. The imperialists are the ones who started the rumour about shooting fugitives.'

'Really?' His words were no surprise. The Khmer Rouge never thought that their killings had been witnessed. It was always supposed to be secret, so they thought it was safe to dismiss reports of killings as imperialist rumour. 'Well, I only say what I'm told. They told me Angkar shot fugitives, so that's what I believed.'

'I understand. We won't shoot you. You have my word,' he said, handing me a cooked banana. 'We need labourers. You must agree to work with us, that's the only thing. That's the condition for your rehabilitation.'

Despite myself, I found myself wanting to believe him. Astonishing – two years of terror should have dissipated any illusion about the value of Khmer Rouge promises. Still, they told me what I wanted to hear and they were feeding me. Reassured – at least for a while – I ate my banana and watched the fire. I was still very cold, and desperately in need of comfort. The man was still talking. 'You're a Cambodian. We need you. You are our comrade, our brother!' Deep down, I wanted to believe him. He really seemed to be considering me as an individual.

Perhaps for that reason, I stood up, and took a step towards the fire. Given his reassuring words, it should have been the most natural thing in the world. But as I moved, I heard behind me the click of a rifle being cocked. I turned, and saw a soldier pointing his rifle at me.

'Where are you going?' he asked abruptly.

'Comrade, I'm going to warm myself at the fire.'

'No. Don't move. Go back to your bed. Stay there.'

The leader said nothing. He seemed totally uninterested in the incident. The guard's words brought me back to reality sharply. I was no comrade, no brother, only a prisoner who could not even go and warm his frozen body near the fire.

After I'd eaten another banana, the leader looked up.

'What's this you were hiding in your water-bottle?' he asked quietly, waving the bills at me.

'Money. American money. Hundred-dollar bills. They're slightly damp, but you can always dry them out.'

'What's a hundred dollars?'

'Enough to get two automatic watches in Thailand. With those three hundred dollars, you would get six watches.'

'And this head, this face, who is it?'

'It's the President of America, or at least one of their Presidents.'

'President. What's that?'

'It's like the King. It's a person who's as important as the King.'

'Oh, imperialists! And this, what's this?'

'French money. Five hundred francs.'

'Who's this?'

'I don't know. Probably a king in France.'

'Oh, more imperialists. They still have classes. The high people, low people. And this?'

'Thai money. With that, you can buy things. Food, for

example. The five hundred French francs are worth as much as the hundred dollars.'

'Oh? You mean this big paper is worth as much as this little paper?'

'Yes. In any case, you do what you like with them. They're yours.'

The leader went away for a short time to speak to another Khmer Rouge guard. I overheard mention of 'another leader'. Apparently the guard was being dispatched to the commanding officer who was on a mission at the border, across the river, a few miles from the camp site. My interrogator was his deputy.

After the interrogation, I was brought to another bed covered by a plastic sheet. I settled down on my bamboo bed, under a jute bag which acted as a blanket. I looked around to try to find my bearings. I couldn't. The sky was overcast. The Me Tuk River, twenty yards down the hillside from our camp and separated from us by a scattering of trees and bushes, seemed to be rising, and was flowing very fast. I was curious to know how the Khmer Rouge would cross. Then I saw, through the trees, a nylon cord stretched across the river, and a little raft tied by ropes to the shore. To cross, the guards sat on the raft and pulled on the cord. It looked a dangerous business. If the water rose much higher, and the current increased much in strength, I didn't see how the cord would hold.

When evening came, they gave me more food, rice this time. I hadn't eaten rice for nearly three weeks. I pounced on it, and ate it voraciously, spooning it up as quickly as I could, thrusting it in to my mouth. Seeing my hunger, the Khmer Rouge even offered me some fish soup, which I downed with equal speed. Then, with typical courteousness, the cook came across, and asked if I was enjoying the food. I thanked him and asked for another bowl of rice.

'Oh, no! Look at the others. They only had one bowl each.'

'But I'm still hungry.'

And with the deputy's permission, I got one.

Content for the moment with this improvement, even if it was to be followed by my death, I lay back on my bed.

Night fell. I tried to guess what the camp leader was like. My life depended on his attitude and character. He would be quite highly placed in the military hierarchy, if the age of his deputy was anything to go by.

As I lay there, half-asleep, a young Khmer Rouge soldier came to me. 'Comrade, I have to tie you up for the night. Angkar orders it.'

'Why? I'm not going to run away,' I protested. 'Why would I flee? I eat well here, and I don't want to get lost in the jungle. There's no need to tie me up.'

'Rules are rules. I have to do as the rules say. If you want to relieve yourself, ask your two guards to accompany you.'

'But why must I be tied up?'

'It's for your own good,' he explained gently. 'If we don't tie you up, you might go to the toilet alone, without telling the guard, and you might step on a mine. There are lots of mines round here, and if you strayed too far from our camp, other guards who do not know you might mistake you for an enemy. So you understand, don't you?'

Better to seem compliant than make a fuss. 'OK. It's not important,' I replied, in equally reasonable terms. 'You can tie me up if you like.'

Even while I was speaking, the Khmer Rouge set to work, pulling my elbows behind me so that the nylon rope bit into my flesh, then forcing me to lie down on the bamboo bed, with my back arched over my elbows. He held me down, slipped the end of the rope under the bed and tied me to the poles beneath so tightly that the nerves in my arms screamed. In less than a minute, I was immobilized, trussed up like meat. Only my legs were free.

The two guards settled down, sitting together on the next bed under a separate plastic sheet, not guarding *me*, they told me carefully, but guarding the camp. Several times, I asked them to loosen the cords, explaining that I was in such pain I couldn't sleep. They were politeness itself. Unfortunately, one of them said, their job was to guard. It was another comrade's task to tie and untie ropes. One of them placed my water-bottle under my head to act as a pillow, but there was nothing else they could do. I implored them, with growing desperation, to ease my pain. 'No, no, comrade, it's against the rules. Sleep. Tomorrow morning Angkar will see about it.'

* * *

During the course of that long and agonizing night, I looked back on my whole life. All my friends and all those I loved came before my inward eye. I saw my father's drawn face muttering, 'Stay alive, my son!' I saw my mother's last moment of happiness, eating the mass of sugar I had found for her. I saw the faces of my lost children, Sudath and little Staud, my sisters – Keng, gentle in everything but the defence of her husband, Vuoch, who tried so hard to disguise her gentleness – and Theng, the sportsman, reduced in the end so quickly I never even knew he was ill. Staud had been the luckiest. He had been the first to die, the first to escape the suffering, dying in his sleep with his parents by his side. But poor Sudath, snatched away to his death, alone, away from his parents, under frightful conditions – and Nawath, left alone at the hospital, without his parents, living in misery. He was alive, I knew it. But the memory of abandoning him still wracked me. And Any, lost in the forest, succumbing to hunger, wild animals, the Khmer Rouge, who knew what terrible death. I thought of my own decisions – would Any now be alive, looking after Nawath, if I had refused to take her with me? I thought of my courageous parents, who had freed me from my responsibility towards them to concentrate on escape. They had given me their goods so that I could go on living. They had bequeathed me the gift of life.

Now all hope had come to nothing. I had the dubious consolation of dying while struggling for my liberty, of being able to eat before dying, of knowing I had done everything possible. But it was such a waste. I had almost reached the frontier. I would have liked to have crossed, to have lived to find Nawath, and to have spoken for all the dead, to have testified to what was happening in Cambodia, for the sake of my children, my wife, my parents, my brothers, my sisters, and all my dead compatriots.

As I lay, my elbows locked behind me, with the bag over my arched body and my head resting on my water-bottle, dreamlike memories alternated with watchfulness. I was aware of the guards changing every two hours. They had the leader's watch with them, and passed it to their successors at each change. There was no light, except for the occasional glow of a cigarette lighter.

The next morning, my two guards untied me. I sat up, hardly

able to move. My two arms below the elbows were dead, white, drained of blood, and icy. As I waited for the blood to restore colour and warmth to my forearms, soldiers stopped and stared at me. I was a great attraction. It seemed to me they had never captured anyone before.

I followed the morning bustle of the camp with only passing interest. Several of the soldiers were sharpening bamboo stakes, which would be jammed inverted into the forest trails to wound the feet of refugees. Some of them were preparing food. Others left on patrol with their rifles and their back packs. A dozen men crossed the river towards Thailand. Eventually, the deputy came across.

'Well, are you all right? Did you sleep well?'

'How do you expect me to sleep tied up like that? The knots were too tight. Look, my hands are numb. They're absolutely icy.'

He looked, and nodded, acknowledging my complaint, but without saying anything, and then left me again.

Strangely, my right eye now began to twitch. When I became aware of it, it seemed particularly insistent. The eyelid flickered incessantly. Why? Clearly it could not presage anything very wonderful. Perhaps, since all normal values were now reversed, my good omens had been transformed into bad ones. My twitching left eye had meant I was about to be captured, and the twitch in my right eye meant I was about to be executed. A pity; but there it was.

All morning, I remained seated, impassive, looking at the river and the jungle around me. There was plenty of time to allow my mind to dwell on my fate. Almost without conscious thought, I found myself repeating my father's Sanskrit prayer. *Neak mo puthir yak. Meak a-uk, meak a-uk, meak a-uk.* I repeated it seven times in my mind, as my father had instructed me.

But what if my eye was trying to tell me something after all? A thought came to me: Since my number was up, why not try to escape? Even if they killed me, it was worth trying.

Suddenly, after a couple of hours, I was seized with a terrible pain in the stomach, the result of eating all the rice and bananas. I told the guards that I needed to relieve myself. I urged them to hurry, for all our sakes. They quickly gave me a spade, and led me out of the camp, up the slope, away from the river. A few yards into the jungle, they signalled me to stop.

'Dig a hole and do your business there!'

I wondered if it was the right time to escape. If I did, they might kill me on the spot, but then I was going to end up dead anyway. Why not chance it? I dug, grimacing, trying to keep my protesting bowels under control, and at the same time scanning the forest uphill and down. Perhaps if the rifles were not yet loaded, I would have a few seconds' grace. But at that moment, I heard the snap and clatter of their breeches as they loaded up. Besides, they were right by me, and remained so while I squatted over the hole. I wouldn't have got ten yards.

While I was there, a group of five soldiers passed by near us. 'How are you, Comrade Chuon?' one of my guards called out cheerily to a soldier.

'I'm all right. How about you? Smells good, does it? D'you like watching an enemy crap?' They all laughed.

Enemy! The word shocked me. In political meetings, an 'enemy' was always someone to be killed. The next few words confirmed my fears.

'You can laugh, friend,' the guard replied, jokingly. 'It'll be your turn to watch him next.'

'My turn? No chance! The chief returns this evening. By tomorrow it'll be over.'

I was horrified. I knew now, with dreadful finality, that I would be dead in twenty-four hours. I stood up, dug in the hole, and returned to my bed between my two guards.

Later, after a midday bowl of rice, my interrogator came to me again. I repeated the same story – I didn't know where Thailand was; a hundred and twenty-five miles away? I must have walked in the wrong direction. I was happy there, happy to be eating at last.

For the rest of the day, I stared round at the jungle. With death approaching, my thoughts were still obsessed by food. Sometimes I dreamed of what I could have done if I'd succeeded in getting into Thailand. But most of the time I was in limbo, thinking that all I wanted was to eat to my heart's content.

That evening, shortly before dusk, the camp leader appeared down the trail out of the forest. He was a solid man of about thirty-five, very fit, walking with his chest out in an authoritative manner, followed by several other soldiers. As he came closer, I saw two ballpoint pens in his top pocket, a sign of his status. He nodded towards me and settled down near the fire, while his deputy explained about me. Occasionally the leader looked across at me with interest and approval. Once again, I had the impression I was the first prisoner here. I heard him say, 'Watch him carefully. Woe betide you if he escapes.' Then it was time for supper – a bowl of rice with a rich fish soup. A feast. Perhaps my last.

At dusk, a different guard came to tie me to my bed. The deputy had apparently told him not to pull the rope so tightly. To improve my lot further, I began to complain, keeping pressure on my cord.

'Don't pull so hard, comrade,' I groaned, 'You are hurting me.'

He didn't wish to appear brutal. 'Is this all right?' he asked. 'Tell me if it's all right.'

When he was done, I was well tied, elbows behind my back, fixed to the slatting as before, but at least I could move my arms a little. I fell asleep at once, as if by magic. All anguish disappeared. I slept like a child, sleeping the sleep of the just.

Until, deep in the night, I was woken by thunder. A storm was brewing. Lightning flickered over the forest. I heard one of the guards say it was eleven p.m. Except when lightning lit up the camp, spotlighting my two guards, the plastic tents and the surrounding jungle, it was impossible to make out anything. Regularly, one of the guards came to check on me, peering at me by the flame of his lighter. I noticed, however, that they didn't bother to look at me at other times. I coughed, and moved around, trying to get comfortable, and they took no notice. Why should they? They knew I was lying there, and knew there was nothing I could do.

Suddenly, again, I was gripped by stomach cramp, the same fearful pain I'd felt that morning. Without warning, instantaneously, I felt as if my stomach was being torn out. I brought my knees up to my chest in agony, and gritted my teeth. For some reason, I didn't want to disturb the guards, hoping to restrain myself until morning. I writhed in agony, telling myself that the pain would go away.

It didn't. I had to call the guards before I let go in my pants.

'Comrades! I have a stomach ache. Quick, quick!'

'What? Another? You went to the bushes this morning.'

'Yes, comrade. But it's agony. I can't hold out. Hurry up, otherwise I'll do it in my pants.'

'All right. Hold on!'

As the thunder rolled closer, and the lightning gave occasional blinding glimpses of the camp, and the wind of the coming storm rustled the leaves of the jungle, one of the guards untied the end of the rope holding me to the bed, without untying my elbows. The other guard meanwhile began to dig a hole about three yards from my plastic shelter. His comrade, holding my rope, leading me as if I were a dog, took me to the hole. But it was difficult to do anything tied like that.

'Comrade, could you untie my arms a little?' I shouted, through a rumble of thunder. 'I can't undo my trousers.'

The soldier loosened the rope slightly so that I could reach the buttons of my trousers, then he let me relieve myself.

While I was rebuttoning my trousers, the storm struck, without warning, a few heavy drops, then a cascade. All three of us leaped for shelter. We weren't quick enough though. In that second or two, we were soaked.

Back under cover, one of the guards quickly tied my elbows together again behind my back, pulling very hard. I resisted, to have as much leeway for movement as possible. Nobody in the dark could see my efforts. Then he tied me back on my bed and put the sack over me, moving by feel and the ever more frequent flashes of lightning, before returning to his place. My world contracted into one of blinding flashes and deafening noise – almost constant thunder and water battering the foliage and the plastic sheets above me.

I tried moving my arms. I found, to my interest, that I could reach across my chest, just enough for my fingers to touch the knots at my elbows. Patiently, persistently, I began to scratch at the rope, with no particular plan in mind. The rope, dampened by the rain, seemed to have some give in it. I was like an animal exploring the limits of my cage.

Suddenly, the knot on my left arm felt loose. My heart began beating violently. For the first time since my arrival I felt a sudden electric tingle of excitement. Perhaps, after all, escape was possible.

Slowly, more methodically now, my fingers continued to explore the rope. I found the rope-end, traced it back through a knot, pulled here, pulled there, and then, still not able to believe what was happening, I realized my left arm was untied. It was the work of a few seconds to unravel the rest of the rope from around my right elbow until I found myself completely free.

I lay beneath my sack, smiling in pure joy, overwhelmed by the beauty of the moment, by that exquisite first hint of freedom. Almost instantly, my head cleared. It was as if I had suddenly been made the guardian of a treasure that must at all cost be preserved. In case the guards came, I quickly wound the rope back around my arms, and lay back under the sack, arched over my elbows, thinking. I coughed, and shifted a little, to preserve the routine of noise and movement.

Not that the guards could have heard. The rain continued to pound down on the plastic sheets. Every now and then – it seemed an infinity of time to me, though it couldn't have been longer than half a minute – lightning flickered over the camp, revealing my two guards sitting cross-legged on their bed, reduced to silence by the teeming rain and the thunder. No light shone anywhere. The rest of the camp was plunged in sleep.

I took my time. At each lightning stroke, turning my head from side to side, staring to catch the vague shapes through the cataract of water, I reminded myself of the position of the tents, the slope up to the jungle, the tree-covered slope down to the river, the rocks that marked the lower edge of the camp, the exact position of the guards, and the beds.

While waiting in agonized impatience for each flash, I thought about what I should take with me – perhaps a bit of rice and a piece of plastic for shelter? No, too much. I would take only my water-bottle, which was acting as my pillow. Perhaps I could gain time by arranging the jute bag into a human form.

There was nothing more to do, no reason to delay.

At the next blinding flash, as inky darkness enveloped us again, I hastily unravelled my rope, seized my water-bottle, and lay back down under my blanket, ready for the next flash. Then, in darkness again, I swung off the bed, bundled the bag up, and squatted down below the level of the bed. Another flash. The guards still sat there facing each other. I coughed to show I was still there. Another flash. Then I was off, down towards the river.

No: a different idea, a better one. I turned and went back up the path I had used the previous day. When the next flash came, I was in among the trees. There, on the path, I trod heavily in the middle of the path, leaving footprints in the soaking mud. I went down on my hands and knees, thrusting my hands as well as my feet into the mud, until I was sure traces of my presence would be clearly visible in the morning.

Then, with another flash to give me indistinct guidance, I squelched and slid back down the hill, at the side of the trail, on dead leaves and waterlogged grass, hoping the rain would eradicate any trace of my passage.

The image of the camp was clear in my mind. By the next flash, I was in amongst the riverside trees. No more thoughts of the guards now, no thought other than the need to get down the slope as fast as possible. The slope increased. I didn't hesitate, and slipped and rolled right down through the trees to the river-bank.

Now I needed to find the cable which was slung between the two banks. I waited for a lightning stroke to catch a glimpse of it. A flash came – and I saw nothing but black overlooming trees, the enclosing gauze of rain and the racing black river. It was impossible to see the cable, even in the lightning. I staggered up the bank, then back down again, waving my arms. Nothing. I began to panic. If they found me gone, and started to search, I was lost. I couldn't wait. I would have to escape along the river bank.

No sooner had I set off, than my shin banged into something, and I tumbled forward, right into the raft drawn up on to the bank. I recovered myself, raised my arms, and felt around. There was the cable, right above me. Panic drained away. I was saved.

Should I use the raft? No – I had to put the Khmer Rouge on the wrong track. Seeing the raft gone, they would be after me. Anyway, I didn't want to waste time untying the raft. I would cross the river by hanging on to the rope.

I grabbed the rope, took the strain, and stepped into the pitchy water. After a yard or two, my feet were swept away from under me. I began to work my way, hand over hand, into the middle of the river, the water swirling around my chest, and my fingers aching. The current became ever stronger. The rope trembled in my grasp. Water broke over me and my body trailed downstream like a flag in a high wind.

As I reached the centre, where the cable was at its slackest, the water began to break over my head like a bow wave. I could breathe only by jerking my head above water, and I knew that my fingers would slip at any moment. With a supreme effort, I hauled the cable under my armpits, and only then did I know that I was safe from being swept away.

I have no idea how long it took me to complete the crossing, but it seemed interminable. At last, exhausted, breathless, I felt solid ground beneath my feet. The current slackened, and I crawled out on to the further bank, too weak to stand. I lay there, almost a free man, happy to die right there, on the brink of freedom.

I glanced back at the opposite bank. Every now and then the jungle appeared in the garish white glare of a lightning flash. The camp was invisible in among the trees. There were no lights.

As I lay there panting in the rain, I thought: I really was lucky to have been captured. How else could I, starving and weak as I was when they found me, have crossed the river, if not with the rope? How could I have managed that crossing without all the food and the enforced rest I had received over the last two days? I was a lucky, lucky man.

After perhaps fifteen minutes, I stood unsteadily, made my way up the bank, and slipped into the jungle. It was still pouring down, and in the darkness progress was slow. Beneath the canopy, even the lightning offered no help. But both the rain and the darkness were also my protection.

Two possible directions were open to me. To the west and to the south-west, there was rolling ground, with vegetation that didn't look too dense. That much had been clear from the camp. Supposing they realized that I had crossed the river, the Khmer Rouge would assume I would go that way, the shortest and the easiest path to Thailand.

I would therefore head north-west, into the mountains. I didn't think they would believe I was strong enough to undertake such a difficult task. In fact, the difficulty itself was another reason to opt for that route. In the darkness, it would be difficult to orientate myself on flat ground, whereas mountains would provide natural guides. If that night I kept climbing, I was on the right track. If I went downhill, I was going wrong. It was simple. Even groping my way through rain and darkness I could assure myself that I was not turning my back on liberty.

Suddenly I felt again that electric surge of exhilaration, and this time there was nothing to hold me back. 'Free!' I yelled, 'Free!' And I began to sing at the top of my voice, bawling out that song, 'Rowing a Boat', that had been popular in Cambodia before the revolution, the one Sim used to whistle in Veal Vong. 'I'm rowing a boat! Rowing a boat!' I sang, as the thunder rumbled, and the rain fell, and the lightning flashed. 'Rowing a boat and going to pluck lotus flowers!' I barged on upwards over rocks, with branches slapping and scratching me, bellowing the song's meaningless, joyful refrain – *Aeu! Aeuy!* – at the top of my voice like a crazy man, exploding with joy.

All night, I climbed through the darkness, determined to establish a comfortable lead. At daybreak, I reached the top. My exhilaration had long since vanished. I was very tired, and fighting for breath. I saw off to one side, just beneath the summit, a shelf of rock sticking out vertically. I collapsed beneath it and slept.

All day I slept, and on through the next night.

When I awoke, it was still raining. I set off, away from the river and the slope, and found myself on a large plateau. The trees were less densely packed here, but the sky was overcast, and I couldn't find my direction. I ran the risk of getting lost, of going around in circles, of turning back without knowing it. But if I waited, I also risked being weakened by hunger and being caught.

Two distant rifle-shots made me eager not to loiter. Fortunately, though it was still raining, a break in the sky came to my rescue. Now I could get my direction westward again. At one point, I followed a stream uphill. It was not easy to walk in, but this way my tracks would not be seen. I kept slipping on the pebbles, and at one point cut the sole of a foot, but I was too eager to cross into Thailand to worry about that.

Perhaps I was already on the other side. After all, my good luck had not abandoned me, as I had first thought in the camp. The twitch of the left eyelid had foreshadowed rest and food, the right-eye twitch had been followed by my escape. But I took no chances, moving forward from tree to tree, glancing round constantly.

Soon it stopped raining. The sun shone. I accelerated my pace, walking straight ahead, westward, with only the sun for company.

Now that I was nearing the end, I became strangely afraid. It is difficult to express the feeling which came over me after the ecstasy of escape and before the attainment of liberty. I felt increasingly that something of supreme importance was about to happen, but I was correspondingly afraid of ultimate failure. My mood swung violently, as I anticipated joy and anguish in equal measure.

Suddenly, as I was walking down a hillside in this rolling landscape, I heard a sound, a distant mechanical roar. As I descended, the noise diminished. As I climbed, it returned. The higher I climbed, the clearer the sound. It seemed to come from straight ahead, from the west. I wondered if I was hallucinating from exhaustion. No: the persistent, distant, muffled roar was real enough.

All at once, I stepped out of trees on to the edge of the plateau. There ahead lay a beautiful sight, the sight I had so long dreamed of, and so long despaired of seeing. More than three thousand feet below, along the foot of a mountain range, beyond the forest, lay a highway, with traffic roaring by, and toy-like houses scattered beside fields, and, in the distance, the sea.

Thailand.

But my problems were not over yet. Before me lay my final climb.

After half an hour of descent, I felt a sharp pain at the side of my foot. I stopped, looked down, and saw beside my foot a sharpened bamboo stake. By pure luck, the stake had cut the side of my foot, instead of piercing it. Ahead on the trail, I saw a carpet of dead leaves, and here and there more of the deadly white points, uncovered by wind and rain. I was not in Thailand yet.

This, undoubtedly, was the frontier itself.

The field of stakes ran diagonally across in front of me, a swath one hundred and fifty yards wide. I wondered if I should follow the line of stakes until I found a gap. No: there would be some other deterrent, and perhaps a worse one – landmines perhaps. I decided to cross the field of stakes. With great care, I pulled out a bamboo, and placed a foot on the vacant spot. Then I reached forward, pulled out another stake and stepped on to the hole it had made.

It took me an hour to work myself into the middle of the field of stakes. If I was spotted now, I would be as helpless as a rat in a trap. But, looking around, I thought there was little chance of being seen. I was protected by screens of trees on all sides. For anyone to see me, they would have to be almost as far into the stakes as I was. Gingerly, I turned, stooped down, and felt for the next stake.

After another hour of this slow and nerve-wracking progress, the way ahead lay clear. I stood, paced forward carefully, and then reassured, strode out. Almost at once, I came to a stream. I walked on downhill in the stream, stepping from rock to slippery rock, to avoid any other traps and at the same time hide my tracks.

After another two or three hours of walking – I was too weak with exhaustion now to care about the passing time – the mountain torrent slowed, and I was clear of the slope. Tottering straight through the remaining trees, I passed a rubber plantation, and approached the highway. I tumbled down into a dry ditch, crawled up the other side and there, ahead, was the highway itself. I crawled forward to the verge and, still kneeling, saw a car go by. A truck came past in the opposite direction.

I rolled over, and lay flat on my back, too exhausted to move, my head turned to the road, watching the magical sight of traffic – motorcycles, taxis, cars, trucks. I felt reborn, as happy as if I had arrived in paradise.

It was June 22nd, 1977, and I was free, at last.

EPILOGUE

I began work on this version of my story in the quiet and comfort of Oxford, surrounded by suburban gardens neatly prepared for spring. It was like a reincarnation. I found it almost impossible to think of myself as the same person who had staggered over the border nine years before.

For a while, I was not noticed by anyone. Then two young Thais on bicycles, whose attention must have been attracted by my living skeleton, hailed a taxi for me, and I was taken to the administrative post of the area, Mai Rut, two miles away. There, an American missionary, Robert Stearns, questioned me in English to establish I was not a Khmer Rouge.

Though now accepted as a refugee, I was still technically guilty of crossing the frontier illegally. I was given a nominal prison sentence of one week, and then moved to a cell in the police station, pending transfer to a refugee camp.

While I was in the police station, three other Cambodians were brought in. They had just been intercepted at the frontier, and I was asked to be the interpreter, to translate their story into English to one of the policemen. To my astonishment, I was confronted by my cousin, Yann, and two others from the group of escapees from Leach, in an equally lamentable condition. Yann and his group had known nothing about the cause of the sudden dispersal either. They had lost trace of the others as quickly as Any, Eng and I, and simply continued on their way. Eventually, they had come across a Khmer Rouge patrol. Two were arrested, while Yann and his two friends had time enough to escape.

A few days later, I was sent to the refugee camp back in Mai Rut. There, several journalists visited me. I began to fulfil my aim to make my story public knowledge.

On October 13th, 1977, I flew to Paris, where I arranged a series of press conferences to describe to Western journalists the real situation in Cambodia. In 1978 I spoke in Paris, Brussels, Montreal, Ottowa, and Washington, demanding Western action against the Khmer Rouge.

Western nations, however, were helpless to intervene. In the end the Khmer Rouge created the conditions for their own downfall. Unable to slacken their iron discipline, seeing enemies everywhere, caught in their own trap, they had only one solution: to kill, and keep on killing, turning in the end on the Ancients and on their own ranks. Estimates of the dead vary between 2 and 3 million out of a total population of about 7.5 million. My own opinion is that in 1975–9 at least one third of the Cambodian population died. Only an objective census will reveal the true extent of the holocaust.

In January 1979, the Vietnamese harvested Cambodia like a ripe fruit. Since then, a Khmer Rouge dissident, Heng Samrin, has ruled Cambodia under the Vietnamese. Since June 1982, these two elements have been opposed by a coalition: the hard-line Khmer Rouge, Sihanouk's National United Front, and the Khmer People's National Liberation Front, headed by Sonn Sann, Sihanouk's former Prime Minister. All three have headquarters abroad and fighters inside Cambodia.

I find it astonishing and intolerable that this opposition, which claims to lead the war of liberation against the Vietnamese and is recognized by the United Nations, operates under the Khmer Rouge name of 'Democratic Kampuchea' and includes the handful of Khmer Rouge leaders who masterminded the policy of genocide. The presence of such monsters only feeds the justifications of the Vietnamese occupiers and weakens the cause of Cambodian nationalism.

Cambodia must cast off, or be released from, the clutches of Vietnamese colonialism. The country's relief when Hanoi's troops expelled Pol Pot should not justify the permanent colonization of Cambodia by Vietnam. But nor should Cambodia ever again fall under the demented rule of the Khmer Rouge. The great powers should do everything to provide a framework for a political solution. Then perhaps we could dress our wounds and be reborn in peace, independence and neutrality, forming a haven of stability from which regional prosperity might spring.

The tragedy of Cambodia has not yet run its course, nor will it for generations. Millions have died, a culture has vanished. The personal consequences of such a tragedy are incalculable, comparable only to the destruction wrought by the Black Death in Europe, by the Jewish Holocaust, and by the Stalinist Gulag.

I was one of the lucky ones. After my escape I resumed work as an engineer, first in France, and subsequently with an international development organization based in the Philippines. As the fortune-teller in Leach foretold, I have indeed travelled 'all the time'. I remarried, and once again have three sons.

Some of my family, too, survived. Thoeun, my second brother, who decided to remain in Koh Thom, escaped with his group – his two children, his wife and her parents. They crossed into Thailand in 1982 after the Vietnamese invasion, and now live in Australia. Any's mother and sister, Anyung, survived, and are still in Cambodia.

Besides those members of my family whose deaths I witnessed personally, though, many others perished. Any's father and Oan both vanished. My great-uncle, the Patriarch Huot Tat, was arrested a few hours after my departure from the pagoda, taken to our native village of Oudong, and executed. Numerous friends, all intellectuals, who joined the Khmer Rouge, vanished or were killed. After the Vietnamese invasion, many of their names were found on a list of victims in Phnom Penh's Tuol Sleng torture centre. Many others must have perished in the mass graves found all over the country. In Leach itself, within a few months of my departure, all those with any education, many of them close friends of mine, were killed. Even though only ostensibly a 'technician', I would have been among them if I had stayed.

My country's tragedy will always remain an open wound for me. I still agonize over the decisions I made. If I had insisted that Any remained in Leach, she would not have been lost in the jungle. Perhaps she would have survived with Nawath. After all, Yann left alone, and his wife and family survived. Sometimes, darker thoughts obsess me: was Any's disappearance some sort of punishment on us both for leaving Nawath? Or my punishment for allowing her to come with me? Did Any's death somehow ensure my survival? Because there are no answers, the questions haunt me still, and always will.

There is one particular, enduring pain: the loss of Nawath. I feel sure he is still alive. I have sought him through every means at my disposal, distributing his picture to surviving relatives in Cambodia and to refugee camps in Thailand, all to no avail.

I pray that Nawath will one day read my testimony, know the truth both of my survival and of our country's bloody history, and that we can find each other once again.

THE AUTHOR

When the Khmer Rouge seized power in Cambodia in April 1975, Pin Yathay was an engineer with a good education and a successful career. Under the brutal new regime, his class and position as an employee of the state made him a prime target for elimination. Two years later he reached freedom in Thailand and his harrowing ordeal came to an end. Pin Yathay then went to France, Canada and the United States where he spoke publicly about his country's plight. He began to rebuild his life and re-establish his career, working for five years as an engineer in France. He also remarried. He now lives with his wife in Manila and they have just added a third son to their family. He still hopes that his son Nawath may be alive and that they will one day be reunited.

THE EDITOR

John Man, who has a particular interest in human survival in extreme circumstances, is the author of *The Survival of Jan Little*, the story of a blind woman alone in the Amazon jungle, and *The Waorani: Jungle Nomads of Ecuador*. He also conducted the interviews for Channel Four's documentary series, *Survive*.